Erie Wrecks East

Second Edition

A Guide to Shipwrecks of Eastern Lake Erie

Georgann & Michael Wachter

Avon Lake, Ohio

Second Edition March, 2003

This book is dedicated to our children

Brendon David Wachter

Kimberly Michelle Wachter

and the memory of our daughter

Courtney Kristen Wachter

May 16, 1974 - January 30, 1993

Erie Wrecks East

Second Edition

A Guide to Shipwrecks of Eastern Lake Erie

Georgann & Michael Wachter

Cover paintings by Georgann Wachter

ISBN: 0-9661312-4-X

Published by **CorporateImpact**
Avon Lake, Ohio
e-mail: Wachter@Eriewrecks.com
web site: www.Eriewrecks.com

CONTENTS

Contents

We could not have produced this book without the help and encouragement of a great many people. In particular, we wish to express our appreciation to:

Christopher Gillcrist, Executive Director, Bill O'Brien, Past Executive Director; Noelle McFarland; Peg Bechtol; and Carla LaVigne of the Great Lakes Historical Society in Vermilion, Ohio.

Bob Graham of Historical Collections of the Great Lakes, Center for Archival Collections, Bowling Green State University.

Our friends who operate dive charter boats around Lake Erie have openly shared information and locations for the shipwrecks they charter. We encourage you to dive with:

Ed McLaughlin, **Days Off Dive Charter**, Port Dover, Ontario Canada

Craig Workman, **Lake Erie Marine Services Dive Charter**, Port Colborne, Ontario Canada

Dixie Greenwood, **Long Point Divers**, Port Dover, Ontario Canada

Wayne Hopper, **North Coast Nautical Services**, Port Stanley, Ontario Canada

Jim Herbert, **Osprey Dive Charters**, Barcelona, New York USA

Many friends and dive partners provided significant encouragement and information or photographs:

Larry and Mary Howard have done what is perhaps the most extensive original research on eastern Lake Erie shipwrecks.

Pat Labadie, author, researcher, historian, friend provided photos, invaluable information and confirmation or rejection of some of our shipwreck identifications.

Ralph Roberts provided rare photos from his extensive private collection.

Dave & Annette Soule, our dive partners and fellow shipwreck research enthusiasts, provided research and moral support.

We also received information and assistance from the following individuals and institutions: Jennifer McLeod of Marsh Collection Society, Amherstberg, Ontario; Jack Messmer, Lower Lakes Marine Historical Society, Buffalo, New York; Matthew Daley, Father Edward J. Dowling Marine Historical Collection, University of Detroit Mercy Library; John Polacsek, Dossin Great Lakes Museum, Detroit, Michigan; Marine Museum of the Great Lakes at Kingston, Ontario; Rocky River Public Library, Rocky River, Ohio; Erie County Historical Society, Erie, Pennsylvania; Buffalo and Erie County Historical Society, Buffalo, New York; Milan Historical Museum, Milan, Ohio; Great Lakes Marine and U.S. Coast Guard Memorial Museum, Ashtabula, Ohio; Rutherford B. Hayes Memorial Presidential Center, Fremont, Ohio; Port Colborne Historical and Marine Museum, Port Colborne, Ontario; Saint Catherines Museum, Saint Catherines, Ontario; Western Lake Erie Historical Society, Toledo, Ohio; Eric Guerrein of Lakeside Towing, Erie, Pennsylvania, Mark Musante of Lakeside Towing, Erie, Pennsylvania, Charles E.and Ricki Herdendorf, Sheffield Village, Ohio, Gerry and Walter Paine, Avon Lake, Ohio; Doug Embler, Erie, Pennsylvania, Doug King, Sr., Blasdell, New York; Bob Turner, Harbor Dive Center, Ashtabula, Ohio; John Veber, Brantford, Ontario; Gerald MacDonald, Dunville, Ontario; Kevin Magee, Fairview Park, Ohio.

DISCLAIMER

The authors have made every effort to assure the accuracy of the contents of this book. However, no warranty is expressed or implied that the information contained in this volume is accurate or correct. In fact we expect to hear from many people pointing out errors in our facts! The authors shall in no way be responsible for any consequential, incidental, or exemplary loss or damage resulting from the use of any of the graphics or printed information contained in this book. The authors disclaim any liability for omissions, errors, or misprints and give notice to all readers that this book is not to be used for dive planning or navigation.

Many of the shipwrecks described in this volume are beyond the limits of sport diving as defined by all major certifying agencies. They should only be attempted by very experienced divers with specialized training and equipment for depths in excess of sport diving limits.

Lake Erie is the fourth largest of the five Great Lakes by surface area, but the smallest in volume. Although this shallow freshwater sea averages only 60 feet in depth, the area off of Long Point reaches 210 feet. In most instances, her shallowness makes Lake Erie ideal for scuba diving. However, the wrecks off Long Point often exceed the recommended depths for sport divers without deep water training and equipment. In general, the visibility on the deeper wrecks in the eastern basin is better than that on the shallow wrecks in the western end. Visibility on these wrecks often exceeds 100 feet in the summer months.

The lake is quick to turn from millpond to white water fury and many vessels have met their end in sudden squalls. The first steam-powered vessel on Lake Erie met her end this way. Built in 1818, The *Walk-In-The-Water* was a trim schooner rigged two master with port and starboard paddle wheels amidships. There is some question if her steam power was augmented by her sails or vise-versa. Regardless, she sailed for three years running from Buffalo, New York to Detroit, Michigan. On October 31, 1821, she sailed out of Buffalo Harbor for the last time. As she approached Point Abino she encountered a gale too powerful for her paddle wheels to overcome. She lost headway and began to break apart. Because her primitive boiler could not supply sufficient steam to run both her engine and her pumps, she was forced to set her anchors. This only worsened the strain on the hull and the captain finally let go the anchors. Drifting free with the gale, the *Walk-In-The-Water* washed toward shore, finally running aground at the mouth of Buffalo Creek.

Other ships were lost by collision or run aground in the fog. In our research we even found references to the "Lake Erie Monster," a sea serpent of giant dimensions. Regardless of the cause of the loss, the lure of a shipwreck is like no other for a diver. As you descend, you leave the present behind and enter a moment in the past. While you explore this unique time capsule, many questions go through your mind. What happened on the fateful day the ship went down? What was she carrying? Did the passengers and crew survive? This book provides the answers to these questions for many of the shipwrecks in eastern Lake Erie. We encourage the reader to join us in learning more of the wrecks we dive and the events surrounding their loss.

We have visited most of the shipwreck sites in this volume, and recorded our own observations and Loran or DGPS numbers. Global Positioning Systems will soon make Loran numbers obsolete. Where we have provided DGPS coordinates, anyone using a differential GPS should be able to go directly to the wreck. Where we have provided Loran coordinates (TDs), recognize that Loran numbers will vary by machine and location on the wreck charted, so you should bring several search markers to aid in locating the wreck.

Our descriptions of the wreck sites are generally from personal experience. We have observed that over the years wrecks change and further deteriorate. Silting, storms, and zebra mussels obscure features. As an example, at one time the entire length of the *Merida* was above the silt and her gunnels cleared the silt bottom by 3 feet. Today, the bow and stern rise above the bottom, but the entire midsection of the vessel is buried beneath the bottom silt of Lake Erie.

Canada and the United States have laws prohibiting the destruction of wreck sites or salvage without permits. Canada has recently considered legislation that would extremely restrict access to wreck sites. The authors believe all divers should have free access to the shipwrecks of Lake Erie. We also believe the quickest way to lose that right of free access is to pillage the wrecks. Many of these sites are the final resting place of the crewmembers and passengers aboard the vessel when she sank. Please show them the respect they deserve and preserve our shipwrecks for future divers.

Take care and good diving!

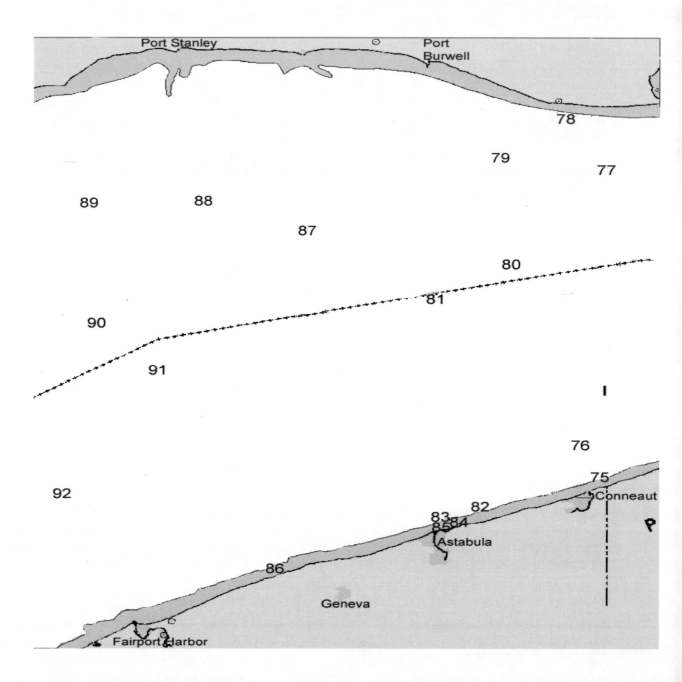

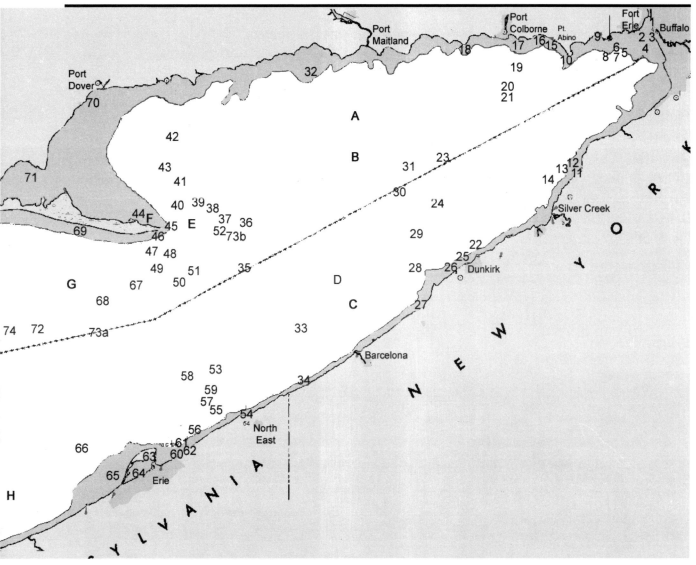

A	Niagara	14	Bishop's Derrick	36	Cracker	58	Indiana	79	Michigan Transpor-
B	George C. Finney	15	Steel Products	37	Persian	59	Gerkin, Howard S.		tation Barge 3/4
C	Hedger, Betty	16	Raleigh	38	Swallow	60	Eldorado	80	Stevens, William H.
D	Barge F	17	Osborn, S.S.	39	Junction 20	61	Canobie	81	Reed, James
E	Mast Hoop	18	Marengo	40	T-8	62	Crete	82	Dixie
F	Pratt, Pascal	19	Dupuis #10	41	Brown Brothers	63	Dow, Neal	83	Joy, James F.
G	Crystal/Hook	20	Cisco	42	Wilma	64	Willis, Hunter	84	Gulnair
H	Susquehanna	21	Benson, C.B.	43	17 Fathom	65	Armour, Philip D.	85	Wonder
I	Carol Sue II	22	Golden Fleece	44	Siberia	66	Foster, Charles	86	Hill, Charles B.
1	U.S. 104	23	McGrath, J.G.	45	Clay, Henry	67	Saint James	87	Nimrod
2	Barge 43	24	Brunswick	46	Elphicke, C.W.	68	Trade Wind	88	O'Neill, Louie
3	Alabama	25	Wilson, Annabell	47	Atlantic	69	Wild Rover	89	Dawn
4	Richardson, W.C.	26	Canadaway Creek	48	Stern Castle	70	Cecil J	90	Merida
5	Acme Tug	27	Manzanilla	49	Andrew B	71	Ontario	91	Killarney
6	Finch	28	Passaic	50	Acme/Arches	72	Aycliffe Hall	92	Lockwood, C.B.
7	Tonawanda	29	Irving, Washington	51	Smith	73	GLM 507	93	? Marquette and
8	Cheney, O.W.	30	Acme Propeller	52	Van Straubenzie, Sir C.T.	74	Drill Rig		Bessimer #2
9	Walk-In-The-Water	31	Carlingford	53	Richmond, Dean	75	Chesapeake		
10	Briton	32	Abyssinia	54	Oneida	76	Lyon, John B		
11	Dacotah	33	Boland, John J.	55	Martin, S.K.	77	Majestic		
12	Diesel Barge	34	City of Rome	56	Isolde	78	Wocoken		
13	Erie	35	Oxford	57	Mud Wreck				

ABYSSINIA

Official #: 107221   **Site #:** 32

Location: Tecumseh Reef, 8 miles southwest of Port Maitland, Ontario

Coordinates: Bow Loran: 44719.7   58805.8   GPS: 42 48.750 79 42.660

                 Stern Loran: 44719.3 58805.3   GPS: 42 48.730 79 42.550

Lies: scattered   **Depth:** 30 feet

Type: wood schooner/barge   **Cargo:** wheat

Power: sail/towed

Owner(s) Lake Transit Company (Hutchinson & Company), Cleveland, Ohio

Built: 1896 at West Bay City, Michigan by J. Davidson

Dimensions: 288'6" x 44'6" x 19'1"   **Tonnage:** 2,037 gross 1916 net

Date of Loss: Thursday, October 18, 1917

Cause of Loss: ran aground

Abyssinia

Great Lakes Historical Society

Story of the Loss:

The *Abyssinia* was the largest of 14 vessels of her type, a barge with schooner rig. They were designed to be towed, but able to maneuver under sail if she lost her tow. These boats were famous for their ability to handle large cargos and notorious for their inability to handle rough weather. Despite this reputation, in <u>Lore of the Lakes</u>, Dana Bowen points out that the steamer *City of Glasgow* ran from Detour, Michigan to Port Huron, Michigan in 21 hours and 40 minutes with the *Abyssinia* in tow. Darn fast for the time.

On October 17, 1917, the *Abyssinia* was under tow of the steamer *Maruba*. Bound for Buffalo, New York from Fort William, Ontario, the two vessels were encountering fairly strong winds out of the northwest and tucked in against the north shore to gain shelter in the lee of the land. As they continued toward Buffalo, they got in too close to shore and both vessels ran aground on Tecumseh Reef.

Abyssinia's captain, T.K. Woodward, initially reported that the vessels were hard aground but were not leaking. All that was required was to lighter the *Abyssinia's* load of one quarter million dollars worth of wheat. As the seas were coming down and the prediction was for good weather, the tugs *Kennedy* and *G.C. Harding* were dispatched with the lighters *Rescue* and *Newman* from Detroit. Regrettably, Captain Woodward's estimate of the damage to his vessel would prove to be badly in error. Through the night, the waves continued to pound the grounded vessel against the rock bottom. By Friday morning, Captain Woodward was reporting that the hull was filling with water through at least three gaping holes, and her sides were bulging out. Since the cargo of wheat was destroyed, one tug and one lighter were called off. Uninsured, the now beaten and battered *Abyssinia* was abandoned as a "constructive total loss." The *Maruba* was pulled off the reef by the tug *Harding* and the lighter *Rescue*.

With her crew gone and left to the unrelenting winter elements, the *Abyssinia* was broken up by the winter ice and scattered to the sea.

The Wreck Today:

Divers located the *Abyssinia* in 1962. Her keelson and hull fragments lay in four parts near the buoy on the east side of Tecumseh Reef. As with many shallow water wreck sites, the *Abyssinia* provides an excellent habitat for fish. She teems with bass and is a favorite fishing site of local sport fishermen.

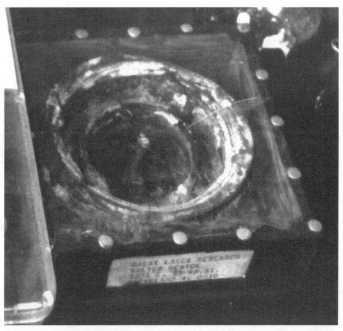

This gauge from the Abyssinia was donated to a private museum by diver Don Ward who had salvage rights to the Abyssinia in the 1960's.

ACME PROPELLER

Official #: 297   **Site #:** 30

Location: 316°T 11 miles off Dunkirk, New York, 16°T 19 miles off Barcelona, New York

Coordinates: Loran: 44639.7 58887.6   **DGPS:** 42 36.607 79 29.853

Lies: bow southwest   **Depth:** 130 feet

Type: hogging arched propeller   **Cargo:** beef, flour, corn, lard,

Power: steam engine   cow hides

Owner(s) Western Transportation Company of Buffalo, New York

Built: 1856 at Buffalo, New York by George Hardison

Dimensions: 190'10" x 33'3" x 12'9"   **Tonnage:** 762

Date of Loss: Monday, November 4, 1867

Cause of Loss: sprung a leak in gale weather

Acme

Loudon Wilson drawing from private collection of Ralph Roberts

Story of the Loss:

While en route from Chicago, Illinois to Buffalo, New York, the *Acme* was nearing the end of her trip when she encountered a classic, Lake Erie November gale. November is a fearsome time on all of the Great Lakes, but it is particularly so on shallow Lake Erie. Captain Dixon and his crew were not surprised at how quickly the winds and seas rose on the lake that day. They were, however, surprised at how quickly their 191 foot steamer filled with water.

As the gale raged on and the water level in the holds continued to rise, Captain Dixon realized his ship would not survive and gave orders to lower the boats. Two boats were launched without incident. As they rowed away, the mate observed that the *Acme* settled to the gunnels and sank about an hour after she was abandoned.

The crew of one small boat was picked up by the revenue cutter, *Commodore Perry,* and taken to the safety of Dunkirk, New York. The second boat with Captain Dixon and 9 crewmen aboard rowed into Dunkirk several hours later. All on board survived without injury.

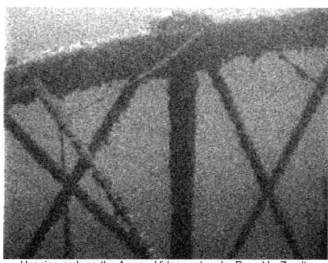

Hogging arch on the Acme. Video capture by Dave VanZandt.

The Wreck Today:

The *Acme* lies embedded in the mud in approximately 130 feet of water. Her upper cabins have been blown off, exposing her engine. The hogging arches rise to about 117 feet. This wreck provides an excellent example of early steamboat construction.

Expect 40° water even in the summer and be aware of a possible current. The tie-in line goes to her port arch.

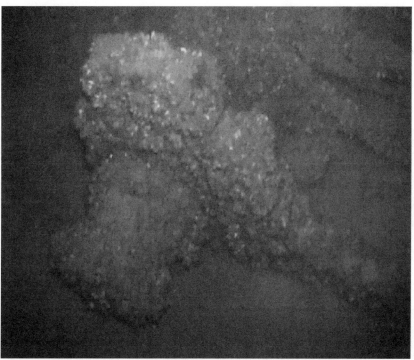

Windlass on the Acme.

ACME TUG

Official #: 107039   **Site #:** 5

Location: 240°T 3.8 miles off Buffalo, New York's north harbor entrance

Coordinates: Loran: 44922.1 59222.7   **DGPS:** 42 50.701 78 57.840

Lies: scattered   **Depth:** 35 feet

Type: wooden tug   **Cargo:** towing *Wilkesbarre*

Power: steam engine, 22" x 26" cylinder

Owner(s) Hand and Johnson, Great Lakes Towing Company, Buffalo, New York

Built: 1893 at Buffalo, New York by O'Grady and Maher

Dimensions: 66'8" x 17' x 9'6"   **Tonnage:** 58 gross 29 net

Date of Loss: Tuesday, April 15, 1902

Cause of Loss: collision with her tow

Acme

Private collection of Ralph Roberts

Story of the Loss:

It was briskly cold and the sun shown down on the pilothouse of the tug *Acme* as she made one of the first runs of the new shipping season. Observers say the tug was cutting through the Lake Erie ice "like it was paper" as Captain Harley H. Vroman, Engineer Fred Ferguson, Firemen James Murray and Fireman Frank Dovey towed the propeller *Wilkesbarre* from Buffalo Harbor.

It was spring and the ice flows prevented the large propellers from leaving harbor under their own power. The *Wilkesbarre* followed lazily behind the little tug on 200 feet of towline. Behind her the propeller, *Thomas Adams,* was enjoying a free passage in the wake of the other vessels.

The crew's joy at being back at sea was cut short when she lurched to a sudden stop, caught fast in the ice. Glancing back, Captain Vroman knew the momentum of the freighter would bring her crashing into the tug. As he made one last ditch effort to power the tug off the ice, he gave orders to throw out the life raft, abandon ship and swim clear. The freighter loomed larger as her momentum brought the two vessels closer and closer to the final impact. Captain Vroman was still in the pilothouse as the *Wilkesbarre,* unable to check herself, crashed into the *Acme,* staving in her port side. He fought with the pilothouse door, unable to open it as the tug was starting to roll over and sink. Finally, breaking through a window, the captain leapt to the water and swam for his life. Burdened by his heavy clothing, Vroman barely kept afloat as he watched the tug roll and sink in 40 feet of water.

Struggling in freezing cold water and heavy clothing, the tug's crew received numerous cuts and bruises from the ice. Captain Dennis Driscol of the *Wilkesbarre* anxiously watched the helpless men as his vessel slid past her sinking tow. Aboard the steamer, *Thomas Adams,* Captain McCallum gave four sharp whistle blasts as he checked his steam down and ordered preparations to board the survivors. Lines were thrown to the men in the water and all were recovered with no major injuries.

On hearing the distress signals issued from the *Acme,* the tug *Gee* had started from Buffalo Harbor. The chilled tug crewmen were put aboard the *Gee* for the return trip to Buffalo. Having seen to it that all of the lost tug's crew were safely aboard the *Gee,* the *Thomas Adams* and the *Wilkesbarre* continued their upbound trip.

The Wreck Today:

The *Acme* lies on a sand and mud bottom 3½ miles off Buffalo's north harbor entrance. The wheelhouse and name board were torn off the tug by the ice in the accident that sunk her and the divers who found her removed her whistle and other artifacts. In 1990, the whistle was donated to the Great Lakes Historical Society's Inland Seas Museum in Vermilion, Ohio.

The primary features of this site are the ship's rudder, wooden hull frame, and boiler. Her hull is entirely gone on the port side and the boiler is rolled on its side beside the wreckage. The steering gear is off the wreck next to the boiler.

Watch for heavy boat traffic.

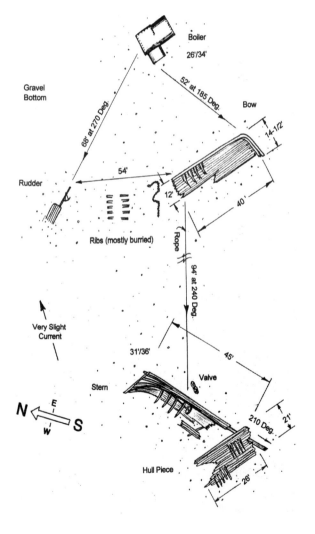

Acme site drawing by Doug King, Sr.

ALABAMA

Official #:	none	**Site #:**	3
Location:	275ºT 0.7 mile off Buffalo, New York's north harbor entrance		
Coordinates:	Loran:	**DGPS:**	42 52.393 78 54.723
Lies:	scattered	**Depth:**	35 feet
Type:	wood sidewheel steamer	**Cargo:**	none
Power:	steam engine		
Owner(s)	Hall Russel and Burton of Sandusky, Ohio		
Built:	1848 at Detroit, Michigan by W. Gooding		
Dimensions:	234' x 29' x 12'	**Tonnage:**	799
Date of Loss:	Tuesday, August 29, 1854		
Cause of Loss:	waterlogged		

Alabama

Drawing by Georgann Wachter

Story of the Loss:

The sidewheel steamer *Alabama* was a mere six years old and already in need of significant repairs. She was a modern design with a steamer's hull and a main deck that extended to the edge of the paddle boxes. Due to the feeble condition of her hull, she had laid in Buffalo Harbor for several weeks trying to get into dry dock for repairs. The dry dock operators feared the required repairs would tie up the dock for an extended period of time and refused to admit her.

On realizing that the dock operators were in no hurry to haul the *Alabama*, the decision was made to take her to the dry docks at Huron, Ohio. At 4:00 a.m. on Tuesday, August 29, the steamer slipped past the Buffalo Harbor lights, bound for Huron and badly needed repairs. She was hardly under way before it was discovered there was two feet of water in the hold. As the water continued to pour through the dilapidated hull, Captain Titus ordered the vessel turned back to Buffalo. Despite being only three miles out, the sidewheeler was unable to make the harbor before the rising waters extinguished her boilers and she settled to the bottom just off the Black Rock Canal.

The water was sufficiently shallow that her smoke stacks and upper works remained above the water, permitting her stranded crew to sit comfortably in the wheelhouse and on the hurricane deck. This made rescue of the crew a relatively easy matter for the tug *Hamilton Morton* which came to the sunken steamers assistance.

Her owners announced that preparations would be made immediately for the raising of the sidewheeler. However, on September 4, large quantities of the *Alabama's* upper works were reported floating up the Niagara River. She continued to sit exposed to the tortures of the winter seas until salvors removed much of her machinery the following year.

The Wreck Today:

One hundred fifty years sitting in shallow water at the bottom of Lake Erie takes its toll on a shipwreck. Not much remains of the *Alabama* except some iron parts of her paddlewheels, her keel, and a toppled capstan. There is a sizable debris field of pieces parts, but very little structure. Don't go looking for her engines, they aren't there and are presumed to have been removed in the 1855 salvage work.

Caution is required due to extremely heavy boat traffic in this area.

Buffalo Harbor circa 1900. Authors' collection.

ANDREW B

Official #:	189887	**Site #:**	49
Location:	4 miles south of the tip of Long Point		
Coordinates:	Loran:	**DGPS:**	42 28.796 80 04.249
Lies:	on its side	**Depth:**	180 feet
Type:	dredge barge	**Cargo:**	crane & 5 ½ cu. yard dredge
Power:	towed		
Owner(s)	Canadian Dredge and Dock, Ltd. of Toronto, Ontario		
Built:	1958 at Port Weller, Ontario by Port Weller Dry Dock		
Dimensions:	120' x 50' x 8'	**Tonnage:**	388
Date of Loss:	Wednesday, November 8, 1995		
Cause of Loss:	storm		

Andrew B

Private collection of Skip Gillham

Story of the Loss:

The derrick scow *Andrew B* was built for use in Russel Construction Company dredging projects. After Canadian Dredge and Dock Company acquired this work vessel, she was equipped with drills for blasting rock and making trenches for sewer outfalls or water intakes.

The *Andrew B* had finished dredging a channel up at Bruce Mines, Ontario, near Sault Ste. Marie. She had ducked into Port Stanley, Ontario because of weather. She was headed for Whitby, Ontario, just east of Toronto, when she left Port Stanley under tow of the tug *Offshore Supplier*. She continued to encounter nasty weather, and, off Long Point, the tow line broke. With no momentum to provide stability, the barge was free to tumble in the storm tossed waters. She soon rolled over and settled beneath the waves in the deep waters off Long Point.

The Wreck Today:

The bulkheads of the barge were crushed so she was not salvaged. The hull is on its side and her crane, surprisingly, is still attached. One spud is suspended horizontally approximately 50 feet above the bottom.

This wreck lies in 180 feet of water. It is well beyond the limits of sport diving as defined by all major certifying agencies. As such this dive should only be attempted by very experienced divers with specialized training for depths in excess of sport diving limits.

East End Lighthouse, Long Point Island.

Long Point East End Light House. Authors' collection.

PHILIP D. ARMOUR

Official #: 150459   **Site #:** 65

Location: 250°T 5.8 miles off Erie, Pennsylvania's harbor entrance

Coordinates: Loran: 44339.2 58434.5   **DGPS:** 42 07.684 80 10.693

Lies: bow northwest   **Depth:** 30 feet

Type: wood barge (converted propeller)   **Cargo:** coal

Power: towed

Owner(s) Boland and Cornelius of Buffalo, New York

Built: 1889 by Detroit Dry Dock Company at Detroit, Michigan

Dimensions: 264' x 40'6" x 21'   **Tonnage:** 1990 gross 1452 net

Date of Loss: Saturday, November 13, 1915

Cause of Loss: storm

Philip D. Armour

Historical Collections of the Great Lakes, Bowling Green State University

Story of the Loss:

At the time she was launched, March 30, 1889, the *Armour* was the largest wood propeller ever built by the Detroit Dry Dock Company. She had been in service a scant five months when, traveling in clear skies and calm waters, she collided with the steamer *Marion* in the Saint Clair Flats. The crew of this fine new ship had no time to dally. All safely abandoned ship. From the point of collision to the time she fell to the bottom of the 70 foot deep waters was barely four minutes. This first sinking foretold her destiny, both as a shipwreck and for her crew's survival.

She was salvaged by the James Reid Wrecking Company for a fee of $45,000. Reid spent 10 months in the effort and is rumored to have lost $10,000 on the contract. Regardless, she underwent the most extensive refitting ever performed by the Detroit Dry Dock Company and continued in service for another 26 years.

By the time she left Ashtabula, Ohio the evening of November 12, 1915, she had been converted to a barge and was in the tow of the tug *Gillen*. Bound for Welland, Ontario with 2,000 tons of soft coal, they were working their way through a building gale as they approached Erie, Pennsylvania. Coming on Presque Isle, the vessels were encountering waves that would soon build to be as high as 25 feet. The captain of the *Gillen* turned to seek safe harbor at Erie and disaster struck. The towline fouled in the tug's propeller. The line severed, casting the *Armour* adrift. The tug, now out of control, had to be beached.

Drifting and tossing wildly in the monstrous seas, the *Armour* sounded continuous distress signals. She struck a shoal and stuck fast as scores of onlookers, unable to enter the towering seas, watched helplessly from the shore. Responding to the distress signals, the Erie Lifesaving crew finally reached the stranded ship. They rescued three of her crew. Seven others, including Captain Joseph Boland, refused to abandon their vessel. The lifesaving crew had no sooner left the scene than the once mighty vessel cracked in two and her stern sank rapidly beneath the waves. The remaining crewmembers huddled in the bow as the waves continued to pound the *Armour* to pieces.

Once again, the lifesaving crew ventured out on the treacherous waters. Passing the tug *Buffalo* en route, they saved the last of the crewmembers as the waves washed away the remaining decks of the devastated ship. The tug *Buffalo*, having ventured out to the rescue carried the crew safely back to Erie.

The Wreck Today:

The *Philip D. Armour* sits on a sand and hard pack bottom with her rudder lying flat at the stern. Working from the stern, you find her propeller and tiller. There are two double boilers on the port side and her engine and some pipe lay amidships. Further toward the bow is a set of bollards. Much of the port bow is missing.

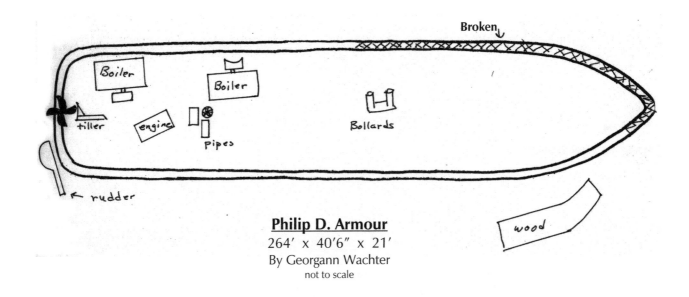

Philip D. Armour
264' x 40'6" x 21'
By Georgann Wachter
not to scale

ATLANTIC

Official #:	None	**Site #:**	47
Location:	358°T 24 miles off Erie, Pennsylvania – 214°T 3.1 miles off Long Point Light		
Coordinates:	Loran: 44522.7 58561.1	**DGPS:**	42 30.620 80 05.086
Lies:	bow west	**Depth:**	155 feet
Type:	sidewheel steamer	**Cargo:**	passengers
Power:	vertical beam engine		
Owner(s)	Samuel Ward & Eber B. Ward of Newport, Michigan with Steven Clements of Chicago, Illinois		
Built:	1849 at Newport (Marine City), Michigan by John Wolverton		
Dimensions:	265'7" x 33' x 14'6"	**Tonnage:**	1155 gross
Date of Loss:	Friday, August 20, 1852		
Cause of Loss:	collision with the propeller *Ogdensberg*		

Atlantic

The Great Lakes Historical Society

Story of the Loss:

Running under charter as part of the Michigan Central rail fleet, the *Atlantic* was one of the largest and fastest passenger steamers on the Great Lakes. A graceful combination of palatial, sleek, and fast, she once made the Buffalo to Detroit run in 16 ½ hours. Her speed may well have been her undoing.

This particular Buffalo to Detroit run was to be very profitable for the *Atlantic*. In addition to a full complement of passengers, she reportedly carried $35,000 of American Express payroll money and some $5,000 in gold. She delayed in Buffalo to board 200 Norwegian immigrants and, as she steamed out of Buffalo harbor, the immigrants and their belongings filled her decks and passageways.

She progressed rapidly toward Long Point with calm water, no wind, and stars visible through a light haze. Captain Petty chose to retire and placed first mate Blodgett in charge of the boat. The *Atlantic* was putting on steam to make up time as she approached Long Point at 1:30 in the morning. Off in the distance both Blodgett and the wheelsman spotted a single white light approaching. Believing the light to be a schooner capable of doing only 3 miles per hour in the light breeze, the *Atlantic* kept her course and speed.

On board the downbound propeller *Ogdensberg*, the wheelsman noticed the lights of the approaching *Atlantic* and advised the mate that the *Ogdensberg* would need to turn as he thought the upbound vessel to be a point off course. The mate on duty is reported to have replied, "Hold your course mister. That's a passenger boat coming up to us and those fellows think they own Lake Erie. You stay where you are and we'll drive that 'expletive' back where he belongs."

With each slap of her 30-foot, paddle wheels the *Atlantic* came closer to disaster. She relied on her speed to safely cross the bow of the approaching propeller she believed to be a schooner. With a heart-stopping jolt, the *Ogdensberg* rammed her just forward of the port paddle wheel. Believing the damage to be minor, both vessels continued on.

Shortly, one of the stokers reported she was taking on water uncontrollably. Captain Petty now ordered more steam and a turn toward shore. Too late, passengers were awakened and told to prepare to abandon the ship. As the in rushing water met the super heated boilers, geysers of steam erupted through the ship's skylights. The ensuing panic on board caused passengers to leap to their deaths in the deep dark waters of Lake Erie. In the melee, Captain Petty was injured and all pretense of control on board the sinking *Atlantic* was lost. The 265-foot pride of the Lake Erie fleet sank bow first in 160 feet of water.

Hearing the screams of the panicking passengers, the *Ogdensberg* came about and picked up survivors of the disaster. Those who had clung to the stern of the ship were saved. Most who leapt to the sea perished. In all, over 250 people lost their lives this night. This sinking is second only to the fiery death of the *G.P. Griffith* for worse loss of life shipwreck in the history of Lake Erie.

The Wreck Today:

One of Long Point's most famous shipwrecks, the *Atlantic* has been the subject of extensive litigation and was closed to diving at one point.

This dive is beyond the limits of sport diving as defined by all major certifying agencies. It should only be attempted by very experienced divers with specialized training for

Paddle wheel of the Atlantic. Photo by Mike Wachter.

depths in excess of sport diving limits. She sits upright in 160 feet of water and you will reach the wreck at about 135 feet. Usually there is a tie-in line attached to her hogging arch. The upper decks have collapsed, but the middle deck and holds are still intact. Commercial diver, Mike Fletcher, who rediscovered the wreck tells of a pioneer wagon sitting in the holds and books that were still legible.

While zebra mussels have covered her, she is an impressive sight with her single mast still proudly erect and the forward rails waiting a passenger's grip. Her paddle wheels stand fairly intact and the double helmsman's wheel has fallen over and can be found protruding from the silt. Peering into the interior of the wreck, one might still see the passenger's belongings and occasional artifacts of the time strewn about the wreck.

Salvage and Treasure Hunters:

The *Atlantic'* story continues to this very day, for you see, she is a "treasure ship." She is known to have been carrying American Express money in her safe and rumors of gold and cash worth over $400,000 have circulated since the day she went down.

Legendary hardhat diver, Johnny Green was the first to attempt to recover the treasures of the *Atlantic*. Working under a salvage agreement with the American Express Company, Green braved the depths of the *Atlantic*, going beyond the reach of the technology of the day. He got himself severely bent (decompression sickness) in the process.

According to Green he had made several dives on the *Atlantic* and on his last dive had managed to extract the safe from the pursers cabin and set it on deck to be raised. Ascending from the dive, he was struck with a crippling case of the bends. This necessitated suspension of diving operations. When he returned to retrieve the safe some two years later, he found that it had already been raised by another hardhat diver of the time, Elliot Harrington.

Green's account describes the difficulty of diving in 160 feet of water using 1850s' technology:

> *"I found great difficulty in moving, the water was so compressed; and with the diminutive air pipe which we used, it was next to impossible to keep the armor inflated below the waist, and often it rose as high as the chest. The pressure was immense. The rush of blood to the head causes sparks of various hues to flash before my eyes, and I had a constant tendency to fall asleep."*

Harrington disputes Green's claim alleging that the safe was not on the deck when he arrived. According to Harrington, he was undaunted by the depth, which many men told him was impossible. He discarded the diving apparatus common to the times and adapted a diving bell to the conditions at the *Atlantic* site. After many trips to "depths of nearly 200 feet," he finally located the purser's cabin. Working in total darkness, he used an axe to break in the window and, enlarging the opening, was able to extract the safe. Much to his chagrin, the first attempt to lift the safe failed, as the safe broke free of its chains and struck Harrington, nearly killing him. Returning to the surface to forge a stronger chain, Harrington was able to successfully raise the safe on his next attempt, June 22, 1856.

Diver Elliot Harrington recovered Atlantic's safe.

When one considers that Green's descriptions of the wreck and her depth are more accurate than Harrington's, one begins to doubt Harrington's account. You tell us whom you think did the lions share of the recovery and who did not. Either way, the inventory provided the courts by Harrington indicated the 28" x 18" x 16" iron strong box contained $5,000 in gold coin, $31,000 in bills, and six gold watches. Also in the box, but not reported by Harrington, were a parcel of Michigan State Bonds and a warrant on the United States Treasury payable to John N. Garns, Paymaster, United States Army for $10,000.

There were other salvage attempts in 1873 and 1910. However, for almost 130 years, the *Atlantic* lay lost and undisturbed, but not forgotten. In 1984, Canadian commercial diver, Mike Fletcher rediscovered the wreck. Fletcher was interested in finding an early submarine lost near the wreck in an 1853 salvage attempt. While he did not find the submarine, he did raise many artifacts from the shipwreck. This ran him afoul of Canadian authorities.

Then, along comes a group of treasure seekers from California, Mar-Dive Corporation. Mar-Dive located the wreck by stumbling onto Fletcher's buoy. They attempted to revive the defunct Western Wrecking Company in order to purchase salvage rights. They also misrepresented material facts to gain an Admiralty judgment in California courts permitting them to take possession of the wreck. Mar-Dive raised many artifacts and removed them to California for sale.

In a long series of court battles, the net result is that Canada owns the wreck. Mar-Dive must return the artifacts taken. And Fletcher is off the hook for having assisted the Canadian government's claim.

May She Rest in Peace:

Today, many believe the *Atlantic* still has enormous potential as a treasure ship. The steamer trunks of hundreds of passengers are rumored to rest intact in her cabins and holds. While, Canadian law prohibits the removal of artifacts from a shipwreck in Canadian waters, there is little to prevent a disreputable diver from removing artifacts from the site. We expect we have not heard the last of the court cases and treasure searches surrounding the sidewheel steamer *Atlantic*.

The authors encourage visiting divers to remember that this site is the final resting place of 250 souls whose last moments were spent in anticipation of a new life in a new world to the west. The new world they found was a watery grave in eternity. Treat it with respect.

Full many a hundred fathoms deep.

Down under the mounting seas,

The drowned their ceaseless vigils keep,

Sad watchers that they be.

They left a life in the world above

When they went down to the sea,

And now like lovers lost they rove

Forever restlessly.

- Cleveland Morning Leader, Friday, July 4, 1856

Aycliffe Hall

Official #:	147800	**Site #:**	72
Location:	316°T 21 miles off Erie, Pennsylvania, 232°T – 19.5 miles off Long Point Light		
Coordinates:	Loran: 44410.4 58393.2	**DGPS:**	42 22.532 80 21.225
Lies:	turtled, bow east	**Depth:**	75 feet
Type:	steel canal freighter	**Cargo:**	light
Power:	triple expansion steam engine with 15-25-40 x 33 cylinder and stroke		
Owner(s)	Hall Corporation of Canada		
Built:	1928 at South Bank-on-Tees, England by Smiths Dock Company, Ltd.		
Dimensions:	253' x 43'6" x 20'6"	**Tonnage:**	1900 gross
Date of Loss:	Thursday, June 11, 1936		
Cause of Loss:	collision with steamer *Edward J. Berwind*		

Aycliffe Hall

Remick Collection

Story of the Loss:

The Canadian owned *Aycliffe Hall* had cleared Port Colborne, Ontario bound for Collingwood at 9:30 Wednesday evening. Traveling light, she steamed at full speed through the night and into a dense Thursday morning fog. The United States owned *Edward J. Berwind* was downbound from Ashland, Wisconsin with a load of iron ore for Buffalo, New York. She too, traveled at full speed through the night and into the Thursday morning fog. The pressure to make time often leads to foolhardy seamanship.

According to the Canadian crew, the *Aycliffe Hall* was proceeding on her course at full speed when they heard fog blasts off the port bow. Mate Clarence Kenney was standing watch and checked the steamer down. He issued a one blast signal and testifies that he received a one blast signal in reply. Accordingly, the *Aycliffe Hall* changed course to starboard. The *Berwind*, however, continued on at full speed. The crew of the *Berwind* contended they were sounding an automated fog signal of three blasts each minute and that no signal was given by the *Hall* until she loomed out of the fog. Collision was unavoidable. The *Edward J. Berwind* rammed the *Aycliffe Hall* amidships at 5:30 in the morning. James Cooney of Rocky River, Ohio was an 18 year old seaman on the *Berwind*. He recalls that they were going about 11 knots. He heard the danger signal sounded, and as the *Berwind* crashed into the *Hall* near her coal bunkers, the watchman flew up into the air. The first mate, who was in charge when the incident happened, got suspended for a month.

Seeing water rapidly filling the *Aycliffe Hall*, the crew lowered their lifeboat at the same time that the *Berwind* lowered a boat to assist the crew of the stricken vessel. The *Hall's* full complement of 19 men was taken aboard the *Edward J. Berwind*. Within 20 minutes, the *Hall* settled to the bottom in 70 feet of water. Her spar marked her grave as the *Berwind* carried both crews on to Buffalo.

The following day, Captain Ross Sinclair, a native of Toronto, told the *Toronto Evening Telegram* that the loss of his ship was an act of God. "An act of God , that's how I see it. Here I've been sailing the lakes every season for 23 of my 39 years, for 12 seasons as captain, and I've never been mixed up in any way with any piece of sailor's bad luck. Then this thing happens to me out of nowhere, and my ship is gone. Yes sir, it was an act of God." We think two ships traveling at full speed through a dense fog is more like an act of stupidity.

In September 1936, the Tom Reid Salvage Company bid $30,000 to raise the *Aycliffe Hall*. They successfully floated her bow and determined the hole in her side was too large to patch. Using pontoons, the ship could be raised. However, the pontoons were lost, and then plans were developed to drag her to shallower water. As preparations were being made to move her, a storm closed in on the site. As the waves built, she rolled over and was lost again. Subsequent efforts to relocate the wreck proved fruitless.

The Wreck Today:

In July 1939 United States Coast Guard divers located her again. The Canadian Department of Transportation considered the vessel to be a hazard to navigation and sent the buoy tender *Grenville* to dynamite the wreck.

Today her remains lay upside down in 75 feet of water. As with most turtled propellers, the most notable feature of the wreck is the large propeller and rudder. The dynamite job has opened large holes in her hull in addition to the tear suffered in the collision. The bottom of the overturned hull has collapsed into the vessel like a large slide at either end. This leaves holes that access her interior. There is a tear at the port stern.

Caution should be exercised at this site due to the temptation to penetrate the wreck. Wreck penetration should only be attempted by divers with the proper specialized training and equipment.

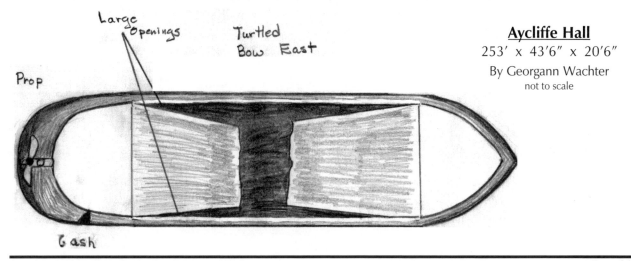

Aycliffe Hall
253' x 43'6" x 20'6"
By Georgann Wachter
not to scale

BARGE 43

Official #: 172728   **Site #:** 2

Location: 300°T 0.2 miles off Buffalo, New York's east harbor entrance, inside western-most breakwater

Coordinates: Loran: 44933.3 59237.9   **DGPS:** 42 52.430 78 54.100

Lies: broken   **Depth:** 30 feet

Type: steel barge   **Cargo:** scrap wood timbers

Power: towed

Owner(s) Great Lakes Dredge and Dock Company of Duluth, Minnesota

Built: 1911 at Manitowoc, Wisconsin

Dimensions: 150' x 36' x 12.1'   **Tonnage:** 546

Date of Loss: Wednesday, May 24, 1961

Cause of Loss: sprung a leak

Barge 43

Lower Lakes Marine Historical Society

Story of the Loss:

Barge 43 was working on Buffalo Harbor improvements recommended by the Army Corps of Engineers. As part of these improvements, the north entrance of the harbor was relocated by creating a 1,100 foot opening in the old breakwater. This required removing the wood cribs used in constructing the breakwater. To dispose of the millions of board feet of scrap timber, *Barge 43* was used as a burning scow. The crib lumber would be loaded on her and then set on fire.

On May 24, 1961, the scow was observed to be leaking. Her pumps were started and the barge was towed to a mooring outside the main breakwater, near the new west breakwater. The idea was to lighten her by setting her load of timbers on fire. Unfortunately, before her load could be torched she rolled and sank.

The following day, an attempt to raise the barge only succeeded in righting the overturned vessel on the bottom. The derrick on the salvage vessel failed when they tried to lift *Barge 43* and no further efforts were made to raise her.

The Wreck Today:

Care should be taken because of the heavy boat traffic in this area and the occasional presence of a strong current. The barge sits mostly intact with 15 to 20 feet of water over her shallowest section. A large number of fish make their home on the wreck. A diver can enter the barge through any of several holes topside. Remember that shipwreck penetration should only be attempted by experienced divers with proper training and equipment.

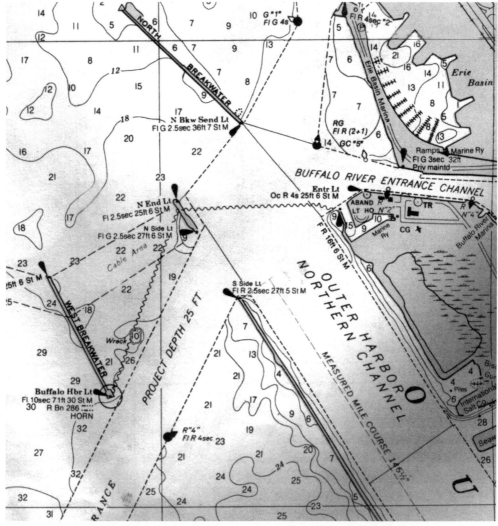

Barge 43 lies slightly to the north of the wreck indicated on the Buffalo Harbor Charts.

BARGE F

Official #:   **Site #:**   G

Location: 333°T 11.7 miles off Barcelona, New York

Coordinates: Loran: 44603.5 58760.5   **GPS:**   42 30.11   79 42.00

Lies: bow north   **Depth:**   145 feet

Type: schooner barge   **Cargo:**   coal

Power: towed

Owner(s)

Built:

Dimensions: approximately 135' x 30'   **Tonnage:**

Date of Loss: unknown

Cause of Loss: unknown

Story of the Loss:

Unknown.

The Wreck Today:

This yet to be identified barge rises eight to ten feet off the bottom. Her rudder is hard to port. As the diver drifts over her rounded and sharply undercut stern, a beautiful ship's wheel becomes visible. Forward of this is a deck opening, and then a pump and capstan.

Five large hatches dominate the mid section of the ship. However, heavy layers of silt inside come to within one or two feet of the ship's deck. On each side of the barge are sets of bollards. Moving forward, the diver discovers a large windlass, another two handed pump, and a tow bit at the blunt bow.

Looking to the starboard bow one finds a fluted, wood stock anchor. This is matched on the port bow by another anchor resting near the winch. There is no railing. However, the gunnel is about a foot above the deck.

Although there are no masts on the vessel, an examination of the sides of the boat finds turnbuckles. This suggests that *Barge F* once had masts. Additional investigation finds metal rings across from each hatch, probably used as part of a system for tying the hatch covers down. The capstan cover is in place, and it reads "J.W. Henry, Quebec and Lawrence Foundry".

As with many wrecks at this depth, lots of burbot make this vessel their home.

Thanks to Niagrara Divers Association, there is a permanent mooring at the bow on the windlass.

Expect bottom temperatures below 45° even in mid summer.

C.B. Benson

Official #:	125226	**Site #:**	21

Location: 175°T 6.2 miles off Port Colborne, Ontario's harbor entrance

Coordinates:	Loran:	**DGPS:**	42 46.259 79 14.609
Lies:	bow east	**Depth:**	86 feet
Type:	barquentine, 3 masts	**Cargo:**	coal
Power:	sail		

Owner(s) E.H. Norton of Toledo, Ohio, A. Andrews of Toledo, Ohio, and John Duff of Port Clinton, Ohio

Built: 1873 at Port Clinton, Ohio by John Duff

Dimensions: 136'5" x 26' x 13'   **Tonnage:** 299 gross 284 net

Date of Loss: Saturday, October 14, 1893

Cause of Loss: storm

C.B. Benson
Buffalo and Erie County Historical Society, Buffalo, NY

Story of the Loss:

The *C.B. Benson* was built specifically to demonstrate the viability of direct bulk trade from the Great Lakes to Europe. Having heavier timbers, a greater sheer, and barquentine rigging designed for the ocean passage, she differed only slightly from normal Great Lakes sailing ships of her time. Launched in 1873, she left Toledo, Ohio in May 1874 loaded with 23,600 bushels of corn destined for Cork, Ireland. Her history-making trip started out well enough as she crossed Lake Erie without incident. However, as she entered Port Colborne and the Welland Canal, the *Benson* ran aground. Undeterred, Captain Duff had his vessel pulled off and continued on his way to Montreal. On arrival in that fair city, insurance inspectors refused to accept the *Benson's* center-board design and cancelled her insurance. Fortunately, Duff was able to find other carriers to insure the vessel, and entered the Atlantic Ocean en route to Cork, Ireland. The ship encountered storms off New Brunswick, and false reports of her loss at sea spread through the Great Lakes shipping community. She finally arrived safely in Cork on July 15, 1874. Cable dispatches electrified the produce exchanges upon her successful voyage.

Having opened the way for direct bulk cargos from Lake Erie to Europe, the staunch craft spent several

C.B. Benson

Post card written by John Duff before the Benson's last sailing.

years trading between the British Isles and South America before returning permanently to the Great Lakes in 1880.

Defying superstitions surrounding sailing on a Friday and the number 13, the *Benson* left Buffalo, New York and loaded coal in Erie, Pennsylvania on Friday, October 13, 1893. While in Erie, John Duff wrote two postcards to his wife. In the second card, he expressed doubt about the advisability of leaving, as the weather did not look good. Unfortunately, Captain Duff chose to put out to sea despite the weather. Sailing from Erie, her destination was Detroit, Michigan. A huge storm swept Lake Erie on October 14. Several ships, including the steamer *Dean Richmond* and schooner *Riverside* were lost or driven ashore in this storm.   Two days later, masts were reported sticking out of the water off Gravelly Bay. First believed to be the schooner *F.C. Leighton* the truth was learned only after the *Leighton* made her way to the Detroit River.

The masts belonged to the *C.B. Benson*. Having taken all that the Atlantic Ocean could throw at her, the *Benson* was overcome by the unpredictable seas of Lake Erie. She took Captain Duff, his son, mate Curtis Duff, the cook and five sailors with her. Only the fact that Mrs. Curtis Duff was pregnant had prevented her from being on this final voyage and joining her husband in his watery grave.

Having sunk on October 14, 1893, the *Benson* became the first of three ships owned by the same company that would meet their fate on October 14. The *Kate Winslow* sank in Lake Huron on October 14, 1897 and the *Nellie Duff* was lost off Lorain, Ohio on October 14, 1895.

The Wreck Today:

The *C.B. Benson* sits upright in 86 feet of water. She is very well preserved. Her wheel sits beside the rudderpost at the stern waiting the steady hand of a new wheelsman. Empty yawl boat davits reach aft of her stern. The bilge pumps look ready to be worked and the belaying pins are in the fife rail surrounding the remains of a mast. Deadeyes, blocks and booms are clearly in evidence and her cargo holds are full of coal.

One anchor off the C.B. Benson is on display in Avon Lake, Ohio.

One of her two anchors is gone. It was removed prior to her sinking and can be found in front of a lakefront home in Avon Lake, Ohio. Descendants of the Duff family reside in Avon Lake and in addition to the anchor have other memorabilia from the glory days of the *C.B. Benson*.

This site has mooring blocks at both the bow and stern.

Pictures from left to right are: Georgann Wachter at the ship's wheel, the broken main mast, complete with fife rail, the capstain, and one of her two pumps. Video captures by Mike Wachter.

C.B. Benson
136.5' x 26' x 13'
By Georgann Wachter
not to scale

In 2002, twelve members of the Duff family , accompanied by members of Niagara Divers Association, held a reunion above the remains of their great-grandfather's ship. The authors were privileged to dive with two direct descendants of Captain John Duff and First Mate Curtis Duff. Named for their ancestors, John Duff and Curtis Duff Paine descended into their family history to observe and touch the vessel built and sailed by their great-great grandfather. Ten other members of the Duff family waited on board the *Charlie E* until the divers surfaced with vivid descriptions of their journey. For the first time in almost 110 years, members of the Duff family had once again roamed the decks of the *C. B. Benson*.

Curtis & John (lower left) share a moment together before their dive. Photo by Bill Duff.

BISHOP'S DERRICK

Official #:   none   **Site #:**   14

Location: 47°T 13.9 miles off Dunkirk, New York Harbor entrance

Coordinates: Loran: 44780.3 59077.1   DGPS: 42 37.76   79 08.56

Lies: see drawing   **Depth:**   55 feet

Type: wooden salvage barge   **Cargo:**   none

Power: towed

Owner(s)   Bishop

Built: 1853 at Buffalo by Bishop

Dimensions: 150' x 25'   **Tonnage:** approximately 300

Date of Loss: Saturday, September 24, 1853

Cause of Loss: foundered in gale

Story of the Loss:

Bishop's Derrick was built for the express purpose of aiding in the salvage of the steamers *Erie* and *Atlantic*. The *Erie* was lost by fire on Monday, August 9, 1841. The *Atlantic* sank in a collision on Friday, August 20, 1852. *Bishop's Derrick* was on her maiden assignment when she was lost.

The steamer *Empire* had traveled from Buffalo Harbor to Grand River to pick up *Bishop's Derrick* and take her to the site of the *Erie*. Lying just off Silver Creek, the *Erie* was considered to be prime for salvage operations because of stories of the immigrants aboard her carrying gold. Intending to raise the ship, Bishop and his aids had placed chains under the *Erie*. The derrick was positioned over the site and made ready for the salvage effort. As they completed this task, a strong gale built across the lake and continued with howling winds throughout the day. The strength of the gale threatened the new derrick and she was lashed between the vessels *Madison* and *Lexington* to provide additional stability.

As night fell, the gale continued to pound away at the small fleet of ships over the salvage site. By the time the crew working the site decided to leave, the waves were too powerful for them to raise anchors. Their only option was to ride it out. Through most of the night, the little fleet held its own. Then, at 4:00 in the morning, calamity struck. The trussels, which had strapped the derrick to the *Lexington*, gave way. As the derrick began to list, her hull rapidly filled with water, drawing *Bishop's Derrick* and the *Lexington* down together. The derrick came to rest on the bottom of Lake Erie approximately a half mile from the site of the *Erie*.

Five men working on the site clung to the sides of a small boat and were picked up by the steamer *Empire*. Several others took to a sailboat, arriving in Buffalo shortly after sunrise. One horse went down with the ship. Among the survivors was famed submarine diver, John Green. Green had assisted in the design and building of the derrick and was working aboard her when she went down.

The Wreck Today:

When she was first found, there were huge blocks and a large wood stock anchor among the wreckage of *Bishop's Derrick*. Today, the anchor and most of the blocks are missing. Off to the side of the wreck is a pony boiler and several sections of planking.

The drawings below are from the Remick Collection and were done by some of the divers who first dove the site in August of 1980.

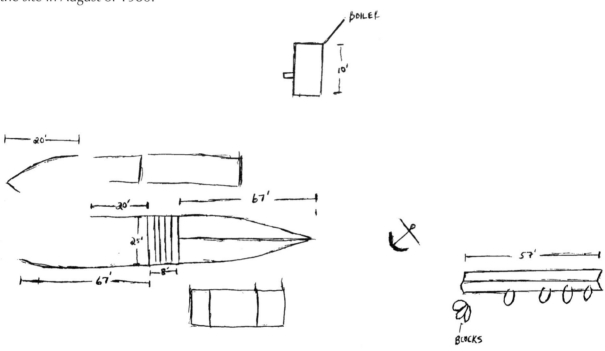

Their correspondence illuminates the mindset of the shipwreck searcher.

8/26/80

Unfortunately, a good portion of the wreck is buried in mud several feet thick. ... We will have to do a lot of digging if we expect to get much from her. ... We did get a few brass valves. If you want, we'll try and raise one of the pulleys for you. They're tough to get because you have to cut through 1½" steel shackles. We got one better than half done.

Jeff and I concentrated our main effort on raising the anchor. We got four 55 gallon drums and all our inner tubes, but she didn't budge.

John J. Boland, Jr. #1

Official #: 149467   **Site #:** 33

Location: 291°T 7.3 miles off Barcelona, New York

Coordinates: Loran: 44545.5 58721.1   **DGPS:** 42 22.794 79 43.929

Lies: bow west   **Depth:** 135 feet

Type: bulk freighter "canaler"   **Cargo:** coal

Power: triple expansion steam engine, cylinder and stroke: 15"-25"-40"x33"

Owner(s) Sarnia Steamships, Limited, Saint Catherines, Ontario

Built: 1928 by Wallsend-on-Tyne in New Castle, England

Dimensions: 252'9" x 43'4" x 17'8"   **Tonnage:** 1939 gross, 1149 net

Date of Loss: Wednesday, October 5, 1932

Cause of Loss: foundered in storm

John J. Boland, Jr.

The Great Lakes Historical Society, Bowen Collection

Story of the Loss:

She was a "canaler", one of many boats built to traverse the small locks of the Saint Lawrence Canals before the advent of the Saint Lawrence Seaway. Sailing in her fifth season, the Boland had brought pulpwood from Montreal, Quebec to Erie, Pennsylvania and had taken on a load of coal at Erie to carry across the lake to Hamilton, Ontario. As was the custom of the time, her holds were filled to overflowing with coal, which continued above the hatches onto the decks until the ship had reached her maximum draft. As the run across the lake to the Welland Canal was a short one, no hatch covers or tarps were fastened to the load.

She cleared Erie by 3:30 am encountering a strong southwest wind from the start of the voyage. She was running to the northeast, making her way to Hamilton, Ontario. As the trip took her further from the protective south shore, the seas grew and began to wash over the decks and open hatches of the *Boland*. Soon, the coal piled on the decks was washed to sea and the crew struggled to stretch tarpaulins over the open holds and passageways. Recognizing his ship was in peril, Captain E.C. Hawman tried to bring his ship around and head for the protective lee of the American shores. His ship would not respond. Being battered by the waves with her rudder not responding, the *Boland* was helpless in the heavy seas. Within 4 minutes she would be gone.

So sudden was her loss that most of the crew had no time to lower lifeboats, choosing instead to leap to the foaming waters. Four crewmen were able to partially lower one boat, but this was capsized as the *Boland* sank. Fortunately it was torn from its moorings and the seamen were able to crawl aboard and save many of their mates. Four, who were below decks when the *Boland* foundered, were not found. Having climbed or been dragged aboard the lifeboat, 15 survivors searched the petulant seas above the *Boland* in vain. Finally giving up the search, the survivors rowed for six hours to reach the shore 11 miles to the south. On landing the boat they were confronted with insurmountable cliffs. Exhausted and battered, they walked the boat another mile along the rocky shore before finding a bank they could climb.

Following the investigation of this loss, Captain Hawman lost his command for a year. More importantly, the practice of overfilling the holds so hatches could not be closed was abandoned by the steamship companies.

The Wreck Today:

The depth, occasional strong current, and the temptation to enter the wreck make this an advanced dive.

This site is an incredible example of a depression era steel canaler. Lying on her starboard side, the wreck rises forty feet off the bottom. Often, a tie in line is attached to her rudder. As you descend the line, you first encounter her large four bladed prop and rudder. Proceeding toward the bow, her aft cabin structure is partially intact, ladders, deck gear, railings, portholes and the pilothouse can all be examined without penetrating the wreck.

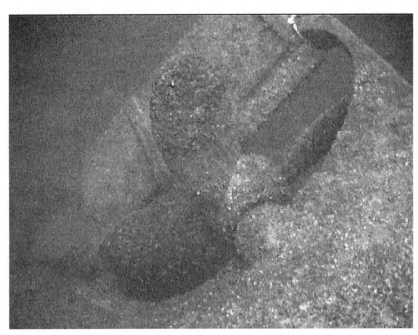

Boland propeller. Photo by Mike Wachter

Her holds invite the diver to enter the wreck. Don't be drawn into penetrating the wreck without proper training and equipment. While she looks inviting, loose cables, aging structures and silt all pose potential life-threatening hazards on any wreck penetration.

BRITON

Official #: 3493   **Site #:** 10

Location: ¼ mile southwest of Point Abino Light, Ontario, Canada

Coordinates: Loran: **DGPS:** 42 49.932   79 06.013

Lies: bow west   **Depth:** 20 feet

Type: steel freighter   **Cargo:** wheat and flax

Power: triple expansion steam engine

Owner(s) Buckeye Steamship Company of Cleveland, Ohio

Built: 1891 at Cleveland, Ohio by Globe Iron Works

Dimensions: 296' x 40' x 24'   **Tonnage:** 2434 gross   1875 net

Date of Loss: Wednesday, November 13, 1929

Cause of Loss: ran aground

Briton

Great Lakes Historical Society

Story of the Loss:

Captain Johnson was in command of a crew of 27 on his first Great Lakes trip as a captain. They had left Buffalo, New York and were headed for Port Arthur, Ontario with a full load of grain. Shortly after leaving Buffalo Harbor, an aging ship, a stormy sea, and a fog horn not working came together to spell the end of the steel freighter *Briton*. She had plied the lakes for 38 years before the brand new master ran her aground on the rocks of Point Abino.

The *Briton* was battling strong winds and heavy seas as she made her final voyage. The crew could not have heard the warning horn from the lighthouse, it was not working. Nevertheless, her captain must have been mortified when he found his ship had come aground on the shallow shoals only 12 miles out of Buffalo. A call for help brought four tugs from the Hand and Johnson Company to attempt her rescue. With the tugs assistance, the crew fought to free her and struggled to keep her afloat against the pounding torrent of the waves. The battle raged for two days before the seas proclaimed their victory as the aging seams of the steel freighter finally gave way to the continual battering of the waves. As water flowed in through the hemorrhaging seams, the vessel shifted and swung on the shoals. This rendered even larger openings and the water level rapidly overwhelmed the boiler and engine. Forced to surrender their ship to the sea, the crew was rescued by a Buffalo Coast Guard cutter at 11:00 a.m. Friday, November 15, 1929. The *Rescue* was dispatched from Cleveland to salvage her cargo, but arrived too late to recover all but 20,000 bushels of grain.

The Wreck Today:

The *Briton* was dynamited a few years after her loss. Combined with years of storm and ice damage, the demolition has left the *Briton's* remains broadly scattered a quarter mile southwest of the Point Abino Lighthouse. Fish find this to be an excellent habitat. On a calm day the shallow wreckage can be seen from the surface. You can also see the huge boulders that form part of the shoals on which the *Briton* went aground.

CAUTION: Many of the boulders in this area are very near the surface. Don't let your dive boat join the bones of the *Briton*. We don't need a new dive site that badly.

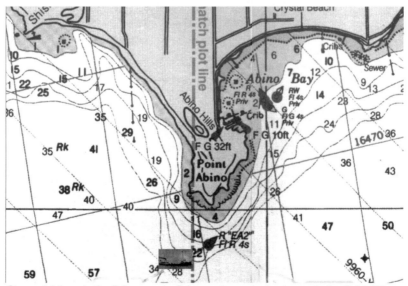

Shore sightings to the Briton require lining up the arched entrance to the Point Abino Light with the edge of the trees behind the light and lining up the chimney of the last house west of Point Abino with the slender tree behind the small shed near shore.

BROWN BROTHERS

Official #:   133792   **Site #:**   40

Location: 313°T 28.8 miles off Barcelona, New York   18°T 5.7 miles off Long Point Light

Coordinates: Loran: 44583.8 58618.1   **DGPS:**   42 37.647 80 00.912

Lies: bow northeast   **Depth:**   120 feet

Type: wood fish tug   **Cargo:**   light

Power: diesel

Owner(s)   Harry Gambel of Port Dover, Ontario

Built: 1915 at Port Stanley, Ontario by Thomas Thurstin

Dimensions: 75'2" x 16'5" x 7'7"   **Tonnage:** 64 gross 44 registered

Date of Loss: Wednesday, October 28, 1959

Cause of Loss: foundered in storm

Brown Brothers

Great Lakes Historical Society

Story of the Loss:

She was built as a steam powered tug designed to fish the waters off Long Point. She did this job well for 44 years, three owners, two names, and two power sources. After the first 31 years she was sold to Thomas Ivey and Sons. They renamed her *Iveyrose* and fished the boat for four years. By 1950, her steam engine was in need of replacement and she was converted to diesel. That same year she took back her original name, *Brown Brothers*, under the ownership of Harry Gambel. To supplement her fishing income, she is rumored to have been used as a "rum runner" during prohibition.

By 1959 the tug had been left to rot on the river bank in Port Dover. Then, on October 28, 1959, the aging wood tug was under tow of the tug *Luke* off Long Point. En route to Port Burwell, Ontario, they were caught in a violent storm. Perhaps the worst place one could possibly be in a Lake Erie storm is off the point. Rising storm seas wash off the point and join to form rogue waves twice the height of the prevailing sea. As the wave heights build, they come from many different directions, creating impossible conditions for a vessel caught in their fury. This proved to be more than the 44 year old fish tug could handle. She took on water that overwhelmed her and sent her to the bottom. Fortunately, no lives were lost in this incident. Then again, local fishermen laugh off the storm story and tell us that the *Brown Brothers* was deliberately cut loose and scuttled!

Wheel of the Brown Brothers. Photo by Tom Wilson.

The Wreck Today:

Also known as the *22 Fathom Wreck*, the *Brown Brothers* sits upright with a slight list to starboard. Her wheel lies in the wreck, toward the bow, against the port gunnel. A fish net trails off the bow post. Much of this tug is intact and she is home to fresh water ling cod (lawyer fish).

Because of her depth and location, this is considered an advanced dive. She lies in 120 feet of water, the maximum depth recognized by most certifying agencies for open water sport divers.

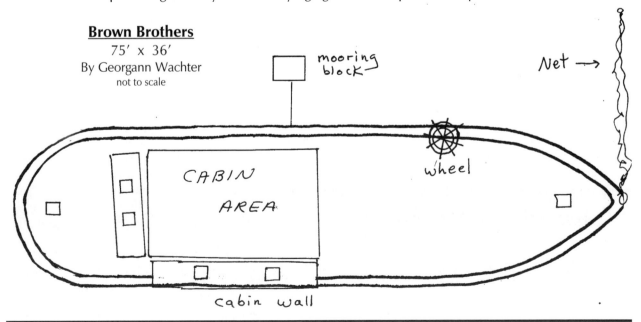

Brown Brothers
75' x 36'
By Georgann Wachter
not to scale

BRUNSWICK

Official #:	3148	**Site #:**	24

Location: 334°T 7.5 miles off Dunkirk, New York harbor entrance

Coordinates:	Loran: 44706.8 58931.0	DGPS:	42 35.465 79 24.546
Lies:	bow northeast	**Depth:**	100 feet
Type:	four masted iron propeller	**Cargo:**	anthracite coal
Power:	steam		

Owner(s) Charles Bewick of Detroit, Michigan

Built: 1881 in Wyandotte, Michigan by the Detroit Dry Dock Company

Dimensions:	235' x 35'6" x 15'6"	**Tonnage:**	1120 gross

Date of Loss: Saturday, November 12, 1881

Cause of Loss: collision with the schooner Carlingford

Brunswick

Remick Collection

Story of the Loss:

First enrolled at Detroit, Michigan on June 11, 1881, the *Brunswick* was on her second voyage when she sank a scant five months later. The trip began with the *Brunswick* leaving Buffalo at 10:00 on Friday night loaded with fifteen hundred tons of hard coal for Duluth, Minnesota. It ended with a run for Dunkirk, New York as the sinking steamer tried desperately to reach shore.

As Captain Chamberlain stood watch in the wheelhouse, the *Brunswick* departed Buffalo with a light snow falling. By eleven o'clock the skies were clear with a light south by southeast wind. Toward midnight, the captain turned the watch over to first mate John Frazer. As he walked the decks to the stern dinning room, Chamberlain could see the lights of Dunkirk twelve miles to the south.

Having satisfied his hunger, the captain settled down by the stove for a smoke in the comforting glow of the ship's brass kerosene lamps. As Captain Chamberlain enjoyed his smoke, First Mate Frazer was working to maneuver the ship around the approaching schooner, *Carlingford*. On a west by southwest course, the *Brunswick* had observed the green light of the *Carlingford* on a northeast by east course. The mate ordered "Starboard your wheel, we'll go under her stern." Some time later, the wheelsman called out, "Mr. Frazer, a schooner is coming in stays." "Port your wheel then," ordered the mate. However, on looking at the schooner through his glass, he ordered "No, keep her starboard; we haven't time to port." Immediately after this command, the *Brunswick* struck the *Carlingford* on her port bow. The combination of observing her green light and striking her toward the bow on the port side indicates the *Carlingford* had luffed her sails directly in front of the oncoming *Brunswick.*

Upon feeling the jolt of the collision, Captain Chamberlain rushed forward to see that the schooner was sinking and her crew was taking to the yawl boats. Learning from the second mate that the *Brunswick* was also taking water, Chamberlain headed his vessel for shore in an effort to save her. Forty-five minutes later, heavy with water, her furnaces went out. The vessel was adrift without power and listing dangerously.

The crew of fifteen launched two boats. On launching his boat, chief engineer Francomb lost his footing, fell into the lake, and was drowned. In the other boat the captain and his crew failed to cut the yawl's bow lose from the steamer and the yawl was dragged down with her, carrying the cook and her daughter to their deaths. The captain and remaining men from his yawl were picked up by the second yawl boat and taken safely to shore. Three lives had been lost in just a few short minutes.

The Wreck Today:

Resting upright in 100 feet of water the top of her boiler and forward decks are reached at roughly 85 feet. Her cargo of hard coal is scattered about the wreck. On her bow you can see her anchors still in place and the hole in her starboard side that sunk her. While all four masts are broken off, a portion of the foremast still remains. Some penetration is possible, but proper equipment and training are necessary. Toward her stern, her boiler and engine are remarkably intact and make an interesting study for the visiting diver. This extraordinary shipwreck has both capstans and her windlass still in place.

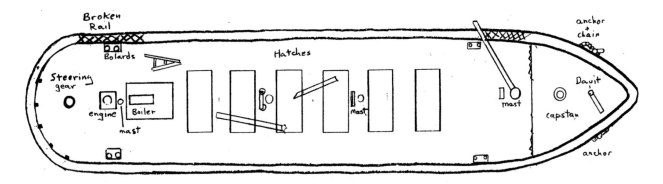

Brunswick
235' x 35'6" x 15'6"
By Georgann Wachter
not to scale

CANADAWAY CREEK

Location: 2 miles west of Dunkirk, New York

Site #: 26

Coordinates: Propeller: 42 28.741 79 22.481   Rudder   42 28.769 79 22.580

Water Intake: 42 29.861 79 21.258   **Depth:** 20-25 feet

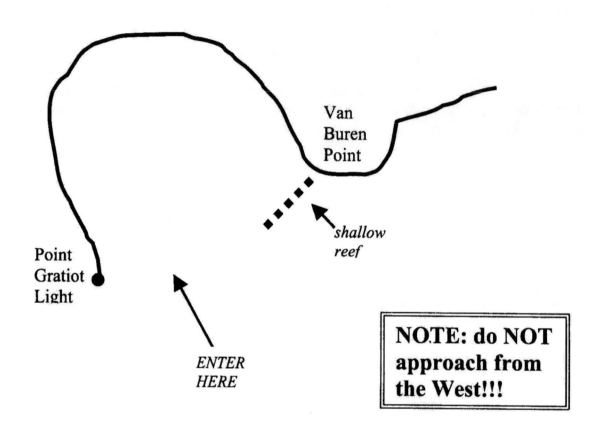

Canadaway Creek

Drawing from Annette Soule

The Wreck Today:

Charter Captain Jim Herbert rates this as a fun dive. The old bed of Canadaway Creek has been flooded and a dive in this area reveals many interesting formations, old tree stumps, and a couple of man made structures. You'll find a propeller and rudders as well as a water intake. These ship parts may be from the *Golden Fleece* or the unidentified tug salvaged by Tom Reed. See page 92 for information on the *Golden Fleece* and on Tom Reid's salvage.

Pay attention to your charts. There is a shallow reef off Van Buren Point.

Point Gratiot Light viewed from land.
Photo by Georgann Wachter

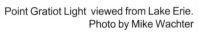

Point Gratiot Light viewed from Lake Erie.
Photo by Mike Wachter

CANOBIE

Official #: C-133826   **Site #:** 61

Location: 70°T 3.0 miles off Erie, Pennsylvania harbor entrance

Coordinates: Loran: 44394.8 58533.9   **DGPS:** 42 10.326 80 00.903

Lies: bow northwest   **Depth:** 15 feet

Type: wood propeller   **Cargo:** none

Power: fore and aft compound engine

Owner(s) Lehigh Coal Company. Ltd.

Built: 1887 at Detroit, Michigan by Detroit Dry Dock Company

Dimensions: 259'3" x 37'4" x 19'8"   **Tonnage:** 1748 gross 1051 net

Date of Loss: Tuesday, November 1, 1921

Cause of Loss: scuttled after storm

Canobie (as Iron King)

Great Lakes Historical Society

Story of the Loss:

Built as the *Iron King*, official number 100412, the *Canobie* sailed under United States registry from 1887 to 1913. She became a Canadian registered vessel in 1913 under the name *Canobie* and Canadian official number C 133826.

After 34 years of service, the *Canobie* was clearly showing her age as she set sail for her final voyage on a blustery fall day in 1921. Her old oak timbers peered through the flaking paint on her sides, and the boat was considered to be difficult to handle due to her dilapidated condition.

As she made the lake crossing on November 1, 1921, a severe storm lashed the lake from the southwest. In this storm, the barge *Thomas Quale* was sunk in Maumee Bay when 40 mile an hour winds pushed her into a crib. The *Canobie* was caught in the open lake and barely made it to Erie, Pennsylvania. She may have been stubborn to handle, but she was also too stubborn to sink. Battered and bruised, this seasoned old war horse was able to limp into Erie under her own power.

Unfortunately, the damage of the storm was too much to repair on a vessel as broken down as the *Canobie*. Her owners stripped her of anything of value and then towed her two miles east of Erie. There she was burned and scuttled.

The Wreck Today:

The huge timbers, engine mounts, and a large propeller of the *Canobie* can be found next to a buoy marking the site.

Lying on a sand and rock bottom, this site is home to numerous fish and occasional fresh water sponges. As she is in only 15 feet of water, both scuba divers and snorkelers can easily enjoy the wreck.

The boiler is a few kicks off the stern and rises close enough to the surface to be a hazard to boat propellers.

Line drawing of the *Canobie*.

CARLINGFORD

Official #: 125024   **Site #:** 31

Location: 329°T 13 miles off Dunkirk, New York harbor entrance

Coordinates: Loran: 44715.7 58905.6   DGPS: 42 39.266 79 28.616

Lies: bow west   **Depth:** 95 feet

Type: three masted schooner   **Cargo:** wheat

Power: sail

Owner(s) John W. Wickham, Captain Oscar B. Smith, Huron, Ohio.

Built: 1869 at Port Huron, Michigan by Fitzgerald

Dimensions: 154.58' x 31.08' x 12.25'   **Tonnage:** 470.40 gross

Date of Loss: Saturday, November 12, 1881

Cause of Loss: collision with the steamer *Brunswick*

Carlingford

Great Lakes Historical Society

Story of the Loss:

It was a seasoned vessel of fourteen years and an experienced crew that braved the 1,000 mile November passage from Duluth, Minnesota to Buffalo, New York. The captain and crew had great faith in the vessels seaworthiness.

Brim full of wheat and battened down well for the long voyage ahead, the *Carlingford* left Duluth before dawn on a cool, crisp morning in early November. Encountering mild weather all the way, the wind filled her sails with a soft breeze through Lakes Superior, Huron, and Saint Clair. The Detroit River carried her into Lake Erie where her trip continued uneventfully and her precious cargo remained dry.

As night fell the evening of November 12, a light snow began falling, but passed quickly as the visibility cleared sufficiently for skipper and crew to see the lights of Dunkirk, New York twelve miles to the south. Knowing Buffalo was only and hour or so away a sense of relief settled over the crew as she held her northeast by east course. Lady luck had been their lookout on this November passage.

Georgann Wachter examines the Carlingford's bow.
Photo by Mike Wachter

The Steamer *Brunswick,* under command of Captain Chaimberlain, was approaching from the east on a west by southwest course. This would bring her under the *Carlingford's* stern if both vessels held course. Not seeing the streamer, the *Carlingford* executed a tacking maneuver as she crossed the bow of the other vessel. With no time to react, the *Brunswick* rammed the *Carlingford* at the bow on the port side allowing water to pour in through a huge hole.

It was just past midnight and confusion reigned aboard the *Carlingford*. All sleeping members of the crew were awakened and they scurried to the small boat for safety. One crewman chose to return to his bunk as the yawl boat pulled away. He was last seen at the forecastle as the *Carlingford* plunged bow first into 100 feet of water.

The Wreck Today:

A pristine example of mid 18th century schooner construction, the *Carlingford* sits with her masts down in 100 feet of water. The gapping hole that sunk her is clearly visible on her port bow. Other than her masts being down and the hole in her port side, this vessel looks much as she did the day she went down. She is perfectly upright with deck gear in place. This includes her windlass, capstan, and rigging winch as well as the fife rails and belaying pins. Her cabins are blown off. With proper training and equipment, penetrating below decks is easy and visibility inside is incredible. This is conceivably the best study in early schooner construction we have ever dove.

Carlingford's capstan
Photo by Mike Wachter

CAROL SUE II

Official #: 225327   **Site #:** 1

Location: 11 ½ miles northeast of Conneaut, Ohio

Coordinates: Loran: 44277.7 58273.8   **DGPS:** 42 07.644 80 28.945

Lies: bow north   **Depth:** 80 feet

Type: wooden fishing trawler   **Cargo:** light

Power: 150 HP diesel engine

Owner(s) John Fresch of Sandusky, Ohio and Randy Francis of Virginia

Built: 1926 at Deltaville, Virginia

Dimensions: 63' x 14.5' x 4.6'   **Tonnage:** 24 gross   16 net

Date of Loss: Monday, October 11, 1999

Cause of Loss: leak

Carol Sue II

Photo courtesy Jim Wilson

Story of the Loss:

The *Carol Sue II* was first named *Olive Virginia*, and hailed from that southern state. As the *Olive Virginia*, she was a working "buy" boat on the Chesapeake Bay. She would haul out to sailing vessels on the bay and bring their catch of clams or crabs to market. She also worked carrying corn and tobacco. At some point, her length was increased from 54'6" to 63 feet.

In 1993, her last owners converted her from a crab dredge to a cruise boat. The cargo hold was converted to a live-aboard cabin and a head and shower were installed. She was not profitable as a cruise boat, so the *Carol Sue II* was used as a private pleasure craft.

On Sunday, October 10, she and her three man crew left Sandusky, Ohio bound for Norfolk, Virginia and her other owner. At 4:00 a.m., Jim Wilson took over the helm in 20 knot northerly winds and four to six foot waves. At 7:00 a.m., Jim noticed two engine gauges had failed, and he awoke Captain John Fresch and Chuck Coykendale. John checked the engine room and found it filled with water. At 7:09 a.m., the bulk carrier *Richard Reiss* received *Carol Sue II's* MAYDAY call and GPS coordinates, and contacted the United States Coast Guard Stations in Erie, Pennsylvania and Ashtabula, Ohio.

Within five minutes the *Carol Sue II* went down, and the men leaped off the bow into the 60 degree water. All were wearing life jackets and clung to the cabin, which had broken free of the vessel and provided a makeshift life raft. Guided by the *Richard Reiss*, Coast Guard Erie found the three men clinging to the radar and light stanchions on the cabin roof. The men had been in the four foot waves and cold water over an hour and Coykendale was briefly treated for hypothermia.

The Wreck Today:

Fortunately, the day we searched for the *Carol Sue II* was flat calm. Otherwise, we may not have noticed her slight rise off the hard pack mud bottom. She has a rounded stern with her name and hailing port (Wilmington, Delaware) painted in blue and white. Part of the cabin walls are present and two portholes are still intact. There are two small pulleys at her stern, some tools, and life jackets are scattered about. The tall helm seat lays beside the port rail. Lakeshore Towing of Erie, Pennsylvania removed her diesel fuel and salvaged part of her mast. The salvaged mast was taken to Erie, and the remaining part lies along her narrow starboard bow.

Recent divers tell us she has settled deeper into the mud and may soon be completely covered over.

One of Carol Sue II's Portholes.
Photo by Georgann Wachter.

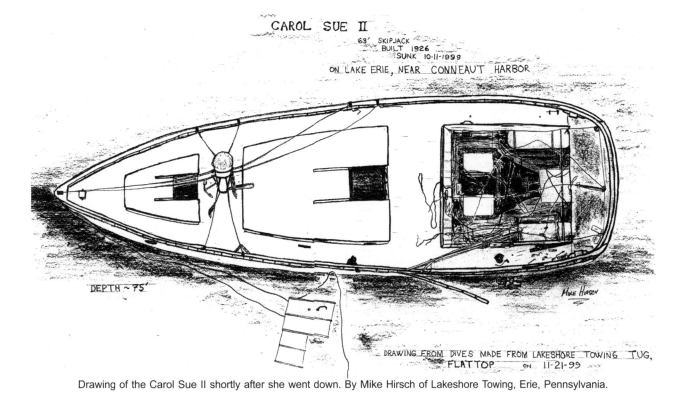

Drawing of the Carol Sue II shortly after she went down. By Mike Hirsch of Lakeshore Towing, Erie, Pennsylvania.

Cecil J

Official #:	170676		**Site #:**	70
Location:	2 miles southwest of Port Dover, Ontario			
Coordinates:	Loran: 44589.3 58529.9		**DGPS:**	42 45.785 80 13.688
Lies:	scattered		**Depth:**	17 feet
Type:	tug		**Cargo:**	none
Power:	gasoline engine			
Owner(s)	William and Cecil Martin of Port Dover, Ontario			
Built:	1915 at Erie, Pennsylvania. Rebuilt 1929 at Port Dover, Ontario by George Gamble			
Dimensions:	47'5" x 12.5' x 3'9"		**Tonnage:**	14 gross 9 net
Date of Loss:	1943			
Cause of Loss:	burned and scuttled			

Cecil J

Remick Collection

Story of the Loss:

She was built with steam power and named *Rambler* by her American owners. At 47 feet, she was small in comparison to the fish tugs of her day. But, she made a name for herself as a "fine little tug." After 12 years of service on the south shore, she was sold to Canadian interests who renamed her *Eureka K*. and moved her to Port Dover, Ontario.

Befitting the superstition that forbade changing the name of a boat, her history from that point is full of misfortune, accidents, and sinkings.   She sank in Port Maitland Harbor after encountering heavy seas rounding the breakwater and dashing back to port. Her owners raised her, repowered her with a diesel engine, added steel ribs to her wooden structure and returned her to service in 1929. She had periodic engine trouble and on occasion stranded her crew in mid-lake. Then she was involved in a collision with the tug *Clara B* and, with a gaping hole in her side, barely made it back to Port Dover. That winter, she laid up at Erieau, Ontario only to sink at the dock when the ice thawed in the spring. Her frustrated owners sold her and the new owners refloated her and towed her back to Port Dover.

Now named the *Cecil M*, the tug continued to break down with great regularity despite installation of a new gasoline engine, strengthening the keelson with steel and rebuilding her decks. In March of 1938 the tug became trapped in ice off Long Point and tugs coming to her rescue also found themselves caught in the ice. After ten days in the ice, the ship was finally rescued. The final insult occurred when customs officials insisted the name be changed again because there was another *Cecil M* already on their books.

Renamed the *Cecil J*, misfortune continued to be her companion until, in 1942, her owners gave up on her. She was replaced by a new and larger steel tug. Considering the boat to be nothing but trouble, her owners towed her into the lake, set her afire, and scuttled her in 1943.

The Wreck Today:

This shallow water site is a popular dive for novice divers boating out of Port Dover, Ontario. Between the fire and the action of ice over the years, she is a scattered debris field. The site is a good habitat for fish and a pleasant shallow water location. Do take care not to run aground in the nearby shallows.

Top: Cecil J under tow to be scuttled. Bottom: Cecil J burning before scuttling. Photos from John Mathews, Port Dover.

O. W. Cheney

Official #:	155034	**Site #:**	8

Location: 247°T 6 miles off Buffalo, New York east harbor entrance

Coordinates:	Loran:	**DGPS:**	42 50.280 79 00.460
Lies:	scattered	**Depth:**	46 feet
Type:	wood tug	**Cargo:**	none

Power: high pressure 21" x 24" cylinder steam engine

Owner(s) Great Lakes Towing Company of Cleveland, Ohio

Built: 1881 at Buffalo, New York by Union Dry Dock Company

Dimensions:	66' x 16' x 9.8'	**Tonnage:**	46 gross

Date of Loss: Tuesday, June 23, 1903

Cause of Loss: collision with *Chemung*

O. W. Cheney

Private collection of Ralph Roberts

Story of the Loss:

The *O.W. Cheney* was made the property of the Great Lakes Towing Company when it acquired the Maytham Fleet in 1889. This acquisition was part of an extensive series of tug line purchases in an effort to form a towing monopoly. Having sold his fleet of five tow boats to Great Lakes Towing, Captain Charles Maytham then participated with others in the formation of the Independent Towing Company, a competing line. The competition between these two lines directly contributed to the loss of the *O.W. Cheney*.

The evening of June 22, 1903, light rains fell on a heavy sea as the *Cheney* and the Independent Towing Company tug *Frank S. Butler* were both stationed outside the breakwater at Buffalo, New York. The competition between the two rival towing firms was such that boats would sit outside the harbor and, on sighting an inbound vessel, race to see who would get the tow. The tow usually went to the first tow boat to arrive. Despite the rain and seas, visibility was good as the *Cheney* and the *Butler* scanned the horizon, alert for the lights of any steamer.

Near 1:30 a.m. on June 23, they spotted their quarry, the steamer *Chemung*. Both tugs raced into the lake competing for the tow. Captain John Whelan and the crew of the *Cheney* reached the *Chemung* first. At the wheel of the tug, Captain Whelan swung around to parallel the steamer's course. Either as a result of an error in seamanship or being pushed by the seas, the *Cheney* failed to come parallel to the *Chemung*. Instead, she crossed into the path of the steamer and was almost cut in two by the subsequent collision.

Two crewmen, Fireman Edward Dugan and Steward Andrew Fritzenshaf, were sleeping below. Both went down with the tug. Fireman McManus and Engineer Byers managed to free a life raft and cling to its sides. They heard Captain Whelan through the darkness. He was obviously injured and they called encouragement to him, but could not find him. By the time the steamer *Chemung* could check down to help, she was already well past the survivors and unable to be of any immediate assistance. Aboard the tug *Butler*, Captain Poor ordered a search for survivors. They saved the engineer and fireman, but after an hour of searching had found no others. Considering further search efforts to be in vain, the *Frank S. Butler* took the *Chemung* in tow to Buffalo.

Efforts to locate the tug and recover the bodies of the crewman proved futile. Her pilot and deck house floated ashore two weeks later and the following day, Fireman Dugan's body was recovered by fishermen. After that, the *Cheney* lay undiscovered for 88 years. She was finally found by sport divers in 1991.

The Wreck Today:

Today, the *Cheney* lies scattered on a rock bottom. Her stern section is all that remains of the hull. It still holds the shaft and propeller. To the north and west of this central feature is a sizable debris field. From the stern section, the boiler lies 100 feet to the southwest and her rudder lies about 100 feet to the west. The rock bottom has many 2 to 3 foot deep cracks which hold many artifacts.

CHESAPEAKE

Official #: none   **Site #:** 75

Location: 10°T 1.75 miles off the old lighthouse, Conneaut, Ohio, position approximate

Coordinates: Loran: DGPS:

Lies: widely scattered, mostly cleared   **Depth:** 40 feet

Type: wood sidewheel steamer   **Cargo:** passengers

Power: vertical beam low pressure steam, 120 nominal horsepower, 28' paddle wheels

Owner(s) Burr Higgins and Company, Sandusky, Ohio

Built: 1838 at Maumee, Ohio by David R. Stebbins

Dimensions: 172' x 24'6" x 10'2"   **Tonnage:** 412.5 gross

Date of Loss: Thursday, June 10, 1847

Cause of Loss: collision with the schooner *John A. Porter*

Chesapeake

Great Lakes Historical Society, Bowen Collection

Story of the Loss:

The *Chesapeake* was well known among the wealthier passenger trade of the 1840's. She had outstanding food and a delightful group of musicians in her band. It is rumored that Captain Waine would spend each winter in New Orleans extolling the virtues of his ship. Wealthy southern patrons filled her summer voyages and the gaming tables are said to have been piled high with gold coins. Perhaps this is merely another treasure tale, but one can imagine the revelry that preceded the chaos that occurred as the *Chesapeake* took her final voyage. Unfortunately, this one ended on the bottom of Lake Erie in 7 fathoms of water.

She had left Buffalo, New York the evening of June 9, 1847, and was sailing in company with the steamer *Constellation*. The revelers aboard had started to turn in as the boats reached Conneaut around midnight. Just off Conneaut, they encountered the downbound schooner, *John A. Porter*. The helmsman on the *Porter* had mistaken the *Chesapeake's* running lights for lights on shore. He made a turn to starboard to pass the *Constellation*, and the schooner struck the *Chesapeake* on the port bow. The *Constellation* sailed on, oblivious to the collision that had just occurred.

Believing their ship to be sinking, the crew of the *Porter* leapt to the perceived safety of the steamer. The *Chesapeake*, thinking there was no consequential damage, continued on her way upbound until Captain Waine was informed he had the crew of the *Porter* on board. He then came about to return the *Porter* crew to their schooner. As a boat was lowered, the schooner *Porter* sank before their eyes. At this same time, Captain Waine was informed by the engine room watch that the *Chesapeake* was also taking on water. All hands were ordered to the pumps and the steamer was headed toward shore. The inrushing water was so strong that it forced the crew from the engine room. This warranted awakening the passengers and putting them to work bailing.

Less than 2 miles from Conneaut, the rising waters quenched the fire in the boilers, leaving the sinking sidewheeler without power. With a freshening breeze coming from the shore, the anchors were lowered to keep the ship in place. Things did not bode well for the people aboard the *Chesapeake*. The boat was sinking quickly and the night was extremely dark. The strong southerly winds argued against any attempt to swim or float to shore. It appeared they would surely die. Captain Waine lashed his wife and other women to the crosstrees in hopes they would survive and advised all to stay with the ship until help arrived. Unfortunately, some, including the chief engineer, disregarded this advice and attempted to reach the shore. They were never seen again.

One yawl boat escaped with four women, some children, ten men and boys. After leaving, they discovered there was only one paddle on the boat. While none of the men aboard knew what to do, one young boy knew how to scull. Working an hour and a half against the strong head seas, this young man landed the yawl boat safely ashore 1½ miles above the Conneaut pier head.

As the ship sank her upper decks separated from the ship and the surviving complement took refuge on this strange raft. At that point, the steamer *Harrison* came in sight and cries for help pierced the night air. All to no avail. She passed the sunken steamer and traveled on to Conneaut, 1½ miles away. However, on arriving in Conneaut, the *Harrison's* skipper, L.B. Parker, was hailed by the young hero who had sculled the yawl boat ashore. Informed of the disaster, he immediately set out to offer assistance. They were successful in rescuing all who had stayed aboard the floating upper decks. The reported death toll ranges from 7 to 18 lives lost.

The Wreck Today:

In June of 1847 the safe of the *Chesapeake* was raised. Copper was salvaged from the wreck in July of 1855. Conneaut has enlarged its harbor and reconstructed breakwaters many times since 1847. The shipping lanes have been deepened and were all cleared for the rail trade from this port. As a result, little remains of the *Chesapeake*. Some scattered iron and railings can be found, but there is no remaining hull structure. If you find any brass spikes east of the harbor, they are probably from the *Chesapeake*.

CISCOE

Official #:	176054	**Site #:**	20
Location:	7 miles south of Port Colborne, Ontario		
Coordinates:	Loran:	**Approximate GPS:**	42 47.18 79 14.54
Lies:		**Depth:**	66 feet
Type:	tug	**Cargo:**	none
Power:	300 horsepower diesel engine		
Owner(s)	Great Lakes Marine Contracting, Ltd. of Port Dover, Ontario		
Built:	1945 at Port Dover, Ontario by W.F. Kolbe		
Dimensions:	75' x 22' x 6'	**Tonnage:**	39 gross 26 net
Date of Loss:	Saturday, December 24, 1983		
Cause of Loss:	towing accident		

Ciscoe

Author's Collection

Story of the Loss:

In her early days as a fish tug, the *Ciscoe* had one other serious mishap before her final loss. On March 22, 1955, while on an early spring fishing trip, she was caught in a hurricane. Unable to return to Port Burwell, Ontario, Captain Buck Young tried to find shelter at Long Point. Before reaching safety, one man was lost. As the tug again tried to make home port, a fuel line burst, leaving the *Ciscoe* at the mercy of the wind, snow, and icy waves. She grounded east of Port Burwell where anxious fishermen spotted her from shore. Heroic efforts of the tugmen on shore led to the rescue of the four remaining, and nearly frozen, crewmen.

In 1980 the *Ciscoe* was lengthened 18 feet and reconstructed for use in offshore drilling work.

Before her final voyage, the *Ciscoe* had undergone another extensive renovation from the keel up. The work was done in Port Colborne and the tug was headed back to Port Dover, her homeport. En route, the newly overhauled engine had to be shut down because of fuel problems. The trouble was probably something as simple as a fuel filter, so the crew dropped anchor while they checked into the problem.

At this point, the Canadian Coast Guard Cutter *Griffin* approached the *Ciscoe*. The skipper of the *Griffin* persuaded the reluctant crew of the *Ciscoe* to leave their tug by offering to tow her into Port Dover. As luck would have it, bad luck that is, the Coast Guard cutter's towline became wrapped around the pilothouse on the *Ciscoe*. As the cutter applied power, the *Ciscoe* was overturned.

For months, as the pack ice held her, the freshly painted blue tug floated bottom up with the winds. As the winds would change, the tug and its encasing ice pack would travel off in a different direction. A couple of months passed and finally, with the spring thaw, the *Ciscoe* dropped to the bottom.

Her owner in Port Dover is still searching for her and still retains ownership of the tug. If you should find her, he'd really like to hear about it.

The Wreck Today:

This one is still lost in the waters off Port Colborne. The approximate GPS numbers given above are at her last known location and the wreck should be somewhere near them. Once again, her owner has not surrendered this one. If you find her, you may be able to claim salvage rights, but he still owns her.

Ciscoe aground as pictured in the March 1955 *London Free Press*.

CITY OF ROME

Official #:	125914	**Site #:**	34

Location: 237°T 7.2 miles off Barcelona, New York harbor entrance – ½ mile off Ripley, NY

Coordinates:	Loran: 44507.8 58710.5	**DGPS:**	42 17.171 79 43.077
Lies:	bow northeast	**Depth:**	15 feet
Type:	wood propeller	**Cargo:**	light

Power: fore and aft compound engines

Owner(s) John Mitchell, Henry, and George M. Steinbrenner of Cleveland, Ohio

Built: 1881 at Cleveland, Ohio by Thomas Quayle and Sons

Dimensions:	268'2" x 40'2" x 20'3"	**Tonnage:**	1908 gross 1594 net

Date of Loss: Thursday, May 7, 1914

Cause of Loss: fire

City of Rome

Author's Collection

Story of the Loss:

The *City of Rome* had a long history of mishaps before she met her end in the predawn hours of May 7, 1914. Rumor has it that Captain Dunn had spent the early evening recalling the 30 plus years the *City of Rome* had worked the Great Lakes. In addition to reminiscing about her many owners and many masters, he had reminisced about her many mishaps. There was the time just one year ago when the aging ship had weathered the great storm of November 1913, one of Lake Erie's worst. There was also the time nine years earlier that she had not faired so well in the great storm of November 1905. During the height of this storm she was blown aground on Lake Erie's Middle Island. In three decades of service, the *City of Rome* had gone from being the largest coarse freight carrier on the Great Lakes, a combination schooner steamer, to being an aging steamer in need of repair. Unfortunately, she was not doing well enough financially to warrant the investment in her. She had seen prosperous years and lean years. She had weathered all of these, just as she had weathered the great November storms. There was talk that her days were numbered. Little did Captain Dunn know how numbered they were when he decided to retire early that fateful night.

The lake was in a good mood as the aging vessel steamed passed the lights of Buffalo Harbor. She delivered her load of grain and was sailing light toward Toledo, where she was to take on a load of coal. As the seas were calm, Captain Dunn retired early to the sounds of a soft spring breeze singing in the ship's rigging. His sleep was to be rudely interrupted when, at about 11:00 pm, first mate John McNamara discovered fire in the dunnage room.

All hands were rousted and put to work fighting the flames. The battle raged for two hours before the captain and crew admitted they were losing the fight. The crew wanted to lower the boats, but Captain Dunn chose to head the flaming ship toward the south shore. At 2:00 am, the blazing ship ran aground near Ripley, New York. Two lifeboats were quickly launched as the flames lapped at the fleeing crew. Finding no safe place to land, the men rowed east into the heavy surf until a beach was spotted at daylight.

The exhausted men landed the boats with no loss of life and walked to a nearby farmhouse. Steward Fred Moore had just survived the second ship fire and fourth shipwreck of his sailing career. Having lost all their possessions, they traveled by interurban to Erie, Pennsylvania where they reported the loss of the *City of Rome*. They then boarded a train for Cleveland, Ohio.

The Wreck Today:

Located on a sand bottom, much of the wooden hull and some of the machinery of the *City of Rome* remain. Her propeller lies at the base of the cliff inshore from the wreck. Divers attempting to salvage it dragged it there. Having dragged it 250 yards through the water, they apparently couldn't figure out how to get it up the cliff. The anchors of the *Rome* were removed and are on display at the Eaton Reservoir.

City of Rome shortly after she burned to the waterline.

This wreck can be done as a shore dive. However, it lies off of private property and permission of the owner is required before entering from the shore.

HENRY CLAY

Official #:	none	**Site #:**	45
Location:	153°T 17.7 miles off Port Dover, Ontario	52°T 0.3 miles off Long Point Light	
Coordinates:	Loran: 44547.7 58589.1	**DGPS:**	42 33.075 80 02.721
Lies:	bow east	**Depth:**	15 feet
Type:	wood propeller, package freighter	**Cargo:**	flour, baled wool, passengers
Power:	steam		
Owner(s)	Captain Aaron Root, Captain G. Callard, G.W. Holt of Buffalo and others		
Built:	1849 at Milan, Ohio by Ruggles and Shupe		
Dimensions:	134'4" x 22'7.5" x 11'	**Tonnage:**	316
Date of Loss:	Friday, October 24, 1851		
Cause of Loss:	capsized in storm		

Henry Clay

Milan Historical Society

Story of the Loss:

When originally built, the *Henry Clay* was 107 feet in length and 221 tons. Her original name was *Erie* and her engine was installed in Cleveland at the Cuyahoga Manufacturing Company. Captain Aaron Root, of Berlin, Ohio, was also a 1/12 owner at the time of her loss. He undoubtedly was involved in her 1851 rebuild at the Black River in Lorain, Ohio. Several vessels bore the name of the famous orator, Henry Clay. As a result, there is often much confusion among these ships. This *Henry Clay* enjoyed the reputation developed by one of her namesake predecessors.

According to an article in the October 14, 1999 *Cleveland Plain Dealer*:

> "In June 1832 the steamer *Henry Clay* left Lake Huron for Buffalo with cholera-stricken soldiers. In Detroit, men armed with cannon refused to let the *Clay* dock for food and medicine. By the time the ship got to Cleveland, six men had died. This town (Cleveland) set up a hospital, quarantine the ship and fumigated the *Clay* before it left after three days. Meanwhile, citizens who were not exposed to the ship became ill. Within two weeks more than 50 people died."

Although not the same *Henry Clay,* it's still a good story.

The *Henry Clay* we're concerned with, the one built at Milan, Ohio in 1849, would meet her end off the tip of Long Point. Captain George Callard was guiding her downbound from Detroit, Michigan to Ogdensburg, New York with a load of flour, bailed wool, and a few passengers. They encountered a severe gale and, as the vessel thrashed about in the gale tossed lake, a portion of her deck load shifted and landed on the engine. The deck load smashed about the engine, finally breaking it. With her engine inoperable, the *Henry Clay* was unmanageable and at the mercy of an angry lake. Her hull breached near Long Point. She fell into a trough as a massive wave ripped her deck from the hull, taking ten of the crew with it to their deaths. She tossed and rolled, drowning all but one of the remaining crewmen. Finally, the battered hulk came aground less than ½ mile from the tip of the point.

Of 17 people on board, there was only one survivor. The survivor made it to shore on an inverted yawl and was then picked up by a passing schooner. The *Henry Clay's* cargo is reported to have washed ashore for months after she was lost.

The Wreck Today:

Commonly known as the "Lighthouse Wreck," charter captain Ed McLaughlin suspects this site is the *Henry Clay*. The wreck rests on a sandy bottom in 15 feet of water immediately off the tip of Long Point. This shallow site is home to large schools of fish. Her keelson and frame members cover a large area. Occasionally horse bones are found at this site. Horses were used to work the deck gear on board the steamer.

Considered an excellent site for newly certified divers, it is also a wonderfully relaxing way to breathe the bottom off your tanks after making some of the deeper dives off Long Point.

This Remick Collection photo of unknown wreckage off Long Point Light is believed to be the remains of the Henry Clay in the mid 1960's.

CRACKER

Official #:
Location: 9.7 miles 86°T off Long Point Light
Coordinates: Loran: 44590.5   58687.1
Lies:
Type: scow
Power: sail, 3 masts
Owner(s) unknown
Built:
Dimensions: 118′
Date of Loss: unknown
Cause of Loss: unknown

Site #: 36

DGPS: 42 33.485   79 51.649
Depth: 190 feet
Cargo:

Tonnage:

Cracker

Watercolor by Georgann Wachter

Story of the Loss:

Apparently constructed before 1860, this three masted scow is yet unidentified. There is no wheel evident, but there is a triangular frame, which could have held one. The question is was she wheel or tiller steered.

The Wreck Today:

A fish net lays across the rudder. Her main mast with the top mast attached has fallen to port. An unusual feature of this wreck is the fact that her cabin, with side windows, remained when she plunged to the bottom. Inside the cabin is a chimney pipe. Other features are her rudder (hard to port), bilge pump, anchors, and blunt bow with carved "figurehead".   Many nets are snagged on this wreck and a mast lays on her port side rail.

This dive is beyond the limits of sport diving as defined by all major certifying agencies. It should only be attempted by very experienced divers with specialized equipment and training for depths in excess of sport diving limits.

The following photos by Tom Wilson provide a visual tour of the wreck. Working clockwise, we see the figurehead, windlass, aft part of the cabin, and cabin companionway entrance.

Photos courtesy of Tom Wilson.

CRETE

Official #:	127180	**Site #:**	62

Location: between the Sun Oil cribs and shore 3 miles east of Erie, Pennsylvania harbor entrance

Coordinates:	Loran:	Approximate GPS: 42 10.30 80 00.94	
Lies:	bow south	**Depth:**	12 feet
Type:	wood barge	**Cargo:**	light
Power:	towed		
Owner(s)	Gravel Products Corporation of Buffalo, New York		
Built:	1897 at West Bay City, Michigan by James Davidson		
Dimensions:	288.6 x 44'6" x 19'1"	**Tonnage:**	2083
Date of Loss:	fall of 1930		
Cause of Loss:	scuttled		

Crete

Great Lakes Historical Society, Bowen Collection

Story of the Loss:

The *Crete* was built to haul iron ore from the Mesabi Range to the steel mills of the lower lakes. This use was found to be unprofitable and the boat was sold to the Hammermill Paper Company of Erie, Pennsylvania. They used it to move pulpwood down from the upper lakes. In 1928, the *Crete* was sold to the Gravel Products Corporation of Buffalo, New York to be converted for use in the sand and gravel trade. However, researcher Mary Howard has determined that the first use of the *Crete* by Gravel Products

Corporation was an effort to salvage their lost vessel *Howard S. Gerkin*. The sandsucker *Gerkin* had been lost in a storm on August 21, 1926. The *Gerkin's* story is told elsewhere in this volume.

Mr. Gerkin had purchased the *Crete* and, in the fall of 1928, he was supervising its use in the attempt to raise his namesake. Divers working off the tug Harry H. Boyd had buoyed the turtled wreck. The *Crete* was to be used to haul pontoons and to help turn and raise the *Gerkin*. Unfortunately for the salvage crew, bad weather defeated their attempt to raise the *Gerkin* and the project was abandoned in November of 1928.

In the fall of 1930, the *Crete*, laying in Erie, was taken in tow and went aground, possibly by design, near the Sun Oil Piers. A local entrepreneur purchased the vessel and began stripping her of fixtures and lumber.

The Wreck Today:

Today, the oak bottom of the *Crete* and a winch is about all that remains at this shallow water site. Because this wreck and the wreck of the *Canobie* lie in close proximity to the old Sun Oil cribs, they are often dubbed the "crib wrecks." The *Canobie* is buoyed, making it easy to find. To locate the *Crete*, go east of the *Canobie*. The *Crete* lies north/south between the crib and shore.

Take care that you don't hit the boiler of the *Canobie* or run aground as this wreck is very near shore.

Crete aground east of Erie, Pennsylvania. Photo from Robert J. MacDonald Collection, courtesy of C. Patrick Labadie.

CRYSTAL WRECK/HOOK

Official #:   **Site #:**   F

Location: 330°T 22.9 miles off Erie, Pennsylvania

Coordinates: Loran: 44458.5   58449.7   **DGPS:**   42 27.135   80 16.536

Lies: bow east   **Depth:**   120 feet

Type: 3 masted schooner   **Cargo:**   grain

Power: sail

Owner(s)

Built: circa 1870 to 1880

Dimensions: approximately 117' x 26'   **Tonnage:** approximately 225

Date of Loss: mid to late 1800's

Cause of Loss:

Crystal Wreck

Watercolor by Georgann Wachter

Story of the Loss:

Unknown

The Wreck Today:

The name *Crystal* is not derived from the glass pieces found on her. Rather, it seems the divers who found the wreck celebrated by consuming a couple of Canadian Crystal beers. At least we're fairly certain they waited until after the dive. She is sometimes referred to as the *Hook* for the fish net snag that located her. Regardless of what she is called, the vessel's excellent condition and the liberal amounts of old hemp fish net draping her make the *Crystal Wreck* one of the prettiest we have encountered.

A tie in line at the bow puts the diver near the vessel's port anchor. She has a beautiful bowsprit, draped in net, rising over 20 feet off the bottom. Aft of this is the windlass and toward the port side a mass of net is held suspended by several floats. A section of her port rail is broken.

Proceeding toward the stern, there is a pump, broken mast rail, mast stump, and the first of her holds. Aft of the capstan is an opening revealing her centerboard. The sheet winch sits forward of her main mast, and then there is another hold and pump. The cabin has blown off but toward the starboard side sits the ship's stove, complete with dishes and a fry pan for the diver to view. Nearby you'll find a shoe and eyeglasses. Hopefully these articles will not disappear! The raised stern is completely covered in net, which protects the intact wheel, steering gear, and a metal pail.

The visibility is often in the 70 to 90 foot range, but the bottom temperature is no greater than 45°.

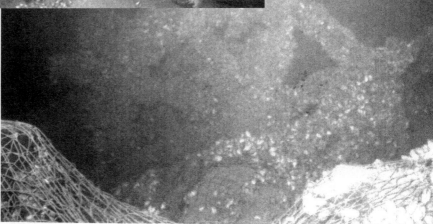

Cook stove and wheel of the Crystal. Photos by Georgann Wachter

DACOTAH

Official #:   none   **Site #:**   11

Location: 151°T 15.9 miles off Port Colborne, Ontario at Sturgeon Point, New York

Coordinates: Loran: 44813.2   59119.2   DGPS:

Lies: scattered   **Depth:**   20 feet

Type: wood propeller   **Cargo:**   general merchandise

Power: oscillating steam engine

Owner(s)   James Clark of Cleveland, Ohio and Dean Richmond of Buffalo, New York

Built: 1857 at Cleveland, Ohio by Luther Moses

Dimensions: 193.39' x 30.29' x 12.5'   **Tonnage:**   698

Date of Loss: Saturday, November 24, 1860

Cause of Loss: storm

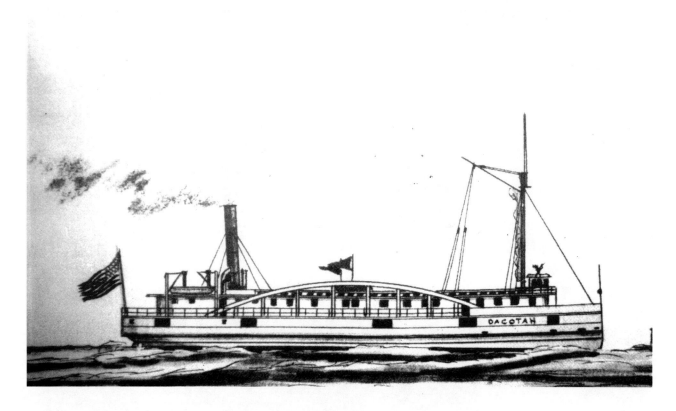

Dacotah

Eric Heyl Drawing

Story of the Loss:

In her enrollments, the *Dacotah* is described as having a round stern, plain head, one deck, and two masts. She operated under charter to the New York Central Railroad Company.

The *Dacotah* left Buffalo, New York the afternoon of Friday, November 23, 1860. She was traveling in company with the propeller *Acme* when they encountered a storm off Dunkirk, New York. The *Acme* turned back to Buffalo and nothing more was seen of the *Dacotah*. She was believed to be sheltering from the storm in Grand River, Ontario until her remains were discovered scattered over several miles of shoreline between Sturgeon Point and Evans Center.

At 9:00 p.m. on Saturday, local residents, Mr. and Mrs. Bennet and their son, heard cries for help. They searched in the snowstorm for an hour and could not find anything. The following morning, the Bennet's son once again went searching. He discovered half the wreck high and dry on the beach. She was believed to have struck a reef and broken up, her topsides washing ashore. Captain William Cross and his entire crew of 23 people were lost.

The *Jersey City* and the schooner *Convoy* were among the other ships lost in the same storm.

The Wreck Today:

Resting in 20 to 25 feet of water, some decking remains of this Civil War vintage wreck site. The debris field is extensive and artifacts are strewn over the bottom. Her cargo consisted of horseshoes, flatirons, ornamental stove parts, pottery, and wheel parts. These have been treasures for divers for many years and some can still be found at the site. At last report, the capstan and rudder were also prominent features of this shallow water dive site.

Pictured on the right is one of the enrollments for the Dacotah. Enrollments are used to document the history of a vessel. They track ownership, official measurements, rebuilds, original commissioning, decommissioning, etc.

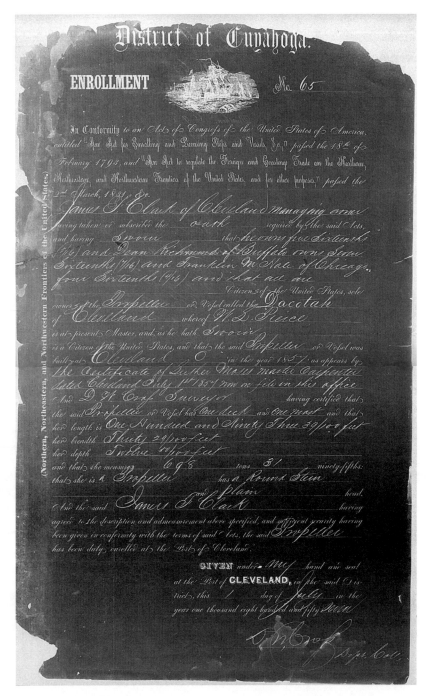

DAWN

Official #: none   **Site #:** 89

Location: 204°T 17.9 miles off Port Stanley, Ontario

Coordinates: Loran: 44233.5 57878.3   **DGPS:** 42 25.247 81 21.497

Lies: bow southwest   **Depth:** 66 feet

Type: schooner, two masts   **Cargo:** light

Power: sail

Owner(s) J.W. Sterling of Monroe, Michigan, F. Waldorf and E. B. Gibson of Buffalo, New York

Built: 1847 at Milan, Ohio by W.S. Lyon & J.P. Gay

Dimensions: 105' x 20'4" x 8'11"   **Tonnage:** 202 37/95

Date of Loss: Friday, October 21, 1859

Cause of Loss: collision

Typical Two Mast Schooner

Merchant Vessels of the Great Lakes

Story of the Loss:

Early in her career, the *Dawn* was owned by J.P. Gay and traded between Milan, Ohio and Oswego, New York. Swayze believes the *Dawn* was sunk by a storm off Madison Dock, Ohio, in July of 1855 and recovered from 25 feet of water a month later.

On her final voyage, the schooner *Dawn* was upbound on the lakes, traveling light for Monroe, Michigan. No one on the schooner saw anything of the 700 ton propeller *New York* until it was too late. According to her skipper, Captain Gibson, the *New York* cut across his bow and rammed the schooner. With a gaping hole forward of the cabin, the small schooner sank in less than ten minutes.

Fortunately for the *Dawn's* crew, they were all able to make it safely to the steamer. As the crew looked back, nothing could be seen of the schooner but the gilt balls on her topmast heads. The crew was landed in Dunkirk, New York. An angry Captain Gibson planned to sue the owners of the *New York* as there was no insurance on the *Dawn*.

The Wreck Today:

The *Dawn* sits with a slight list to starboard. Looking at the amidships section of the wreck, one can see clear evidence of the collision that sunk her. The stern is silting over and the bow has about a seven-foot rise off the bottom.

A survey in the mid 1980's discovered a coin with the dates 1827 – 1835 on it. It was common practice to place a coin under the base of the mainmast when a ship was first constructed. This coin may have been carried by a crewman or, it could be the mast coin.

Dawn
105' x 20'4" x 8'11"
by Georgann S. Wachter
not to scale

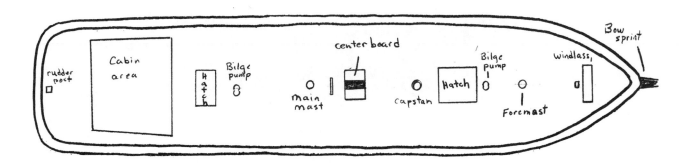

DIESEL BARGE/HYDRAULIC DREDGE

Official #:   **Site #:**   12

Location: 4 miles west of Sturgeon Point, New York – 17 Miles NE of Dunkirk, New York

Coordinates: Loran: 44803.3   59106.5   **GPS:**   42 38.910   79 05.520

Lies: **Depth:**   35 feet

Type: barge   **Cargo:**   light

Power: towed

Owner(s)

Built:

Dimensions: **Tonnage:**

Date of Loss: about 1951

Cause of Loss: storm

Toledo
Similar to Diesel Barge

Private collection of Ralph Roberts

Story of the Loss:

This underwater structure was originally thought to be part of another vessel. However, we have since learned it was a pontoon based hydraulic dredge. The dredge was enroute from Buffalo, New York to Dunkirk, New York when it was caught in a storm stronger than the pontoons could handle and the dredge flipped over in the storm.

The Wreck Today:

There is approximately 30 feet of water over the remaining structure and divers can swim through the girders that composed the dredge's steel frame. The framework of the pump platform with attached large motors and pumps lies upside down. Rumor has it that visibility at this site is usually on the poor side, and it is tough to get a good day unless you are in the area for a while. Other than the girders and winches, no hull structure is evident.

Power winch located at the Marine Museum of the Great Lakes, Kingston, Ontario.

DIXIE

Official #: 175285

Location: 64°T 3.8 miles off Ashtabula, Ohio

Coordinates: Loran: 42120.0 58108.0

Lies: east – west

Type: dredge derrick

Power: none

Owner(s) Price Brothers of Detroit, Michigan

Built: 1941 at Cheboygan, Wisconsin

Dimensions: 88'1" x 28' x 6'5"

Date of Loss: Friday, December 4, 1964

Cause of Loss: storm

Site #: 82

DGPS: 41 56.597 80 43.578

Depth: 47 feet

Cargo: light

Tonnage: 152 gross 152 net

Dixie

Bowling Green State University, Historical Collections of the Great Lakes

Story of the Loss:

With the winds of November behind them and having extended the season as far as it could be stretched, the tug *Superior* left Buffalo, New York and headed for Toledo, Ohio to lay up for the winter. In her tow were the dredge barge *Three Brothers* and the barge *Dixie*. As the small convoy approached Ashtabula, the weather was rapidly deteriorating. The tug made a turn for the protection of Ashtabula Harbor.

Struggling through 8 foot waves, the three vessels made steady progress until the tow cable to the *Dixie* snapped against the strain. Free of her tether, the *Dixie* was out of control and adrift in the building storm.

The *Superior*, with the *Three Brothers* in tow, was unable to recover the *Dixie* and proceeded to the safety of Ashtabula Harbor. At 1:30 in the morning, Ashtabula Coast Guard and Army Corps of Engineers vessels spotted and tracked the *Dixie*. The eight foot seas prevented them from taking her under tow. As the barge tossed and drifted in the winter storm, two Coast Guard boats followed the vessel and warned other ships in the area. Finally, in the middle of the dark night on a storm tossed sea, the *Dixie* gave up her struggle, rolled over, and sank.

The Wreck Today:

The *Dixie* sits on a mud bottom with her pipe crane to the east. There are fittings and pipe parts all around the barge and her intake piping protrudes from the west end of the wreck.

Her 27 foot launch, *Surveyor,* once lay to the east. However, several years ago some local divers attached lift bags in an attempt to raise the launch. The weather turned bad and the attempt was abandoned. When they returned to the site, the divers were unable to locate the *Surveyor*.

There are several large holes in the hull of the *Dixie*. We would caution divers not to penetrate the wreck unless they are properly trained and equipped for penetration diving.

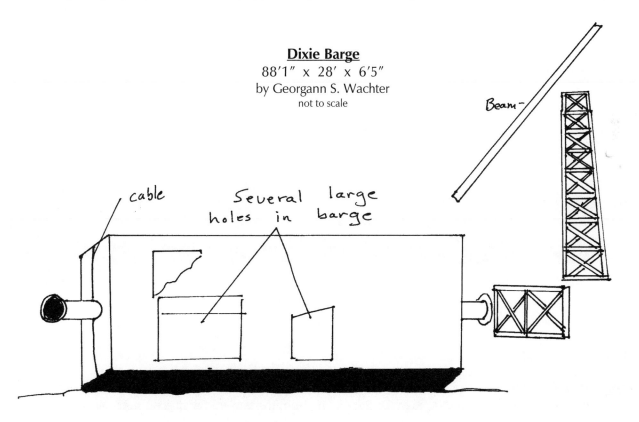

Dixie Barge
88'1" x 28' x 6'5"
by Georgann S. Wachter
not to scale

NEAL H. DOW

Official #: 130445   **Site #:** 63

Location: north end of Misery Bay off Erie, Pennsylvania

Coordinates: Loran: **DGPS:** 42 09   80 06

Lies: **Depth:** 8 feet

Type: wood fish tug   **Cargo:** none

Power: twin 32 horsepower steam engines

Owner(s) Starkweather of Youngstown, Ohio

Built: 1889 at Buffalo, New York by Hingston and Woods

Dimensions: 39.5' x 11' x 4.9'   **Tonnage:** 11 gross 8 net

Date of Loss: around 1910

Cause of Loss: abandoned

Neal H. Dow

Remick Collection

Story of the Loss:

Many of the craft lost in the waters of and off Lake Erie gained no notoriety in the newspapers. They were simple vessels used by people to make their living from the water. Small schooners were often built and operated by the owner's family. If the ship was lost, the entire family would be lost with it. Fishing tugs would work the waters until they were no longer profitable. Then they would simply be beached and abandoned. These vessels leave behind no news articles and limited official documentation. Their tales can only be told through the memories and anecdotes of those who knew them. Such is the story of the *Neal H. Dow.*

The following notes on the *Neal H. Dow* are from a letter by her namesake, Neal H. Dow. Neal was the son of the original owner.

"The engines on her were by my brother, James M. Dow, in a small engine shop he had on Beaver Street, Dunkirk, New York. They were double engines. My brother was for years Superintendent of the Dunkirk Engineering Company, a prominent firm of its day, they made logging engines for lumber camps.

"In the vessel – or in common – just a tug, the forehold as I call it was lined with zinc sheets, this was where they dumped the fish as they came from the nets.

There was a timber used in the construction, from some old battlefield of the Civil War, as several lead minie bullets were imbedded in the timber.

She was sold to Starkweather of Youngstown, Ohio, after my father lost plenty in the nets.

She ended in Misery Bay at Erie, Pennsylvania."

The vessel takes on added significance in light of another letter where Neal Dow says, "The timbers used in the construction of the *Neal H. Dow* came from a forest near Antietam, there were musket bullets in some of the timbers used, so the *Dow* was a Civil War relic in a way." The reference to "some old battlefield of the Civil War" is to the bloodiest day in American history. Antietam was the worst battle of the Civil War. It is reported that 3,620 people died, 17,365 were wounded, and 2,598 were listed as missing or captured. One small piece of this epic battle, the *Neal H. Dow*, now rests on the bottom of Misery Bay, abandoned by her owners because she was no longer profitable.

The Wreck Today:

Very little remains of the *Neal H. Dow*. What little there is lies buried in the sand and silt on the north end of Misery Bay.

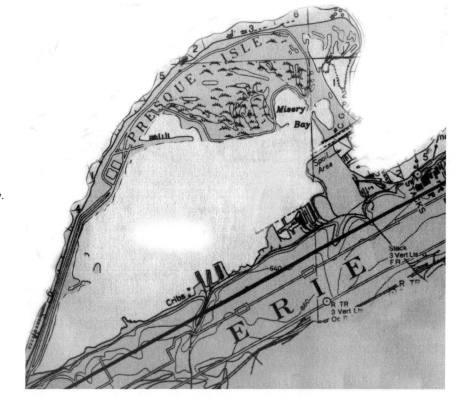

Chart of Misery Bay.

DRILLING RIG

Official #:   **Site #:**   74

Location: 310°T 23.2 miles off Erie, Pennsylvania

Coordinates: Loran: 44397.0 58359.4   **DGPS:**   42 22.471   80 25.108

Lies: scattered   **Depth:**   80 feet

Type: drill platform   **Cargo:**   stacked pipe

Power: towed

Owner(s)   Underwater Gas Development Limited, Port Elma, Ontario

Built:

Dimensions: 40' x 40'   **Tonnage:**

Date of Loss: Wednesday, November 5, 1958

Cause of Loss: storm

Typical Drill Rig

Although years newer, this rig is typical of Canadian gas drilling platforms.

Photo by Georgann Wachter

Story of the Loss:

The *Drilling Rig* was leased to Underwater Gas Explorers and the steel-footed, 40 foot square platform was placed in the center of Lake Erie, near the shipping lanes. The platform had been drilling for gas since the middle of August, but, as winter approached, the rig was being dismantled for the season. Five men were aboard, quartered in a small shed on the platform. They were geologist Jack Brogan, and crewmembers William Marsh, Jr., Leroy Bauwen, Walter Kozloff, and George Mitchell. The crew had already brought in some 4,270 feet of drill pipe and partially completed the transfer of the rig's equipment to shore when they settled in for the evening on Wednesday.

That night, a severe storm with fifteen foot seas wracked the area. One can hardly imagine the terror of fifteen foot waves washing over a 40 foot square platform in the middle of Lake Erie. Sometime during the night, the men attempted to save themselves by donning life jackets and boarding a rubber raft. We will never know exactly what happened as the five men battled the tempest. None survived the ordeal.

The United States freighter *Sumatra* was first to raise the alarm. She radioed that the tower was missing. The gas company sent two tugs to the area and found no trace of the rig. This launched an extensive search involving U.S. Coast Guard cutters and aircraft, aircraft from the Royal Canadian Air Force, and ships in the area. The Coast Guard reported by radio that if there were survivors, they would have to be clinging to the wreckage as none were found at the site where the rig went down. The drilling corporation held scant hope that any would survive. Twenty-four hours had passed since the rig was last known to be in place, but the search went on. The aircraft and cutters were joined by the tanker *Polaris* which radioed it was making maximum speed to join the search effort. Reports that the rig carried a 12 man life raft and a smaller raft gave some hope to cling to as relatives anxiously awaited news of the crew's fate.

On November 7, all hope faded when the Cleveland Coast Guard cutter, *Kaw,* recovered the body of one crewman lashed to a raft eight miles northeast of Erie, Pennsylvania. A second body, supported by a life jacket was pulled from the water amidst debris that had been driven as far as 77 miles from the wreck site.

The Wreck Today:

Located on a mud bottom in 80 feet of water, the steel remains of the drilling rig are scattered with pipe over a broad area. The rig was about 40' by 40' and the retrieved pipe had been stacked under the permanent platform. In addition to the shed that housed the men, there was a drilling tower. The splintered wreckage of the shed was recovered by the Coast Guard. Six other towers in the area survived the storm.

DUPUIS No. 10

Official #: 166284

Site #: 19

Location: 4 miles 155°T off Port Colborne, Ontario

Coordinates: Loran:

DGPS: 42 49.094 79 13.301

Lies:

Depth: 60 feet

Type: steel barge

Cargo: light

Power: towed

Owner(s) Leo Shotte of Toronto, Ontario

Built: 1915 at Nicholson Terminal & Dock Company, Ecorse, Michigan

Dimensions: 143' x 32' x 6.4'

Tonnage: 316

Date of Loss: Wednesday, December 24, 1997

Cause of Loss: foundered

Barge similar to the Dupuis No. 10

Author's Collection

Story of the Loss:

Dupuis No. 10 was one of several barges built in the early 1900's for the A.J. Dupuis Company of Detroit, Michigan. She was owned in Cleveland shortly before transferring to Canadian registry.

The barge had been sitting idle in Buffalo Harbor for several years. Her new owner planned to have her refitted in Toronto, Canada. In preparation for the trip to Toronto, she had been hastily patched and nine rental pumps were placed on board to keep her afloat. The rental pumps were powered by a generator, which was also rented equipment.

Now ready for the short trip across the lake, *Dupuis No. 10* was taken in tow by the *Techno St. Laurent* and they headed out of Buffalo Harbor en route to Toronto. The throb of the generator powered the pumps and all was working fine until the rented generator ran out of gas. Apparently no one had thought to bring extra fuel. Without power, the pumps failed. Without pumps, the hastily repaired hull began taking on water and gradually settled deeper and deeper. Four miles short of the entrance to the Welland Canal, she went down. The *Dupuis No. 10* never made it to Toronto for her refit.

Her owner, Leo Shotte, lost more than a barge that day. The rented pumps and the rented generator were secured against his wife's MasterCard. She was about to be the proud owner of all that equipment lying at the bottom of the lake with his barge.

The Wreck Today:

All but one of the rented pumps were salvaged. Salvaging the pumps went a long way toward clearing the charges levied against the MasterCard. Today, the barge sits pretty low in the muck and silt has covered much of her structure.

Had her pumps run for another four miles, the Dupuis No. 10 would have made it safely to Port Colborne, the Lake Erie entrance to the Welland Canal. Here a salt water freighter is approached by the pilot boat J.W. Cooper.
Photo by Georgann Wachter.

ELDORADO

Official #:	135117	**Site #:**	60

Location: 77°T 2.3 miles off Erie, Pennsylvania, just east of Four Mile Creek

Coordinates:	Loran:	DGPS:	
Lies:	north/south	**Depth:**	15 to 20 feet
Type:	barge	**Cargo:**	light
Power:	towed		

Owner(s) L.L. Slyfield of Saint Clair, Michigan

Built: 1857 by F.N. Jones of Buffalo, New York rebuilt 1871 at Sheboygan, Wisconsin

Dimensions:	189' x 32' x 11'	**Tonnage:**	489

Date of Loss: Saturday, November 20, 1880

Cause of Loss: storm

Story of the Loss:

She was originally built as the steamer *Equator*. In November 1869 she was attempting to pull the schooner *Southwest* off a reef. In the midst of this attempt, she foundered in the very gale that had driven the schooner aground.   Although she was thought to be unsalvageable, the steamer was refloated in 1870. In 1871, her engines were removed to the tug *Bismark* and the hull was extensively rebuilt at Sheboygan, Wisconsin. Following the rebuild, she was renamed the barge *Eldorado* .

Under tow of the steamer *James Donaldson*, the *Eldorado* had left Buffalo, New York and was traveling light for Saginaw, Michigan. Other consorts of the *Donaldson* that day were the barges *George W. Wesley* and *Bay City*. Their passage from Buffalo had not been a pleasant one. Snow had been falling all day and, due to a strong westerly wind, the seas had been rough.

As the convoy approached Erie, Pennsylvania, the seas were worsening as the westerly winds built to gale strength. Unable to manage the towering waves with her consorts in tow, the *Donaldson* cast her consorts adrift and made for Erie. The three barges tried to anchor. However, with neither power nor sail, they were left to drift with the whims of the savage lake. Near 9:00 p.m. the *Eldorado* and *Wesley* washed ashore approximately 4 miles east of downtown Erie. The crews were able to leave their vessels and scramble up the rocky coast to safety.

The *Bay City*, heavily loaded with coal, went aground some distance from shore. As Sunday morning broke, there was still no sign of help for the freezing men and one woman aboard the *Bay City*. With increasing anxiety, the crew could only watch as the waters rose in the holds. As dusk approached, a new terror appeared. The *Bay City* was on fire in the forecastle. Surely, they were all about to die.

Fortunately, the lifesaving crew had finally seen the plight of the *Bay City* and her crew. Captain Clark and his lifesavers rigged a breeches buoy. First to shore was the cook, Minnie Lafrey. She was followed by Captain Sheppard and his dog and then by four crewmen. All were taken to a nearby farmhouse where they were treated for the effects of their ordeal.

The three barge captains had only harsh words for the captain of the *James Donaldson*. They were not happy with his seamanship or his lack of concern for the safety of his consorts.

Having no insurance, the *Eldorado* was considered too costly to refloat and salvage. She was burned and scuttled very close to the point at which she went aground. The *Westley*, though uninsured, was salvaged and returned to service, as was the *Bay City*.

Before leaving for home after the incident, Captain Slyfield of the *Eldorado* thanked the local people for their gracious hospitality.

The Wreck Today:

The charred remains of this once proud vessel rest in shallow water just east of Four Mile Creek. Lying in 15 to 20 feet of water, she, like most shallow wrecks, presents minimal relief, but provides a wonderful habitat for fish. The bass are very friendly unless you disturb them in spawning season. Then they become "attack bass" and defend their nesting spots.

From 1871 until her loss in 1880 the Eldorado worked as a consort barge under tow of a steamer. Pictured above is the steamer John Pridgeon with two consorts. Photo from authors's collection.

C.W. Elphicke

Official #:	126568	**Site #:**	46

Location: 00°T 26.2 miles off Erie, Pennsylvania – 229°T 1.2 miles off Long Point Light

Coordinates:	Loran:	**DGPS:**	PA 42 32.18 80 03.97

Lies:	bow west	**Depth:**	20 feet
Type:	wood propeller, bulk freighter	**Cargo:**	wheat
Power:	triple expansion steam		
Owner(s)	Kinney Transportation Company of Cleveland, Ohio		
Built:	1889 at Trenton, Michigan by Craig Shipbuilding		
Dimensions:	273' x 42' x 22'	**Tonnage:**	2406 gross 1764 net
Date of Loss:	Tuesday, October 21, 1913		

C.W. Elphicke

Great Lakes Historical Society

Story of the Loss:

When the bulk freighter, *Elphicke*, left Fort William, Ontario loaded with 160,000 bushels of wheat, her captain was not expecting to be the first victim of the savage storm season of 1913. The skies were clear, the water was calm, and the breezes were light as the propeller eased her way out on Tuesday, October 14 for the journey to Buffalo, New York. Her journey through the upper lakes was uneventful, and she entered the passage to Lake Erie on Sunday, October 19, confident she would make Buffalo by nightfall on Monday.

As she exited the Detroit River, she bottomed out on an obstruction. The October 23, 1913 *Mail and Empire*, conjectures that this obstruction was part of the wreckage of the steamer *City of London*. Captain Alonzo B. Comins ordered an inspection of the holds and, on finding no significant damage, proceeded down the lake.

Downbound on Lake Erie Monday morning, she encountered a freshening breeze with moderate waves. Still unconcerned, Captain Comins and his crew of 18 continued east. The winds continued to grow to 60 miles per hour. As the 273 foot freighter neared Long Point she was battling a full blown gale. In the mounting seas, a report came from below that there was 46 inches of water in the holds. The pumps were manned, but they were unable to stay ahead of the incoming water. On inspection, the crew discovered a large hole on the ship's starboard side. Every hand now was assigned to work the pumps as Captain Comins navigated for shelter on the lee side of Long Point. The crew engaged in a losing battle with the incoming water through the night. By daybreak there was 7 feet of water in the hold. Not wanting to lose his boat in the deep water trench, Captain Comins ordered a turn to port so the *Elphicke* could be beached on the south side of the point.

Suddenly aground some 2000 feet from shore, the waves continued to wash over the steamer. A yawl boat was launched and immediately overturned by the raging winds. Fortunately, help was on the way. The Long Point Lifesaving Station had seen the ship's distress and sent her surfboat to rescue the crew. Working their way to the *Elphicke* through the pounding waves, the lifesaving crew helped launch the steamer's second yawl, which carried seven survivors to shore. The remaining eleven seafarers were taken aboard the surfboat and brought to safety. As the surfboat was pulling away from the stricken steamer, she broke in two.

Still hopeful that the ship could be salvaged, the Kinney Company sent surveyors to site. They determined that her back was broken, and she was a total loss.

The Wreck Today:

Much of the time the lake's currents wash sand over her remains, covering them. Following a strong south wind, the timbers will uncover, and she can still be explored. Even today, a strong south gale will send pieces of this wreck to shore.

The Elphicke aground south of Long Point.

ERIE

Official #:	none	**Site #:**	13
Location:	48°T 14 miles off Dunkirk, New York	8 miles off Silver Creek, New York	
Coordinates:	Loran: n/a	**DGPS:**	n/a
Lies:	raised	**Depth:**	
Type:	sidewheel steamer	**Cargo:**	passengers and miscellaneous freight

Power:	low pressure vertical beam steam engine		
Owner(s)	General Charles Reed of Erie, Pennsylvania		
Built:	1836 at Erie, Pennsylvania by M. Creamer		
Dimensions:	176' x 27'5" x 10'10"	**Tonnage:**	497 gross
Date of Loss:	Monday, August 9, 1841		
Cause of Loss:	fire		

Erie

Great Lakes Historical Society

Story of the Loss:

Although her machinery was salvaged in 1844 and the hull was raised in 1854, no book of shipwrecks in eastern Lake Erie would be complete without including the terrible loss of the sidewheel steamer *Erie*.

It was Monday, August 9, 1841 and Buffalo Harbor was filled with ships waiting newly arriving immigrants coming off the Erie Canal. Among these was the steamer *Erie*. She was a fine ship, well known for her light weight and fast speed. Having been freshly overhauled and varnished, the *Erie* looked like she was straight out of the ways as she boarded 30 to 40 cabin passengers and some 140 Swiss and German immigrants. She also carried 8 painters on their way to paint the steamer *Madison* at Erie, Pennsylvania. The painter's demijohns of oil, varnish, and turpentine were taken below and stowed along with the assorted household goods and dry goods of the immigrants.

Standing outside the wheelhouse, 33 year old Captain T.J. Titus gave the order to get under way and 28 year old wheelsman Luther Fuller headed the paddle wheeler for the open lake. Both men had held their positions since the *Erie* was launched. Both would distinguish themselves before this historic trip was done. As the ship exited the harbor, one of the firemen on the inspection detail observed that the demi-johns of turpentine had been stowed on a ledge above the boilers. He immediately moved them to safer storage on the promenade deck. Following shortly behind him, one of the painters was surprised to see their equipment had been put out on the open deck and hastened to return the demijohns to their prior storage location.

On the lake a fresh wind from the south was causing a bit of rough water. Two hours out of Buffalo, the shipboard meal had been served and the combination of a cool lake breeze and rough water encouraged many of the passengers to retire early. It was shortly after 8:00 when the calm of the evening was shat-tered by an explosion below decks. One of the demijohns of turpentine had overheated, exploded, and spilled its flaming contents across the holds. Fed by the turpentine and the *Erie's* own fresh varnish, flames rapidly engulfed the ship. As Captain Titus rushed to the ladies lounge for life jackets, he gave wheelsman Fuller orders that would create one of the great folk heroes of the lakes, "Fuller, put the wheel hard to the starboard, remain at your post, and keep the boat headed for shore!"

Panic seized the passengers. Skylights exploded from the searing heat of the flames. Smoke poured from the holds. Despite the valiant efforts of Captain Titus to maintain control, all semblance of order was lost. Three lifeboats were lowered. Each was so overloaded that it capsized instantly upon entering the water. Scores were trapped below decks, and their screams filled the night. Many passengers tore parts of the ship off, cast them in the water, and leapt in behind them. Most drowned for their efforts.

Blocked by the flames from reaching the life jackets, Captain Titus ordered the chief engineer to stop the engine. Desperately he hoped that stopping the boat would lessen the fanning of the flames and slow their spread. All his efforts were to no avail. The heat and flames prevented even this last gesture. Once again, Titus yelled to the pilothouse for Fuller to keep her headed to shore. And keep her headed to shore he did. As the flames burst forth all around him, he headed her for shore. As mothers watched their children die in their arms, he headed her for shore. As the Captain finally leapt to the water, he headed her for shore. Such was his courage and dedication to duty that he was immortalized in song and poem.

Of the 240 or so passengers and crew aboard the *Erie* that fateful night, only 50 survived.

The Wreck Today:

The boilers and shaft were removed during the 1844-1845 season and the hull was raised and towed to Buffalo for stripping on June 30, 1854. A small portion of the hull was abandoned in 30 feet of water at Point Abino, Ontario. It is said that the coin and specie in the hull paid for the salvage and contributed a tidy profit.

Occasional parts of the *Erie* might still be found at Silver Creek, New York. Perhaps some of that coin and gold specie still remain on the bottom of Lake Erie. Today, her true treasure is in the rich folklore that has developed around the events of her sinking.

The Legend of Luther Fuller

At the accident inquest, Titus testified, "He (Fuller) remained at the wheel and never left it until he was burned to death." This is the stuff of legends, and the Fuller legend grew. Lake men and canalers told the story over and over. With each telling the tale was embellished until it was almost unrecognizable. Fuller's name was somehow changed to John Maynard, the *Erie* became the *Comet* and then the *Ocean Queen*. The following poem was attributed to none other than Horatio Alger. Due to the large number of Swiss and German immigrants lost on the *Erie,* this poem was very popular in Switzerland and Germany.

Twas on Lake Erie's broad expanse
One bright midsummer day,
The gallant steamer Ocean Queen
Swept proudly on her way.
Bright faces clustered on the deck,
Or, leaning o'er the side,
Watched carelessly the feathery foam
That flecked the rippling tide.

Ah, who beneath that cloudless sky,
That smiling bends serene,
Could dream that danger awful vast,
Impended o'er the scene, -Could dream that ere an hour had sped
That frame of sturdy oak
Would sink beneath the lake's blue
Blackened with fire and smoke?

A seaman sought the captain's side,
A moment whispered low;
The captain's swarthy face grew pale;
He hurried down below.
Alas, too late! Though quick, and sharp,
And clear his orders came,
No human efforts could avail
To quench th' insidious flame.

The bad news quickly reached the deck,
It sped from lip to lip,

And ghastly faces everywhere
Looked from the doomed ship.
"Is there no hope - no chance of life?"
A hundred lips implore,
"But one," the captain made reply, -
"To run the ship on shore."

A sailor, whose heroic soul
That hour should yet reveal,
By name John Maynard, eastern born,
Stood calmly at the wheel.
"Head her southeast!" the captain shouts,
Above the smothered roar, -
"Head her south-east without delay!
Make for the nearest shore!"

No terror pales the helmsman's cheek,
Or clouds his dauntless eye,
As, in a sailor's measured tone,
His voice responds, "Ay! Ay!"

Three hundred souls, the steamer's freight,
Crowd forward wild with fear,
While at the stern the dreaded flames
Above the deck appear.
He grasped the wheel, and steadfastly
He steered the ship to land.
"John Maynard, can you still hold out?"

He heard the captain cry;
A voice from out the stifling smoke
Faintly responds, "Ay! Ay!"

But half a mile! a hundred hands
Stretch eagerly to shore,
But half a mile! That distance sped
Peril shall all be o'er.
But half a mile! Yet stay, the flames
No longer slowly creep,
But gather round that helmsman bold,
With fierce impetuous sweep.

"John Maynard!" with an anxious voice
That captain cries once more,
"Stand by the wheel five minutes yet,
And we shall reach the shore."
Through flame and smoke that dauntless heart
Responded firmly still,
Unawed, though face to face with death,
"With God's good help I will!"

That flames approach with giant strides,
They scorch his hand and brow;

One arm disabled, seeks his side,
Ah! he is conquered now!
But no his teeth are firmly set,
He crushes down his pain,
His knee upon the stanchion pressed,
He guides the ship again.

One moment yet! one moment yet!
Brave heart, thy task is o'er.
The pebbles grate beneath the keel,
The steamer touches shore.
Three hundred grateful voices rise
In praise to God that he
Hath saved them from the fearful fire,
And from the engulphing sea.

But where is he, that helmsman bold?
The captain saw him reel,
His nerveless hands released their task
He sank beside the wheel.
The wave received his lifeless corpse,
Blackened with smoke and fire.
God rest him! Never hero had
A nobler funeral pyre!

John Gough, famed temperance leader, turned the poem into an oration titled "The Pilot". And, Abraham Lincoln's Secretary of State, John Hay used the story as the basis of his poem "Jim Bludso".

Little did they know that Luther Fuller had escaped the blaze aboard the *Erie*. He stayed at the wheel until the steering ropes burned through. With nothing more he could do, badly burned he cut away a piece of paddle wheel fender and floated ashore. Under the name James Rafferty, he lived a life of crime and alcohol. But on the night the *Erie* burned, he was a hero worthy of song and poem. Luther Fuller died on November 22, 1900 at the Erie County Hospital in Erie, Pennsylvania. Make that 51 survivors.

FINCH

Official #: 9261

Location: 6 miles west of Buffalo, New York

Coordinates: Loran: 44940.9   59191.9

Lies: bow southeast

Type: barge

Power: towed

Owner(s) K&MF Company of Montreal, Quebec

Built: 1871 at Quebec City, Quebec by Cantin

Dimensions: 105' x 22.6' x 7.9'

Date of Loss: Thursday, August 2, 1883

Cause of Loss: rough seas

Site #: 6

DGPS: 42 50.956   78 59.029

42.50.930   78.58.990

Depth: 45 feet

Cargo: sand

Tonnage: 178 gross 164 net

Barges at Hudson River Terminus of the Erie Canal

Gleason's Pictoral

Story of the Loss:

K&MF Company operated a series of Saint Lawrence River barges with home ports in Kingston, Ontario and Montreal, Quebec. The *Finch* was based in Montreal.

The tug *A.I. Holloway* was engaged to tow the barge *Finch* to Buffalo, New York. Surprisingly for the time, the tug's owner was listed as a woman, Mary A. Holloway. According to the August 3, 1883, *Buffalo Morning Express*, the *Finch* sprung a leak in heavy seas before sinking off Windmill Point.

At the time of her sinking, the barge was rumored to have been overloaded. However, a later article in the *Buffalo Morning Express* stated that the *Finch* was "<u>not</u> down to within a foot of her loading line."

The Wreck Today:

The remains of the *Finch* are fairly broken up on the bottom. The bottom is silt and gravel. The rudder lies about 90 feet northwest of the main body of the wreck. The ship's stove is on the starboard side near the stern. A pile of chain is off the starboard side and her capstan is on a section of wreckage off the port side amidships.

You need to watch for heavy boat traffic in this area. Also, there is a slight current coursing over her wooden hull.

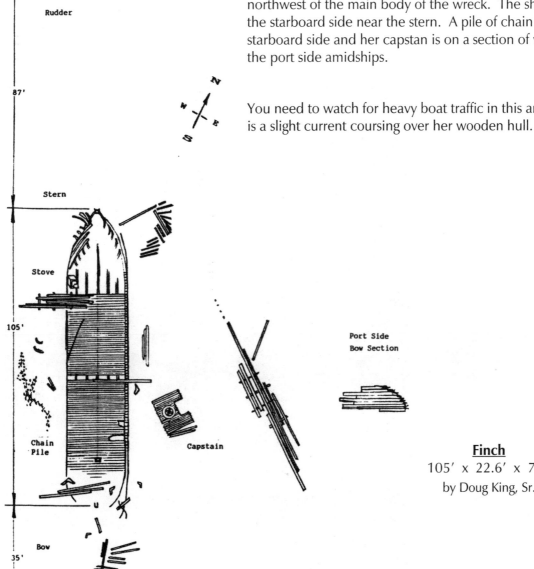

Finch
105' x 22.6' x 7.9'
by Doug King, Sr.

George C. Finney

Official #: 10545

Location:

Coordinates: Loran:

Lies:

Type: 3 masted schooner

Power: sail

Owner(s) Captain Thomas Riordan of Buffalo, New York

Built: 1866 at Oswego, New York by G. Gobble

Dimensions: 136.7' x 26' x 10.8'

Date of Loss: Tuesday, November 17, 1891

Cause of Loss: storm

Site #: B

DGPS: 42 40.087   79 36.250

Depth: 100 feet

Cargo: wheat

Tonnage: 300.66 gross   285.63 net

George C. Finney

The Finney can be seen partially obscured by tugboat steam in this photo from the

private collection of Ralph Roberts.

Story of the Loss:

Two years prior to her tragic loss, the crew of the *George W. Finney* had watched as the fifth waterspout of the day tore up all but her main sail and left her barely afloat. She loaded wheat in Toledo, Ohio and made it almost to Port Colborne, Ontario before encountering the waterspout's vengeance. Her fore-mast was taken down to the deck, half of the main mast was broken off, and the jibboom was wrenched from its mounting. She would live to tell the tale of this treacherous trip only to eventually succumb to the waves of Lake Erie in almost the identical location.

On November 14, 1891, her final voyage would leave no survivors. However, she would leave the hand written testament of a crew member that brings poignancy to the horror of lives lost at sea. Once again, the *George C. Finney* would depart from Toledo, Ohio, this time for Buffalo, New York. Once again she carried wheat, 21,000 bushels. Her crew consisted of Captain Thomas Riordan, five seamen and a woman cook. The following Friday, Captain Fitzgerald of the *Pueblo* arrived in Buffalo with a report of having passed blue painted wreckage below Long Point. Captain Quigley of the schooner *M.J. Cummings* was apparently the last to see the *Finney*. He had followed her out of Toledo, and the two vessels traveled in company of one another until November 17, when Quigley lost sight of the *Finney* during a snow squall just to the east of Long Point.

In July of the following year, a man walking the beach on the north shore of Long Point discovered a bottle containing a pencilled note. It read

> "I Pat McCarty on this awful night in November, write this letter to inform the one who finds it that the boat I am on is about to flounder (sic). Her name is the *Finney* and I am going to Dave Jones Locker. Tell my wife that I leave all my possessions to her. She lives in Michigan. The waves are so high now that I can hardly write. The captain was washed overboard just now, Good bye."

The Wreck Today:

The *Finney* sits upright in 100 feet of water. Her masts are down and much of her decking is gone. Otherwise, she is largely intact. The ship's wheel sits slightly to starboard. Other notable features of the wreck are her windlass, anchors, pump, and sheet winch. The stern is broken and some of the deck is missing.

The *Finney* was originally constructed as a three master and later her masts were relocated to permit greater cargo capacity. The fact that two mast steps aft of the main hold are boarded over, prove that this wrecked schooner had been reconfigured. This bit of information was critical to helping identify the wreck.

CONCERNING THE FINNEY.

Capt. Quigley of the schooner M. J. Cummings gives the most circumstantial account of the lost schooner Finney that has yet been learned of. He left Toledo behind the Finney but came up with her off Point Pelee and the two kept in sight of each other until well past Long point on Tuesday. There was one of the heaviest gales blowing by that time that ever lashed Lake Erie. Some time during the day a snow squall came up and when it passed by nothing could be seen of the Finney. Capt. Quigley missed her and went aloft to look for her but could see nothing. He is sure that she went down in the squall.

The Cummings was very badly handled herself, but being a newer boat she weathered the gale. She had about 975 bushels of wet wheat in her cargo when it was unloaded here.

Report from the *Cleveland Plain Dealer*, November 25, 1891.

CHARLES FOSTER

Official #: 125581   **Site #:** 66

Location: 9.2 miles at 277°T off Erie, Pennsylvania Harbor entrance

Coordinates: Loran: 44345.2 58406.2   **DGPS:** 42 10.445 80 15.007

Lies: bow south   **Depth:** 75 feet

Type: schooner barge   **Cargo:** iron ore

Power: tow, sail

Owner(s) Captain James Corrigan of Cleveland, Ohio

Built: 1877 in Milan, Ohio by Valentine Fries

Dimensions: 227' x 36' x 15'9"   **Tonnage:** 997

Date of Loss: Sunday, December 9, 1900

Cause of Loss: storm

Charles Foster

Great Lakes Historical Society

Story of the Loss:

The steamer *Iron Duke* was making a late season run from Duluth, Minnesota to Erie, Pennsylvania with the *Charles Foster* trailing 600 feet behind her. They encountered not one, but two terrible gales on

Saturday night, December 8. The first thundered in from the south, kicking up the seas and forcing the two vessels to hug the south shore as they proceeded to the east. About midnight, the winds suddenly shifted and a tremendous gale developed from the northwest. The vessels were compelled to move farther from the shore as massive waves and blowing snow engulfed them. Seeing the lights of Erie through the blowing snow, Captain Ashley of the *Iron Duke* made the turn for Erie, Pennsylvania. The vessels continued to roll in mountainous northwest seas when the *Foster*, perhaps struck by a rogue wave, suddenly plunged to the lake bottom without warning. She carried Captain John Bridge, cook Mrs. E.C. Morse, first mate James Burns, seaman Robert Burns, wheelsman Barney Hawkins; and three other seamen to their deaths.

Asked the cause of the sudden loss, the crew of the *Iron Duke* all believed she had lost a hatch or sprung a leak. Captain Ashley reported his conviction that Captain Bridge had perhaps been ill for some time as he had not been seen on deck for three days. The master of the *Iron Duke* felt it was useless to attempt a search in the blinding, stinging snowstorm. "In those tremendous seas no one could have lived a minute, even if the water had not been cold. I would have turned and risked my ship, but it was no use. I had all I could do to make port in safety myself."

Venturing out the following day, the Erie lifesaving crew located the masts of the *Foster* and searched the area for several hours. Nothing was found of the lost crew. The ship's yawl boat and other wreckage washed ashore as the day progressed.

The Wreck Today:

Located on a silt bottom, the iron ore cargo has caused the vessel sides to splay outward. Proceeding from the bow there is an anchor, metal tank, windlass to port, pump, second metal tank, and the first of two capstans. Off the broken stern you will find the ship's stove and some china scattered about. Also look for her wheel off the stern on the starboard side in the mud grooves.

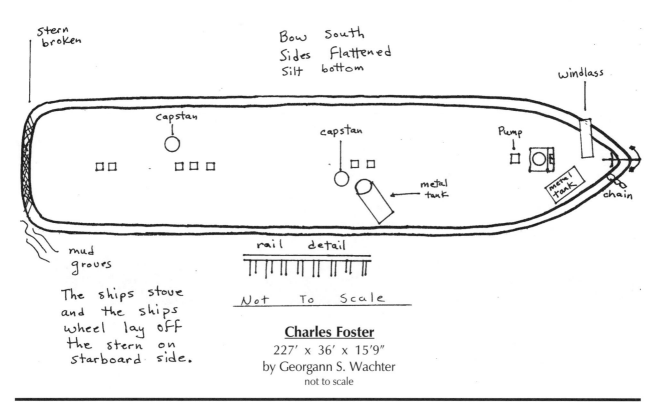

Charles Foster
227' x 36' x 15'9"
by Georgann S. Wachter
not to scale

HOWARD S. GERKIN

Official #: 225429   **Site #:** 59

Location: 9.13 miles 40 °M off Erie, Pennsylvania Harbor entrance. Position approximate.

Coordinates: Loran: DGPS:

Lies: turtled   **Depth:** 70 feet

Type: sandsucker   **Cargo:** sand

Power: twin steam propeller

Owner(s) Gravel Products Corporation of Buffalo, New York

Built: 1917 as *Rosamond Billett* finished 1918 at Trois Rivers, Quebec by Tidewater Ship building

Dimensions: 241′ x 41′ x 14′   **Tonnage:** 1322 gross 803 net

Date of Loss: Saturday, August 21, 1926

Cause of Loss: storm

Howard S. Gerkin as T.P. Phelan

Great Lakes Historical Society, Bowen Collection

Story of the Loss:

The *Gerkin* was launched as the freighter *T.P. Phelan*. In 1926 the Buffalo Shipbuilding Company converted her to a sandsucker and she changed nationality from Canadian to United States. She was renamed *Howard S. Gerkin* for the brief period before her loss. She had just completed some work at Presque Isle and was returning to Buffalo when she was lost.

Howard S. Gerkin who was aboard his ill-fated namesake described the loss as follows:

"We traveled to Erie from Buffalo during the day Friday and were just setting out on the return at 8:00 that night. A thirty mile wind which was blowing when we pulled out of the harbor increased to fifty miles at 8:30. Water poured over the decks and imperiled all aboard as the gale, blowing from the southeast, rose to eighty-two mile an hour around 9:30. We sent out distress signals by radio and lights which were not seen in the Erie port.

We turned back to port, but the rain and hail was so heavy that it was impossible to get our bearings. With death staring us in the face, we soaked a mattress with kerosene and set it on fire atop the engine house. It brought the *Maitland* to our aid, and only through the heroic bravery of its captain and crew were we brought to safety."

The car ferry, *Maitland,* running from Ashtabula, Ohio to Port Maitland, Ontario had seen the flames from the burning mattress and gone to the aid of the sandsucker. At 1:30 a.m., the sandsucker gave up. Having sprung a leak, she rolled on her side. The men aboard managed to launch three lifeboats with nine men in one, four in a second, and seven in the third. At that moment the *Maitland* appeared on the scene and picked up the lines of the three lifeboats. Unfortunately one line snapped in the wild waves and driving hail and the boat disappeared into the night. The car ferry searched the waters for three hours. Nothing was to be found of the missing lifeboat.

The 16 men skillfully rescued by the *Maitland* were taken to Ashtabula, Ohio. The following day, one occupant of the missing lifeboat, Fireman Norman Wageman, was later plucked, semiconscious, from the lake by the Coast Guard 15 miles northwest of Erie. The fish tug *Uranus* recovered the lifeboat at noon that day. It was overturned and empty. Three men, mate George McMinn, watchman Richard Freeman, and engineer William Logan had lost their lives amidst the hailstones in a storm tossed sea.

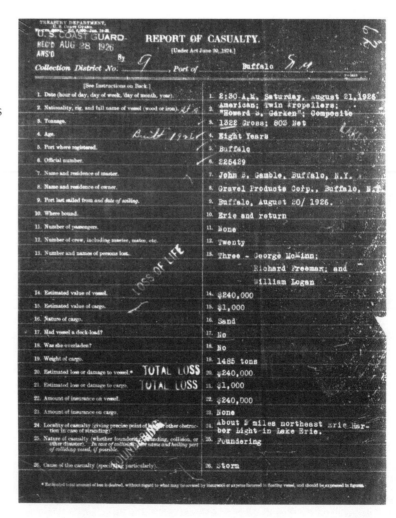

The U.S. Coast Guard Report of Casualty provides details of the loss of the sandsucker *Howard S. Gerkin*.

The Wreck Today:

This wreck has been found and is being dove. The wreck is upside down, and a debris field lies 50 to 100 feet to the west of the hull.

As of this writing we have not dove this wreck, and are relying on discriptions provided by those who have.

GLM 507

Official #: Former US# 291051   **Site #:** 73s and 73b

Location: 316°T, 20.5 miles off Erie, Pennsylvania Harbor entrance

Coordinates: Loran: 44409.9 58395.5   **DGPS:** stern: 42 22.289   80 20.922

                                                        bow: 42 36.497   79 54.443

Lies: broken and scattered   **Depth:** 70 feet

Type: steel barge   **Cargo:** 1600 tons of pig iron

Power: towed

Owner(s) Great Lakes Marine Contracting, Ltd. of Port Dover, Ontario

Built: 1963 at Mobile, Alabama

Dimensions: 240' x 50' x 11'   **Tonnage:** 1,100 gross and net

Date of Loss: Wednesday, November 18, 1981

Cause of Loss: foundered

GLM 507

John "Dooner" Misner

Story of the Loss:

The 90 foot long tug, *Elmore M. Misner*, took the *GLM 507* in tow at Port Colborne, Ontario. She carried 50 to 60 bars of pig iron from the dock of the now defunct Algoma Steel Plant. The two vessels were headed for Cleveland, Ohio when foul weather forced them to take shelter under Long Point and she bottomed out on a bar. They waited out the weather for a period of time and then decided to venture out into the open lake.

In the middle of the night, the towline slackened. When the tug crew investigated, they discovered they were only towing the forward portion of the barge! Somewhere along the way, they had lost the stern portion. The decision was made to return to Long Point. Unfortunately, before they could reach safety, the remaining portion of the barge had to be abandoned in deep water off the point.

It is suspected that when she struck bottom rounding Long Point, she was damaged. This caused her to fracture from the bottom up, dropping her 50 pound bars of pig iron to the floor of the lake.

The Wreck Today:

GLM 507 was owned by John "Dooner" Misner and is commonly known as *Dooner's Barge*. The stern portion of the barge rests on a mud bottom in 70 feet of water. Some of her cargo is scattered about the remains of the barge. The bow rests in 165' of water close to Long Point. We have not visited the site but have been given these GPS coordinates: 42° 36.497' 79° 54.443'.

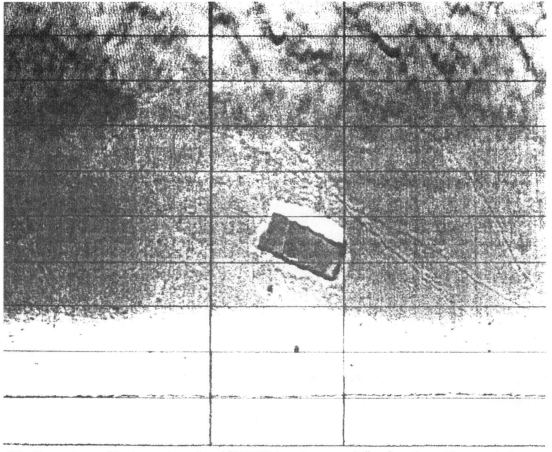

This sidescan image of the deep water portion of GLM 507 shows her squared off configuration and the ragged edge where the barge spli in two.

GOLDEN FLEECE

Official #: 10197   **Site #:**   22

Location: east of Canadaway Creek

Coordinates: Loran: DGPS:

Lies: scattered   **Depth:**   on shore

Type: schooner, 3 masts   **Cargo:**   light

Power: sail

Owner(s) Porters of Lorain, Ohio

Built: 1862 at Cleveland, Ohio by E.M. Peck and Masters

Dimensions: 161' x 30.5' x 12.2'   **Tonnage:** 452 gross 429 net

Date of Loss: Tuesday, October 14, 1890

Cause of Loss: storm

Golden Fleece

Aground at Canadaway Creek, Remick Collection

Story of the Loss:

Built as a barquentine in 1862, the *Golden Fleece* was converted to a schooner in 1869. Of note in her history is an incident in November 1884. According to newspaper reports, one of the captains of the *Golden Fleece* shot the wheelsman on Thanksgiving Day. The paper doesn't give a reason for the shooting. Perhaps the wheelsman wasn't holding a steady course.

The *Golden Fleece* left Buffalo, New York light. She was bound for Erie, Pennsylvania to take on a load of coal, which was to be delivered to Escanaba, Michigan. She encountered a gale out of the southwest and was holding her own until she broke her rudder chains. With no steering, the anchors were both lowered and set to hold the ship in place until the gale blew out. Her anchors strained to hold against the wind driven waves as the ship dragged inexorably toward the beach. Her port anchor chain parted and then, left to hold on its own, the starboard anchor chain also parted. With no steering and no anchors, the *Golden Fleece* was driven on the beach west of Dunkirk, New York. The revenue cutter *Commodore Perry* came to her aid. Seeing that the crew was in no grave danger, the *Commodore Perry* assisted the crew in retrieving their clothing and personal effects.

One crewman lost three fingers in the incident. The other five crewmembers and the female cook were uninjured.

In the aftermath of the wreck, famed salvor Tom Reid bid $5.000 for the *Golden Fleece*. Using oil barrels and a few jacks, he prepared to refloat the ship. Just as final preparations were being completed, a violent storm came in and dashed the *Golden Fleece* to pieces. At this point, Reid had lost $7,500. To his good fortune, he heard stories of a tug sunk and abandoned earlier in the year. Going door to door, he sought the location of the sunken tug. Finally, a farmer was able to show Reid where the tug lay. By salvaging the tug's boiler and engine, Reid was able to recoup his investment and make a small profit.

The Wreck Today:

The scattered remains of the *Golden Fleece* are buried beneath shifting sands just east of Canadaway Creek. After a storm, parts of the vessel are occasionally exposed, only to be buried by sand once again.

Remains of the *Golden Fleece* circa 1934.

GULNAIR

Official #: C 71157   **Site #:** 84

Location: inside the outer break walls of Ashtabula Harbor, Ohio

Coordinates: Loran: 44123.2 58067.8   **DGPS:** 41 54.77   80 46.89

Lies: north/south   **Depth:** 12 feet

Type: schooner, 3 masts   **Cargo:** millstones

Power: sail

Owner(s) Thomas Myles and Sons of Hamilton, Ontario

Built: 1873 at Port Robinson, Ontario by J. Abbey

Dimensions: 142' x 24' x 11'   **Tonnage:** 391

Date of Loss: Friday, July 15, 1892

Cause of Loss: storm

Ashtabula Harbor circa 1885

Author's Collection

Story of the Loss:

News accounts are very sparse on the loss of the Gulnair. Despite the fact she went aground at Ashtabula, the July 17, 1892 *Ashtabula Sentinel* gave the incident a mere three sentences:

> "A severe storm prevailed on Lake Erie Friday afternoon and night. The Canadian schooner Gulnair went ashore at Woodland Beach Park, just east of Ashtabula Harbor. She is valued at $5,000 and will be a total loss.

She belonged to Thomas Myles and Sons who were coal merchants in Hamilton, Ontario. The schooner had been sunk at least one other time. In 1882 she sank in the channel at Kingston, Ontario. She was successfully raised and sailed for ten more years before her final loss at Ashtabula, Ohio.

The Wreck Today:

Located on a sand bottom inside the outer breakwaters of Ashtabula Harbor, the *Gulnair* forms a triangle with two other shipwrecks, the *Joy* and *Wonder*. Known commonly as the "Harbor Wrecks", these three vessels are home to many fish. Due to their proximity to the harbor and shallow depth, the "Harbor Wrecks" make an excellent night dive. Divers who discovered the James F. Joy in 1960 developed the map on page 209. They thought the wreck was in three sections. In reality, there are three wrecks, *Joy*, *Gulnair*, and *Wonder*. These three "Harbor Wrecks" can all be covered in a single dive. The *Gulnair* lies furthest to the south. *James Joy* is the furthest east. Furthest west is the *Wonder*.

A dive flag float and a good lookout are necessary due to the heavy boat traffic at this site.

CARL FEATHER / The Star-Beacon

Divers and other volunteers who retrieved the two-ton millstone from Lake Erie pose with their bounty in front of the Marine Museum. The volunteers are (from left) Chris Brooks, Richard Gould and son Richard, Bruce Watson, David Marsh and son David JR. and Rick Lenart. The stone will become a permanent part of the museum's collection.

Photo and caption from *Ashtabula Star-Beacon*

BETTY HEDGER

Official #: 169396

Location: 352°T 5.1 miles off Barcelona, New York

Coordinates: Loran: 44571.2 58791.5 16522.1

Lies: bow west

Type: barge

Power: towed

Owner(s) New York Scow Corporation

Built: 1927 at Kingston, New York

Dimensions: 113.2′ x 30.1′ x 12.7′

Date of Loss: Tuesday, November 2, 1937

Cause of Loss: foundered in a storm

Site #: C

DGPS: 42 25.110   79 36.528

Depth: 115 feet

Cargo: sulfur

Tonnage: 460

Ballenas

Private collection of Ralph Roberts
Betty Hedger was in tow of the Ballenas when she foundered.

Story of the Loss:

Along with the barges *Lizzie Harvey*, *American Sailor*, and *American Scout*, the *Betty Hedger* was in tow of the steel tug *Ballenas*. Reputed to be one of the most powerful tugs on all of the Great Lakes, the *Balenas* did not have the might needed to overcome the stormy seas that swept over Lake Erie as she and her sulfur laden barges progressed from Buffalo, New York toward Cleveland, Ohio.

When about 12 miles off Dunkirk, New York, the *Ballenas* sent out distress calls and turned for the protection of Erie, Pennsylvania. The Coast Guard surf boat from Erie removed eight men, two from each barge, as the intensity of the storm grew. Strained by the mounting seas, the towlines of three of the barges parted, leaving only one, the *Betty Hedger*, in tow of the *Ballenas* as she continued toward Erie.

The Coast Guard cutter *Tahoma* barged through heavy seas and the cold northern winds from Cleveland to provide assistance to the Coast Guard cutter *Petrel* from Erie. However, everyone feared the *Tahoma* would not arrive before the following morning. Thus she would not be in time to render assistance. For the barges, this fear proved true. The following day the *Tahoma* reported all four barges accounted for, three being broken up and washed ashore and the fourth sinking while still in tow some fifteen miles off Dunkirk Light. Fortunately no lives were lost in this incident.

The Wreck Today:

The mooring line for the *Hedger* is attached to a collapsed bow beam of the wreck. Although the starboard side has fallen to the outside and the port side has fallen to the inside, beams still support part of the decking and the hatch frames, some twelve feet off the bottom. The deck at the bow has several tow bits, a capstan, a small winch, and an anchor. The seven hatches are rimmed by a low wall with cleats at regular intervals. At the east end, there are the remains of a small cabin whose sides still have two portholes, complete with screens. There is a canted section of deck on the starboard stern with a small capstan. Large piles of sulfur remain inside the framework of the wreck.

Divers should check out the 460 ton marking carved on her forward beam. This tonnage mark was used to establish the identity of the wreck. A running light remains on the port bow and is one of the highlights of the wreck.

Visibility often exceeds 70 feet. However, the bottom temperature hovers no higher than 40°. Divers should watch for current on this site.

Tonnage marking and sulfur cargo. Photos by Georgann Wachter.

Deck, cabin window, and bow equipment. Video captures by Mike Wachter.

CHARLES B. HILL

Official #: 6961   **Site #:** 86

Location: 66°T 12.8 miles off Fairport, Ohio harbor entrance ½ mile off Madison, Ohio

Coordinates: Loran: 44042.4 57909.2   **DGPS:** 41 50.585 81 03.140

Lies: bow south   **Depth:** 18 feet

Type: wood propeller   **Cargo:** coal

Power: compound condensing engine

Owner(s) John Boland of Buffalo, New York, M.J. Galvin and others

Built: 1878 at Cleveland, Ohio by Thomas Quale's Sons

Dimensions: 252' x 36' x 16'   **Tonnage:** 1732 gross 1527 net

Date of Loss: Friday, November 23, 1906

Cause of Loss: seams opened in storm

Charles B. Hill

Great Lakes Historical Society

Story of the Loss:

The *Hill* was originally named *Delaware* and operated by the Anchor Line until 1905.

All seamen on Lake Erie learn to respect the gales of November. These treacherous storms form a common thread among many of the shipwrecks in this inland sea. As often happens, it was a nasty November blow that proved to be the undoing of the *Charles B. Hill*, the package freighter *Conemaugh*, and several other lake vessels in 1906.

Captain Coleman and crew were towing the barge *Commodore* from Buffalo, New York when they were caught in a ferocious gale. The *Hill* began to leak, and a decision was made to cut the *Commodore* loose so the *Hill* could make a run for Fairport, Ohio. As the propeller attempted to make Fairport, her port seams opened, allowing water to pour into the boat. Now, a desperate run to shore began. As the waters rose in her holds, the *Hill* rushed to shore near Madison, Ohio. Although the crew managed to run her aground on a North Madison beach, the distance to shore and pounding surf prevented them from leaving the vessel. The lifesaving crew left Fairport aboard the tug *Annie* at approximately 10:00 a.m. It took them two hours to reach the beached *Hill*. Struggling against a heavy sea, the 20 member crew of the *Charles B. Hill* was safely transferred to the *Annie*. All reached Fairport unharmed by 3:30 p.m.

The *Commodore* had set her anchors three miles off Madison and simply waited. She was picked up by a tug and taken to Ashtabula. In June of 1918, the *Commodore* and her steamer tow, *Jay Gould,* foundered at the west end of Lake Erie.

The Wreck Today:

Much of the *Charles B. Hill's* cargo was lightered in an attempt to save her. The bottom is shale and bedrock. The large wood hull is in three sections and provides a home for many fish. Steam pipes and metal pieces litter the area. The boiler lies about 300 feet east of the wreck and comes close enough to the surface to be a hazard to your boats propellers. There is also a smaller boiler.

The day we last dove this site there was a strong current from the west. To the northeast of the coordinates given (wood hull) there are several sections of the wreck, which lie in an east/west orientation. Metal plates and parts lie scattered throughout the site.

Many bass inhabit the area and it is often frequented by recreational fishing boats.

Line up the gable of the third house west of Hubbard Road with the tree and head out about ½ mile to 18 to 20 feet of water.

Charles B. Hill as the Steamer Delaware.
Great Lakes Historical Society Bowen Collection

INDIANA

Official #: 12086   **Site #:** 58

Location: 21°T 10.3 miles off Erie, Pennsylvania harbor entrance

Coordinates: Loran: 44451.7 58564.8   **DGPS:** 42 17.760 79 59.898

Lies: bow northeast   **Depth:** 90 feet

Type: barkentine   **Cargo:** curbing stone

Power: sail

Owner(s) Palmer and Pennington of Cleveland, Ohio and Captain A. McAdams

Built: 1852 at Oswego, New York by G.S. Weeks

Dimensions: 136'9" x 25'2" x 11'   **Tonnage:** 260.75

Date of Loss: Saturday, September 24, 1870

Cause of Loss: storm

Typical Barkintine Rig

Merchant Vessels of the Great Lakes

Story of the Loss:

Under Captain McAdams' watchful eye, the *Indiana* had been loaded with 25 cords of paving stone and flagging at Buffalo, New York and was bound for Cleveland, Ohio. The stone had been carved from the Niagara Gorge and was to be put to use as curbing stone on its arrival in Cleveland. Regrettably, the stone would never arrive. The bark encountered more storm than she could handle as she approached Erie, Pennsylvania. The ship began to leak at 10:00 a.m. and the crew was forced to abandon her by 10:00 p.m. Shortly thereafter, she nosed into the lake and never recovered, diving bow first to the bottom. Her crew were all saved and attended to in Erie.

The Wreck Today:

For several years after her discovery, the *Indiana* was known simply as the "stone wreck." Her cargo of stone still sits in place below and above decks as it was stowed at Buffalo, New York before she departed on her final voyage. The bow is broken and the masts are down.   One lies off the starboard bow, the other off the port stern. The ship hosts belaying pins still in their holders and her capstan and rigging winch are in place. Deadeyes line her gunnels in three locations indicating the rigging for her three masted, barkentine configuration. Two wood stock anchors can be found amongst the timbers at her bow. The ship's stove lies in the debris field off the stern of the wreck.

Lying in 90 feet of water, this is an excellent dive within the range of sport diving limits.

Indiana
138' x 30'
by Georgann S. Wachter
not to scale

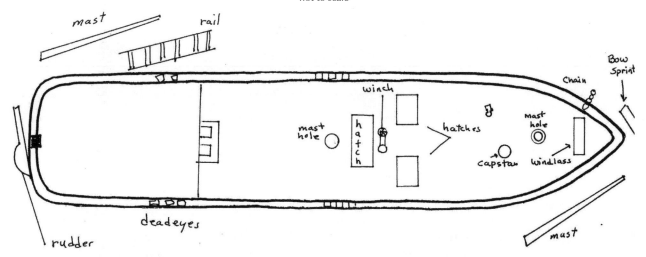

WASHINGTON IRVING

Official #:   none

Location: 299°T 6.7 miles off Dunkirk, New York

Coordinates: Loran: 44674.2   58895.3   28916.8

Lies: bow north

Type: schooner, two masts

Power: sail

Owner(s)   Scott and Marshall of Erie, Pennsylvania

Built: 1845 by B.B. Jones of Cleveland, Ohio

Dimensions: 81'1" x 20'1½" x 7'7½"

Date of Loss: Saturday, July 7 or Sunday, July 8, 1860

Cause of Loss: unknown

Site #:   29

DGPS: 42 32.371   79 27.636

Depth: 120 feet

Cargo: coal and pig iron

Tonnage: 111 44/95

Schooner Glen Cuyler is similar to the Washington Irving

Story of the Loss:

When searchers first discovered this beautiful schooner with her two masts still standing, they named her *"Schooner B"*. Charter operator Jim Herbert of Barcelona, New York believes the wreck to be the *Washington Irving*.

The *Washington Irving* was built with a scroll figurehead and a square stern by one of the noted ship masters of the day, B.B. Jones. She sailed fifteen years before her tragic loss. Unfortunately for the *Irving*, she became one of many vessels that went missing and unnoticed. She had left Erie, Pennsylvania on Saturday, July 7th and was bound for Buffalo, New York. The first clue that she was missing occurred when the tug *J.B. White* discovered her provision chest floating near Dunkirk, New York the following Monday. When she sank , she took the lives of Captain Steven Vannatta, Mate Antonia Veary, passenger Cornelius Leary, and Before the Mast (crewmen) Henry House, Owen Keep, and Peter Silvey.

Divers explore her upright masts.

None knew why she sank. None knew when she sank. All anyone knew was she was gone and had taken her crew with her. The *Erie Weekly Gazette* reported "We have nothing to add to the account of the loss of the schooner *Washington Irving*. No other conclusion can be reached than that the vessel, from some unknown cause, suddenly sank to the bottom of the lake." Perhaps the vessel sprung a leak or perhaps her load of pig iron shifted and pulled her under. As there were no survivors to tell the tale, we will never know.

The Wreck Today:

The mooring for the *Washington Irving* lies off her port side. Both masts are still standing, but canted to port as the wreck lists in that direction. Her stern is partially buried on the port side. The bow is quite rounded and boasts an intact bowsprit. There is often a current on this site and the water temperature is generally below 50° under the thermocline. For those who want to see a schooner with her masts still standing, this may be the only opportunity to do so on a wreck that is still in the depth range of a sport diver. At 120 feet she is at the maximum depth certifying agencies recommend for sport divers.

Anchor at the bow. Video captures by Mike King.

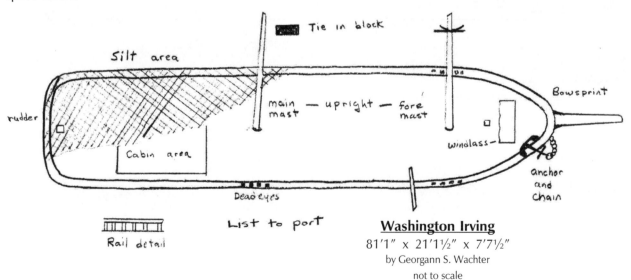

Washington Irving
81'1" x 21'1½" x 7'7½"
by Georgann S. Wachter
not to scale

ISOLDE

Official #: 126722   **Site #:** 56

Location: east of Erie, Pennsylvania, 300 yards west of 7 mile creek ¼ mile offshore

Coordinates: Loran: 58555.0   28883.2   44408.0   **DGPS:** 42 11.88   79 58.67

Lies: east/west   **Depth:** 10 feet

Type: wood barge   **Cargo:**

Power: towed

Owner(s) Lake Chelan Steamship Company - Cornelius-Boland Line

Built: 1891 at West Bay City, Michigan by James Davidson

Dimensions: 298' x 41' x 21'   **Tonnage:** 2140 gross   2058 net

Date of Loss: Thursday, April 27, 1933

Cause of Loss: storm

Isolde as C.W. Jacob

Private collection of Ralph Roberts

Story of the Loss:

The *Isolde* was built as the steam powered freighter *City of Paris* in 1891. She became the *C.W. Jacob* in 1914. Fourteen years later, in 1928, her rig was changed to a barge at the Great Lakes Engineering Works in Ashtabula, Ohio. She was given the name *Isolde* on completion of this change.

The *Isolde* operated as consort of the propeller, *Tristan*. The vessels were named for two lovers in the Richard Wagner opera, Tristan. The *Isolde* had wintered in Erie, Pennsylvania. The day of the loss, the *Tristan* had arrived from Buffalo, New York to take the *Isolde* in tow to Detroit, Michigan. This would be their first (and last) voyage of the new season. Leaving the protection of Presque Isle, the boats were assaulted by a strong northwest wind. The hawser broke against the strain and the *Isolde* careened toward the beach east of Erie, coming aground in the turbulent seas at Seven Mile Creek.

As the *Tristan* stood off shore, the Erie Coast Guard came to the rescue. Headed by Captain M.G. McCune, the coasties were able to save the six crewman aboard the stranded barge before the former Hammermill Paper Company vessel broke up.

The Wreck Today:

Local residents used the *Isolde* as a fishing platform for years until it eventually burned. Time, waves, and ice have taken their toll of this wreck and today the site is fairly barren. There is a large quantity of wood and some anchor chain on a stone bottom. The boiler lies approximately 1500 yards to the west of the wreck and slightly further out. It is awash when the lake is low and presents a hazard your dive boat should avoid. Farther east, towards Shade's Beach, is a small boiler and about a 20' x 40' section of the wreck that the boiler was attached to.

This Remick Collection photograph shows a copper sink and other artifacts recovered from the Isolde in 1968.

JAMES F. JOY

Official #:	12788		**Site #:**	83
Location:	inside the breakwaters of Ashtabula Harbor			
Coordinates:	Loran:		**GPS:**	41 54.77 80 46.89
Lies:	east/west		**Depth:**	12 feet
Type:	3 masted schooner		**Cargo:**	iron ore
Power:	sail/towed			
Owner(s)	R. O'Brian of Erie, Pennsylvania			
Built:	1866 at Detroit, Michigan by McDonald			
Dimensions:	175' x 35'3" x 12'7"		**Tonnage:**	582 gross 553 net
Date of Loss:	Sunday, October 23, 1887			
Cause of Loss:	storm			

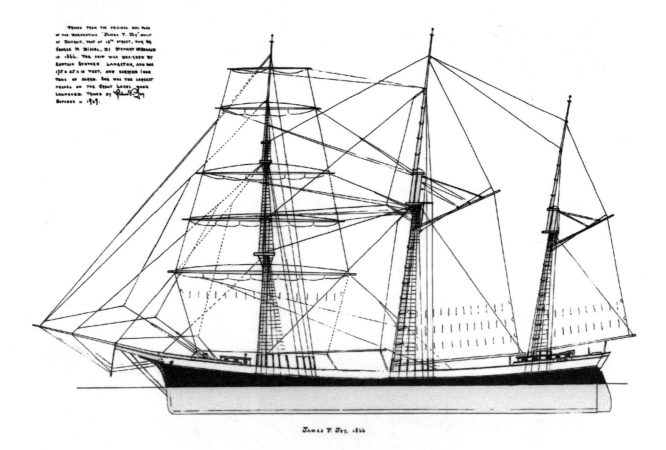

James F. Joy

Sail plan courtesy of Ralph Deeds, Birmingham, MI

Story of the Loss:

The *James F. Joy* was downbound from Escanaba, Michigan to Erie, Pennsylvania under tow of the tug *Winslow*. The common practice in rough seas at the time was to cut the tows loose and let them fend for themselves. Such is the story of the loss of the *Joy*.

The *Joy* had been having problems with leaks during the Lake Michigan passage. As a result, she had taken on additional crew as she transited the Detroit River. As the two boats made their way down Lake Erie, they encountered a storm. Believing they could not manage the storm with their consort in tow, the *Winslow* chose to cast the *Joy* loose.

Drifting down the coast, the *Joy* let her anchors down just east of Ashtabula, Ohio. Her double crew was hard at work attempting to contain the waters driving through her seams. Two tugs, the *Lucy Gordon* and *Red Cloud* attempted to bring her inside the harbor, but had to give up the effort as she was leaking too badly. When she sank, Captain Christie was almost washed from the fore top. The thirteen members of her crew had climbed the rigging and were rescued by a small boat. They had lost everything they owned save the clothes on their backs.

Also lost in this storm were the barge *Oriental,* the schooner *Zach Chandler,* and the propeller *Delaware.*

As an obstruction to navigation, twice in 1888 bids were requested to have her removed. All bids were deemed to be too high and no action was taken other than to buoy the wreckage. In September 1889 bids were again requested to have her removed and an offer of $2,475 was accepted. The wreckage was dynamited and the cargo was clamshell salvaged.

The Wreck Today:

The remains of the *Joy* form part of what is commonly called the "Harbor Wrecks" that lay inside the Ashtabula breakwaters. In addition to the salvage noted above, her 22 foot high rudder, pictured at right, was removed by divers in 1961. All that remains today are some timbers and a few metal parts laying among the weeds on the sandy bottom of the harbor.

Because it is shallow and attracts lots of critters, this is a popular night dive for divers in the Ashtabula Harbor area.

The map on page 209 was developed by divers who discovered the *Joy* in 1960. They thought the wreck was in three sections. In reality, there are three wrecks, *Joy, Gulnair,* and *Wonder.* These three comprise the "Harbor Wrecks" and can all be covered in a single dive. The *James F. Joy* is the furthest east. Furthest west is the *Wonder.* Furthest south is the *Gulnair.*

A dive flag float and a good lookout are necessary due to the heavy boat traffic at this site.

Jack Phelps stands beside the rudder from the James F. Joy in this photo from the October 12, 1974 *Ashtabula Star Beacon.*

The Tug *Champion*, towing sailing vessels through the straits at Detroit. This lithograph is made from the Whipple painting. From front to rear, the vessels in tow are: *Wells Burt, Michigan, Elizabeth A. Nicholson, James F. Joy, Francis Palms, Sweetheart, Sunnyside,* and *Emma L. Coyne.*

Great Lakes Historical Society, Captain H.C. Inches Collection

JUNCTION 20

Official #:   **Site #:**   39

Location: 312°T 25.5 miles off Barcelona, New York – 54°T 4.9 miles off Long Point Light

Coordinates: Loran: 44578.4   58633.8   DGPS: 42 35.402   79 58.378

Lies: bow west   **Depth:**   162 feet

Type: **Cargo:**

Power: sail

Owner(s)

Built:

Dimensions: **Tonnage:**

Date of Loss:

Cause of Loss:

The Wreck Today:

Nicknamed J*unction 20* because of its proximity to a gas well junction this unknown shipwreck has been heavily damaged by the gas pipeline. The site was found when a pipeline was dragged through the wreck as the line was being laid. Sitting in 160 feet of water, this dive is beyond the limits of sport diving as defined by all major certifying agencies. It should only be attempted by very experienced divers with specialized training and equipment for depths in excess of sport diving limits.

The ship is almost buried by silt. She is badly broken up and her foremast has fallen forward. It now lies beside and slightly to the port of the bow sprint.

Gas well tug Nadro Clipper

Author's Collection

Tugs like the one pictured above are used to tend the many gas pipe junctions in Canadian waters. The "Junction 20" wreck got its name by being close to one of these gas pipe junctions.

KILLARNEY

Official #: 229118   **Site #:** 91

Location: 28 miles north of Fairport, Ohio - position approximate

Coordinates: Loran: PA: 44147.7 57882.0 16496.4   **GPS:** PA: 42 09.502 81 14.588

Lies: **Depth:** 71 feet

Type: tug   **Cargo:** none

Power: 12 cylinder diesel engine

Owner(s) Gaelic Tug Boat Company, William Hoey of Gross Isle, Michigan

Built: 1929 at Mariners Harbor, New York by United Dry Docks

Dimensions: 91'5" x 22' x 10'   **Tonnage:** 176 gross 119 net

Date of Loss: Thursday, September 12, 1974

Killarney as the Bruce A. McAllister

Remick Collection

The steam ocean-going tug *Killarney* was built for the Standard Transportation Company and originally named the *Socony 23*. In 1960 she was sold to McAllister Brothers, Inc. of New York and renamed *Bruce A. McAllister*. Shortly before her loss, she was sold to Gaelic Tugboat Company of Grosse Isle, Michigan and renamed, *Killarney*.

Story of the Loss:

The tug was en route from New York City to her new home in Grosse Isle, Michigan when the five man crew issued a distress call. They were taking on water and sinking fast. Responding to her calls were Coast Guard units from Ashtabula, Fairport, and a helicopter from Detroit. The forty-foot Coast Guard cutter from Fairport was within one mile of the tug when the Canadian tug *C. West Pete* reported having taken the *Killarney* crew on board. Shortly after their rescue, the *Killarney* sank almost exactly on the U.S. Canada boundary line. The *C. West Pete* took the *Killarney* crew members to Port Burwell, Ontario.

Following the loss, the United States Coast Guard Cutter *Kaw* circled the site looking for oil leakage. None was reported. Due to pollution concerns, current U.S. law requires the owner of a lost vessel to salvage the wreckage. Failing that, the Coast Guard or Army Corps of Engineers will do the salvage work and bill the owners. It is estimated that 12,000 gallons of fuel were aboard the *Killarney* when she went down.

The Wreck Today:

Known on some wreck lists as the *Unknown USA*, this wreck sports a beautiful ship's wheel.

Killarney as the Bruce A. McAllister. Private Collection of Ralph Roberts.

C.B. LOCKWOOD

Official #: 126650   **Site #:** 92

Location: 13.3 miles at 337° from Fairport, Ohio position approximate

Coordinates: Loran: **P.A. GPS:** 41 56.56 81 23.50

Lies: bow west   **Depth:** 75 feet

Type: wood propeller   **Cargo:** wheat

Power: Hodge triple expansion 23"-37"-62" diameters x 40" stroke steam engine

Owner(s) Gilchrist Transportation Company of Cleveland, Ohio

Built: 1890 at Cleveland, Ohio by Thomas Quayle and Sons.

Dimensions: 285'2" x 45' x 19'9"   **Tonnage:** 2323 gross 1918 net

Date of Loss: Monday, October 13, 1902

Cause of Loss: storm

C.B. Lockwood

Great Lakes Historical Society

Story of the Loss:

The *C. B. Lockwood* had set out from Duluth, Minnesota with an uninsured cargo of wheat and grain. The lakes would not be kind to her. For two days the *Lockwood* was lashed by rain and sleet as she made her way toward Buffalo, New York.

As the pounding waves took their toll, the *C.B. Lockwood* began to labor in the seas. Captain Cassius Saph kept a nervous eye to the holds as the water in the ship's bowels slowly rose. The ship became more and more difficult to manage in the stormy waters of Lake Erie. Finally, when her steam pipe was broken, a massive leak threatened to overwhelm the boilers. Unable to keep up steam, the anchor was lowered and the captain ordered everyone aft to launch the yawl boats.

The larger of the two yawls was launched first. First Mate John Fritz and 9 crewmen hauled about 100 feet away and appeared to be riding the waves well as the second boat was lowered. In this boat were the captain, his wife, Mrs. Davis the cook, and 6 crew. As the yawl was lowered, it pounded so hard against the *Lockwood* that Mrs. Saph was certain the sides would be stove in.

Through the night the captain and his crew bailed and pulled for shore. In the darkest hours, one crewman was washed overboard. With great difficulty, the others were able to rescue him. In the process, an oar was lost. Left with only one oar the small yawl boat struggled on as the crew gradually lost hope for survival. At dawn, when they had all but given up hope, they were spotted by the steamer *G.J. Grammar* and taken aboard to be landed in Ashtabula, Ohio.

The larger yawl was found overturned near Ashtabula, Ohio. None of the 10 people on board survived the night's terrors. The steamers desk, containing $30.00 in silver, washed up off Madison, Ohio.

The Wreck Today:

The cabins and masts of the *Lockwood* floated away and are in a debris field well off the ship's hull. The hull sits on a mud bottom and offers about a 15' rise. In the debris field you'll find the *Lockwood's* railing and mast sticking out of the bottom as though the main body of the wreck is buried in the mud beneath them.

MARINE REVIEW.

VOL. I.   CLEVELAND, OHIO, THURSDAY, JUNE 26, 1890.   No. 17.

Launch of the C. B. Lockwood.

From the upper yard of Thomas Quayle's Sons their No. 141, built for B. L. Pennington and others, was launched, Wednesday afternoon, and was christened C. B. Lockwood by Miss Kent. The Lockwood is the largest wooden boat ever built in Cleveland, her dimensions being 303 feet over all, 285 feet keel, 45 feet beam, and 21 feet depth of hold. Her 13-foot 6-inch wheel, 16 feet lead, will be turned by Hodge triple expansion engines, 23, 37 and 62 inches with 42-inch stroke. The engines deck planking will give good dispatch in receiving and discharging cargoes. Her cabins are in imitation mahogany and cherry and the wide beam has been utilized to make the crew's quarters roomy and comfortable.

The No. 141 does not represent all the ships built by Thomas Quayle, who located his yard here in 1847, for there are a number of which no record was made. But even at that this yard leads the list of lake ship yards in the number of vessels turned out. Among them are the Neosho, Neshoto, A. P. Wright,

Drawn by H. F. Sprague.   STEAMSHIP C. B. LOCKWOOD.

combine the latest improvements found on sea going ships. The placing of the high pressure cylinder between the intermediate and low pressure will give good results. There is probably no better arranged engine room on the lakes. Three 11½ by 12 Lake Erie boilers will furnish the steam at 160 pounds pressure. She is fitted with the "Providence" ship windlass, furnished by Upson, Walton & Co.

It is expected that there will be room in her for 2,500 tons of ore, and her medium fullness and easy lines will combine to give her satisfactory speed. Her eight hatches and absence of main

Olympia, Yakima and J. C. Lockwood, some of the best boats in the larger fleets. In each some improvement has been made, so that the Lockwood should be very nearly a perfect boat. Mr. B. L. Pennington and other gentlemen who are interested in her were present and expressed their satisfaction and pride.

Capt. Jollie will be in command, while James F. Williams will have charge of the engines, with James Williams as second. The boat was so nearly completed when she went into the water that it is expected she will get away for Duluth with coal some time, Saturday.

The June 26, 1890 *Marine Review* announced the launch of *C.B. Lockwood*, "the largest wooden boat ever built in Cleveland."

JOHN B. LYON

Official #: 76199   **Site #:** 76

Location: 357°T 4.1 miles off Conneaut, Ohio harbor entrance

Coordinates: Loran: 44222.4 58212.0   **DGPS:** 42 02.375 80 33.753

Lies: bow east   **Depth:** 50 feet

Type: wood propeller   **Cargo:** iron ore

Power: 2 compound steam engines

Owner(s) J.C. Gilchrist of Cleveland, Ohio

Built: 1881 at Cleveland, Ohio by Thomas Quayle

Dimensions: 255'9" x 38'8" x 20'   **Tonnage:** 1710 gross 1330 net

Date of Loss: Wednesday, September 12, 1900

Cause of Loss: storm

John B. Lyon

Remick Collection

Story of the Loss:

When originally built, the *Lyon* carried 2 masts with sails. She generally operated with one or more tow barges. Before her eventual demise, the *Lyon* was involved in more than her fair share of fires, groundings, and collisions. She sank in the same storm as the schooner *Dundee*.

The *Lyon* began her final journey in Marquette, Michigan loaded with ore for Cleveland and towing the barge *F.A. Georger*. After leaving the barge in Ashtabula, Ohio the steamer continued on toward Cleveland, but put into Fairport for coal. The quality of fuel at Fairport was poor and the chief engineer felt that no suitable fuel could be found in Cleveland. As a result, the *Lyons* headed toward Erie, Pennsylvania — away from Cleveland. She encountered a storm, with 60 mile per hour winds, which caused the boat to take on water.

Seeing that no headway could be made against the mountainous waves, Captain Senghas ordered the ship brought about. He hoped that, by running before the sea, he might reach the safety of Ashtabula, Conneaut, or Erie harbors. Second Engineer David Brown was tending the engines. About one o'clock, he noticed the ship was becoming sluggish. With a draft of 20 feet, the ship had been loaded to 18 feet. This left only 2 feet of freeboard. She was overloaded and taking water at an alarming rate through her battered hatches. Tons of water were pouring in her, yet the ship's engine room floor was bone dry until the actual moment of sinking.

The captain sent several men below to cut drains in the ore to carry the water aft. At some point, the deck broke under Captain Senghas and he fell through into the hold. The lake had tormented the *Lyon* for hours with a terrific northwest sea. The waves had smashed off her pilot house, broken down her amidships deck house, and crushed in her deck, but the *Lyon* struggled on. Recognizing it was inevitable that the boat would be lost, fourteen men and one woman prepared themselves to wage the last fight. They donned their life belts and fastened themselves to lifeboats. Finding that one crewman had no life belt, the captain gave him his. The crewman who donned the captain's life belt survived. The captain, Mate Carlson, Chief Engineer Willows, Steward Alastona, and five other crew perished when the ship went down. She hung bow first with her stern high in the air when a final wave smashed off her stacks and she disappeared into a watery grave.

Anchor of the John B. Lyon on display at Conneaut lakeshore park. Photo by Georgann Wachter.

Six of the crew of 15, including the wife of the steward were rescued. Five of them had lashed themselves to a mast which came ashore near Girard, Pennsylvania. The sixth survivor, David Brown, was found unconscious on the beach. He had floated for 16 hours in the furious seas that sank the *John B. Lyon*.

The Wreck Today:

The *Lyon* lies on a sand and gravel bottom. Her four bladed prop is intact and makes a wonderful photo background. There are two boilers on her starboard side and the anchor chain extends from the bow. The anchor was salvaged by divers in the 1960's and donated to the city of Conneaut. Its recovery is featured in a March 1969 *Skin Diver Magazine* article. Today, the anchor sits in a lakeshore park dedicated to sailors lost on Lake Erie.

MAJESTIC

Official #: 92116   **Site #:** 77

Location: 128°T 18.6 miles off Port Burwell, Ontario

Coordinates: Loran: 44418.1 58325.8   **DGPS:** PA: 42 28.392 80 31.270

Lies: **Depth:** 55 feet

Type: propeller   **Cargo:** light

Power: 1800 horsepower triple expansion engine 20″ x 32″ x 42″ cylinder

Owner(s) J & T Hurley of Detroit, Michigan

Built: 1889 at West Bay City, Michigan by James Davidson

Dimensions: 291′ x 40′ x 21.1′   **Tonnage:** 1985 gross 1610 net

Date of Loss: Thursday, September 19, 1907

Cause of Loss: fire

Majestic

Remick Collection

Story of the Loss:

It was mid September of the 1907 season. The *Majestic* was upbound on Lake Erie, traveling light from Buffalo, New York to pick up grain in Toledo, Ohio. They had cleared Long Point and were off Port Burwell shortly after 1 o'clock in the morning when the alarm was sounded. Fire had broken out in the steering engine room.

According to Captain Hugh Hagen, "the fire was discovered in the steering room in the forward part of the boat shortly after 1 o'clock. We were then about ten miles west of Long Point. The fire alarm brought all hands on deck, and two streams of water were at once turned on the flames. The fire however, gained headway, and the heat became intense. Few of the men were fully dressed, but they all stuck to their posts and worked like Trojans to save the ship. Chief Engineer Thomas Purvis did not leave the engine room until we found that the ship was doomed. Second Mate Davis was clad only in trousers and shirt and his feet were scorched before he gave up.

"After fighting the flames for about an hour, the steamer *Tower* came to our assistance. The *Majestic* was swinging all around in the wind, and it was some time before the *Tower* could give us a line. The *Tower* finally came along side and helped fight the blaze. The fire seemed to gain greater headway, aided by a strong wind, and I saw that there was no chance of saving the boat. Our men were then taken aboard the *Tower* and we started for port. I don't know the cause of the fire because the flames were so fierce when discovered that it was impossible to investigate."

Captain Hagen credited the timely arrival of the steamer *Charlemagne Tower* for saving his crew. "We are extremely grateful to Captain Ellis and the crew of the steamer *Charlemagne Tower, Jr.* for the gallant fight made to save the burned steamer and for the kind treatment given the captain and crew of the *Majestic* on the trip into Buffalo."

The Wreck Today:

Much of the wood hull of the *Majestic* was consumed by fire. Her huge propeller makes a nice photo backdrop. Look for her exposed engines, scotch boilers, windlass, and steering gear.

Majestic at Riess Coal Dock, Ashland Wisconsin from private collection of Al Hart.

MANZANILLA

Official #:	C 85412	**Site #:**	27
Location:	225° 6.5 miles off Dunkirk, New York		
Coordinates:	Loran: 44625.9 58877.9	**DGPS:**	42 25.13 79 27.11
Lies:	southwest/northeast	**Depth:**	8-15 feet
Type:	3 masted schooner or bark	**Cargo:**	block stone and grindstones
Power:	sail		
Owner(s)	Captain Williamson of Hamilton, Ontario and John Murphy of Quebec		
Built:	1873 at Saint Catherines, Ontario by Louis Shickluna		
Dimensions:	137' x 26' x 12'	**Tonnage:**	340 gross 320 net
Date of Loss:	Thursday, October 13, 1887		
Cause of Loss:	sprung a leak in storm and run ashore		

Prince of Wales

Built by Shickluna and of approximately the same dimensions as the Manzanilla.

Remick Collection

Story of the Loss:

In the late 1800's, sailing traffic on Lake Erie was very heavy. Downbound vessels carried grain, lumber, stone, furs, and other natural resources to the east. Upbound vessels carried coal and immigrants to a new life in the west. In the crush of traffic, many vessels were lost with little or no notice. Among these is the schooner *Manzanilla*. She was the sistership of the *Magellan*, which went missing off Two Rivers, Wisconsin November, 1877. The *Manzanilla's* former captain, named Sheldon, is reported to have eloped with a "strange woman", leaving his wife and three children destitute.

Bound from Cleveland, Ohio to Toronto, Ontario, with a load of stone, the *Manzanilla* rode deep in the water. Passing vessels had reported seeing her in distress off Brockton, New York the evening of October 12, 1887. As is all too often the case, she was caught in a storm and proved no match for it. Sometime before dawn on October 13th she was driven ashore and wrecked by the gale winds blowing from the southwest.

Fortunately, seven members her crew were able to make it to shore on the *Manzanilla's* small boat. True to his position, her skipper, Captain George O'Brien, stayed with the boat as it was broken to pieces by the waves. The crew notified the lifesaving stations at Erie and Buffalo of the captain's predicament and neither station responded. Three men in the fishing boat *Beecher* braved the waves to rescue the captain, landing him in Dunkirk, New York at 8:30 p.m.

The Wreck Today:

The *Manzanilla* lies on a slope from eight to fifteen feet, just off the Lake Erie State Park. The large grindstones she carried are still in evidence. Most of the keel and lower ribs are there, but not much else. There is a small amount of anchor chain trapped under several block stones that were a part of the original cargo. The wreck lies parallel to shore (southwest to northeast). At one time there were two bilge pumps at the site.

Visitors to Lake Erie State Park can view the site of the Manzanilla from the shoreline. Photos by Georgann Wachter.

MARENGO

Official #: 17456   **Site #:** 18

Location: west of Port Colborne, Ontario near Morgan's Point

Coordinates: Loran: **DGPS:**   42 51.178   79 20.569
                                             42.51.112   79.20.600

Lies: broken in two parts   **Depth:** 22 feet

Type: schooner/barge   **Cargo:** coal

Power: sail/towed

Owner(s) G. B. Taylor of Erie, Pennsylvania

Built: 1873 at Milwaukee, Wisconsin by Wolf and Davidson

Dimensions: 189' x 32' x 14'   **Tonnage:** 648 gross   616 net

Date of Loss: Saturday, October 12, 1912

Cause of Loss: storm

Marengo

Private collection of Ralph Roberts

Story of the Loss:

The storm that swept Lake Erie on October 12 spanned the entire lake. It carried sustained winds of 50 miles per hour and did damage to vessels the length and breadth of the lake. Among its victims were the steamer *S.K. Martin* and the schooner/barge *Marengo*.

The *Marengo* was in transit from Erie, Pennsylvania to Port Colborne, Ontario when she was destroyed by this fierce storm. She was consort to the steamer *Lloyd S. Porter* and they had made it most of the way to Port Colborne before both vessels were driven aground late Friday evening. The vessels were only six miles off Port Colborne when the continuous working of the wind driven seas caused the towing hawser to break. Shortly thereafter, both vessels were driven on the beach at Morgans Point.

The *Porter* was able to free herself and steam on to Port Colborne. The *Marengo,* however, was driven further on the rocks and broken to pieces. Captain Joseph Dove and his crew of 4 men escaped in the ship's yawl boat. They managed to reach shore only after an exhausting battle with the towering waves.

The Wreck Today:

The *Marengo* rests in two parts, to the north and south of one another, in shallow waters off Morgans Point. As is common with all shallow water wrecks, the ice, wind, and waves have taken their toll on the remains of this once proud schooner. Coal and ship parts lie scattered across a large area and the remaining structure attracts many fish.

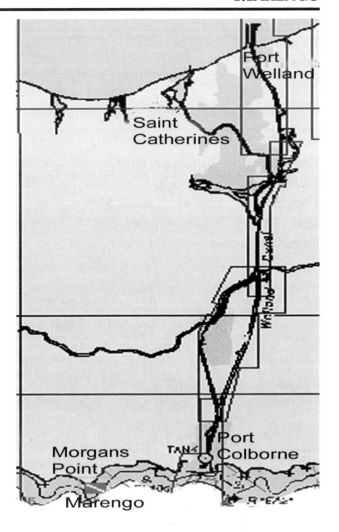

The remains of the Marengo lie off Morgan's Point, just to the west of Port Colborne, Ontario..

Had she made six more miles, the Marengo would have found safe harbor at Port Colborne. This 2001 photo of the port was taken by Georgann Wachter.

MARQUETTE & BESSEMER NO. 2

Official #: 202514   **Site #:** none

Location: Lake Erie

Coordinates: Loran: unknown   **DGPS:** unknown

Lies: unknown   **Depth:** unknown

Type: steel twin screw car ferry   **Cargo:** 30 rail cars of coal, steel, and castings

Power: 2 triple compound direct acting vertical steam engines, 19" - 31"- 52" x 36" cylinders

Owner(s) Marquette & Bessemer Dock and Navigation Company of Conneaut, Ohio

Built: 1905 at Cleveland, Ohio by American Shipbuilding Company

Dimensions: 338' x 54' x 19' 6"   **Tonnage:** 2514 gross

Date of Loss: Wednesday, December 8, 1909

Cause of Loss: foundered in storm

The second Marquette & Bessemer No. 2 at Port Stanley

Port Stanley Train Depot Museum

Story of the Loss:

On December 7, 1909, the four year old car ferry, *Marquette and Bessemer No.2* left Conneaut, Ohio, bound for Port Stanley, Ontario at 10:40 in the morning. She was loaded with 26 rail cars of coal, 3 rail cars of steel, and 1 rail car of castings. As the morning passed, she sailed into ferocious weather and was never seen again. Once she left Conneaut, there is much conjecture about where she went and what happened to her, but little that is known to be factual. The storm she sailed into would claim not only the M&B #2, but also the steamers, *Clarion*, *W.C. Richardson*, and two barges. The steamer *Josiah G. Muir* would go aground attempting to rescue sailors from the *Clarion*.

Nearly two hours behind schedule, the ferry pulled away from her berth, only to be hailed by a throng of onlookers pointing out that a man had missed the boat. Much to his misfortune, the big ferry reluctantly stopped, and permitted Albert Weiss, treasurer of the Keystone Fish Company of Erie, Pennsylvania, to scurry aboard. Traveling to Port Stanley to consummate the purchase of another company, Mr. Weiss is rumored to have carried $50,000 in his briefcase. As a result, *M&B #2* is considered to be one of Lake Erie's "treasure ships."

Though storm signals were posted, she navigated past the harbor light. Captain Bob McLeod was last seen waving a cheerful farewell to the lighthouse keeper as his vessel entered Lake Erie. The ship could do 12 miles an hour in the worst of conditions and the 60 mile trip to Port Stanley was normally no more than a five hour cruise. It is likely that, had she departed on time, she may well have made it safely across the lake.

Marquette & Bessemer No.2 trapped in the ice off Conneaut. Remick Collection

Many people recounted either seeing or hearing the ill-fated car ferry during the night. Mrs. Adam Large, who lived 10 miles east of Conneaut, said she had seen the car ferry from shore shortly before midnight on Tuesday. She tells of talking about it with her family and then going to look again only to find the lights were gone. At 1:30 in the morning on December 8, ore handler William Rice and his co-workers at Conneaut Harbor, heard distress signals they recognized as coming from the ferry. At about the same time, the master and chief engineer of the steamer, *Black*, claimed to have seen the *Marquette & Bessemer No.2* silhouetted by the Conneaut skyline. At 7:00 a.m. a Canadian from Bruce, Ontario claimed to have heard the car ferry's whistle 7 miles east of Port Stanley. These multiple sightings have led to extensive speculation and much confusion about where the *Marquette & Bessemer No.2* sank.

Two days after the *Marquette & Bessemer No. 2* sailed, the steamer *William B. Davock*, having survived the gale, sighted wreckage off Long Point on a course for Buffalo. This would prove to be the first confirmed sighting of the *M&B #2*. The following Sunday, the fish tug *Commodore Perry* recovered a ten man lifeboat 15 miles off Erie, Pennsylvania. Partly filled with water, the boat held the bodies of 9 members of the *Marquette & Bessemer No. 2's* crew.   None of these men were dressed for the elements. This generated supposition that the car ferry had gone down quickly, leaving no time for her crew to prepare to abandon ship. Four months later, on April 17, 1910, the ice encased body of first mate John McLeod washed into the intake slip of the Niagara Falls Power Plant. It was not until October 7, 1910 that captain Robert McLeod's body was found washed onto the beach on Long Point.

Captain Robert McLeod

Until the wreck is found, no one can know what actually happened to the long missing car ferry. One month before she sank, Captain McLeod had complained of almost losing her in a storm as the seas washed over her open stern and flooded her holds. The rising waters had nearly extinguished her boilers. The company had promised to add stern gates to the ship after the season ended. Many speculate that waves rushing over the open stern filled her holds and sunk her. While this may be true, she is known to have been built with 6 watertight bulkheads in her holds. Others speculate that the tie downs on one or more of the rail cars broke loose causing them to roll about the ship in the heavy seas until the *M&B* finally capsized. Still others insist Captain McLeod, knowing his vessel would take water over the stern on rough water, would have headed her into the storm and piloted her toward Erieau, Ontario. Only the 31 folks who died when she went down know for sure.

Compounding her difficulty was the fact that Port Stanley did not have proper navigation lighting. One scenario holds that she made it across the lake only to be unable to enter the harbor safely due to the seas and lack of lighting. If this were the case, she could well have returned to Conneaut to seek safe harbor from the storm. This would explain the reported sightings late in the night. Several petitions for lighting had been submitted to the Canadian government well before the loss of the *Marquette & Bessemer No.2*, but none were acted upon. Following the sinking, Port Stanley established navigation lights, a harbor of refuge, and a lifesaving station.

In a final insult to the ship and her crew, the Marquette & Bessemer Dock and Navigation Company replaced the lost ship with one of very similar design and the exact same name, *Marquette and Bessemer No.2*. Often the second *M&B #2* is pictured in articles about the lost original. They are best differentiated by their pilothouses. The older boat had an enclosed pilothouse with an open bridge above. As shown on the next page, the new boat had two enclosed pilothouses. The new boat was also wider by two feet. She also had stern gates and wireless communications.

The original Marquette & Bessemer No. 2 was replaced by this vessel, which also carried the name Marquette & Bessemer No. 2

Great Lakes Historical Society

The Wreck Today:

One of the last great secrets held by Lake Erie, the *Marquette and Bessemer No. 2* has yet to be found. After she sank, wreckage was found from Port Burwell to Long Point in Canada and from Conneaut past Erie on the US side. Many have looked for her without success. We suspect someone has found her, but is keeping the find to themselves.

A false report had the crew of the steamer *Black* sighting her heading east off of Conneaut at 1:30 the morning of the 8th. As a result, some believe she attempted to return to Conneaut, but was unable to enter the harbor. She could have attempted to anchor off Conneaut and ride out the storm until daylight. When her anchors failed to hold, she may have tried to make her way to the lee side of Long Point, a 50 mile run in a mountainous following sea. However, her debris fields and the location of her lifeboat argue against this theory.

We believe she'll eventually be found in the central basin of Lake Erie. However, your guess is as good as ours. One thing is for certain, she's well worth finding.

S. K. Martin

Official #:	126125	**Site #:**	55
Location:	50°T 9.2 miles off Erie, Pennsylvania harbor entrance		
Coordinates:	Loran: 44441.8 58587.3	**DGPS:**	42 14.546 79 56.004
Lies:	bow southeast (158°)	**Depth:**	56 feet
Type:	wood propeller	**Cargo:**	coal
Power:	350 horsepower high pressure steam engine		
Owner(s)	Captain W. J. Jock of Marine City, Michigan		
Built:	1883 at Benton Harbor, Michigan by J.H. Randall		
Dimensions:	152'5" x 28' x 11'	**Tonnage:**	302 gross 240 net
Date of Loss:	Saturday, October 12, 1912		
Cause of Loss:	storm		

S. K. Martin

Remick Collection

Story of the Loss:

When she was launched in 1883, she was the passenger ship, *City of Saint Joseph*. In 1888 she was converted to a bulk freighter and assumed the name *S. K. Martin*. Regardless of her name board, she was best known as *Skinny Martin*, the nickname given her by the boatmen of the time. The *Skinny Martin* left Buffalo, New York for Erie, Pennsylvania, fully loaded with coal. In Erie she was to pick up her consort, the barge *Melvina*, also loaded with coal. She sailed into a northwest gale that would claim several other vessels, including the schooner *Marengo* lost west of Port Colborne.

The *S. K. Martin* was struggling through the gale toward Erie when, close to 1:00 in the afternoon, Captain Jock noticed the ship was filling with water. A close examination revealed she had sprung a seam. Knowing his vessel would not survive, the captain ordered the female steward, Mrs. Bertha Knopf, to don a life jacket and sit in the watertight compartment of the yawl boat while the rest of the crew lowered the boat to the water. Boarding the yawl, they had barely gotten the boat clear when the *Martin* foundered. As the crew took to the oars, water rushed over the sides of the small boat and lines had to be fastened to each person and to the sides of the craft.

The tale told by a fireman whose face was still covered by the black dirt of the firehold is fascinating:

> "And we were just as gallant as the gentlemen on the **TITANIC** who received so much praises. When it was found that we must abandon ship, we stepped aside and Mrs. Bertha Knopf, the stewardess, was helped into the yawl and made as comfortable as the circumstances would permit. She had been sleeping and was suddenly awakened when the captain abandoned hope after the boat sprung a leak, the two anchors failed to hold the boat in the sandy bottom and the pumps refused to throw out the water as fast as it poured in. Our cook was brave throughout. She lost all her personal belongings, except a light dress she wore when she lay down after dinner. Mrs Knopf did not attempt to run back to her cabin to get her diamonds, gold watch, and rings, also her clothing, but said 'Boys, let us hope for the best', as she crawled into the yawl. All the way to the shore, she and the captain's young son were the bravest of the brave. We regret that our pleasant association on the boat must now be at an end. She was good to all of us and she showed that she was made of the real stuff."

By 4:00 p.m., at the height of the gale, the yawl was spotted from shore. An attempt was made to go to the aid of the survivors in rowboats. However, the seas were too turbulent and those on shore called the Erie Lifesaving Station. As more and more people gathered on shore, the 10 men and one woman aboard the yawl boat continued their battle with the raging sea. Their struggle ended when the boat was blown onto the beach. Surrounded by scores of people, the exhausted and chilled crew of the *S. K. Martin* were taken to a nearby house and treated by local physicians.

The Wreck Today:

The *Martin* lies on a hard mud and sand bottom and a west to east current is often present at this site. Her large boiler is in place. One anchor lies near her starboard bow along with an unidentified piece of the wreck. Near the stern on the port side are many engine parts and a capstan. The ship's mainmast was pulled out and towed to Erie.

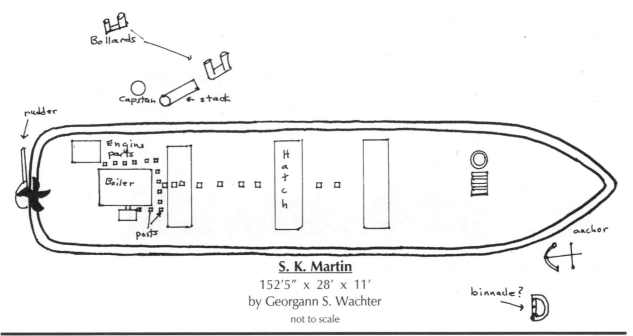

S. K. Martin
152'5" x 28' x 11'
by Georgann S. Wachter
not to scale

MAST HOOP/BOB POWELL'S

Official #:   **Site #:**   D

Location: 146°T 18.8 miles off Port Dover Ontario

Coordinates: Loran: **DGPS:**   42 33.418   79 59.524

Lies: **Depth:**   170 feet

Type: schooner   **Cargo:**

Power: sail

Owner(s)

Built:

Dimensions: approximately 145′   **Tonnage:**

Date of Loss:

Cause of Loss:

Mast hoops on the L.A. Dunten at Mystic Harbor, Connecticut

Photo by Georgann Wachter

Story of the Loss:

Unknown

The Wreck Today:

This unknown shipwreck recieved its dual names for the mast hoops at the site and for the tip from a commercial fisherman, Bob Powell, that provided her location.

The stern of the vessel rises from the bottom of the lake a mere five feet and the starboard side is buried in the sand. A thirty foot long piece of her mast layes to the port side.

In addition to the depth, which is beyond sport diving range, strong currents from the tip of Long Point make this an advanced dive.

The bowsprit and the mast off the port side are clearly visable in this sonar image of the Mast Hoop/Bob Powell Wreck. It is also clear that the starboard side of the wreck is buried in the silt.

Image from Ed McLaughlin, Days Off Dive Charters

J.G. McGrath

Official #:	none	**Site #:**	23
Location:	348°T 12.3 miles off Dunkirk, New York		
Coordinates:	Loran: 44739.7 58949.8	**DGPS:**	42 40.083 79 23.764
Lies:	bow west	**Depth:**	90 feet
Type:	schooner, 2 masts	**Cargo:**	stone
Power:	sail		
Owner(s)	North Shore Transportation Company, H.C. Dunlap of St. Catherines, Ontario		
Built:	1870 at Saint Catherines, Ontario by Louis Shickluna		
Dimensions:	104' x 26' x 12'	**Tonnage:**	219
Date of Loss:	Monday, October 28, 1878		
Cause of Loss:	storm		

Story of the Loss:

Sailing regularly off the waters of Long Point, the *J.G McGrath* had tempted fate once in November of 1873 when she went ashore at Long Point. On that occasion she was recovered and managed to sail for five more years.

On October 28, 1878, under command of Captain McAuley, the *McGrath* was carrying a load of cut stone from Rondeau Bay to Port Dalhousie, Ontario. From some distance away, the crew of the schooner *George W. Holt* saw the final moments of the *J.G. McGrath*. They observed the ship to lurch twice and then go down. There was no distress flag, but a propeller was very close by and the crew of the *Holt* assumed the propeller had rescued the crew of the ill fated schooner.

Captain Murray of the propeller *Araxas* reported that he had seen the schooner go down, but she appeared to have no crew on board. He further reported that his vessel came about and conducted an unsuccessful search for survivors. Believing the crew to have gone down with the ship, the *Araxas* steamed away. However, his story does not agree with the tale told by Captain McAuley.

As reported in the *Buffalo Commercial*:

> "Captain McAuley, of the schooner *J.G. McGrath*, which foundered off Long Point Monday morning, condemns the conduct of the captain of the *Araxes*, and tells a very different story from Captain Murray. He says the *Araxas* was in close hailing distance, and made no efforts to respond to the cries of the wrecked crew. The sea was running very high at the time and there was scarcely a possibility that the small boat, into which the crew managed to get, could weather the storm. With perfect indifference the propeller went away, allowing the suffering crew to be exposed to death. Fortunately the small boat did weather the storm and the crew arrived at Port Colborne in an exhausted condition."

We will never know whose story is true. We do know that the crew of the *McGrath* all managed to board their yawl boat. Rowing in huge seas, they traveled 16 miles from the site of the sinking to Port Colborne. Imagine the horror of rowing a small boat through towering seas for sixteen miles. This fight for their lives was made all the worse by a firm belief that the *Araxas* had intentionally left them at the mercy of the sea.

The Wreck Today:

Sitting in 90 feet of water with both her masts down, the *McGrath* shows heavy damage from her collision with the bottom. Propelled to the bottom by the overwhelming weight of her cargo, she was broken on impact. She is a beautiful dive with most of her working gear in place and her stone cargo scattered about the wreck.

Bowsprint

Bow

Starboard side

Windlass and pump

Cargo hatch

Videocaptures by Mike Wachter

Hold below decks

MERIDA

Official #: 92514   **Site #:** 90

Location: 25 miles east of Erieau, Ontario

Coordinates: Loran: 44160.1 57844.0   **DGPS:** 42 13.955 81 20.788

Lies: bow southeast   **Depth:** 85 feet

Type: steel propeller   **Cargo:** iron ore

Power: triple expansion steam engine

Owner(s) Valley Camp Steamship Company of Cleveland, Ohio

Built: 1893 by F. W. Wheeler in West Bay City, Michigan

Dimensions: 360′ x 45′ x 25′8″   **Tonnage:** 3329 gross 2389 net

Date of Loss: "Black" Friday, October 20, 1916

Cause of Loss: storm

Merida

Remick Collection

Story of the Loss:

At the time of her launch, in May of 1893, the *Merida* was the largest vessel on the Great Lakes. She also held a record for the biggest cargo. American Steamship Company rebuilt the vessel in 1909. She had a double hull and five watertight bulkheads. These proved insufficient in the wicked waves of Lake Erie.

The *Merida* was downbound from Fort William to Buffalo, New York when she ventured into the teeth of the great Lake Erie storm of 1916. The steamer *Frank Billing* followed the *Merida* out of the Detroit River that fateful Friday. However, before reaching the Southeast Shoal, the *Billings* could no longer see the *Merida*. The steamer *Briton* last saw her about 12:30 Friday afternoon. At that time she was 25 miles past Southeast Shoal, rolling heavily, and shipping heavy seas over her stern. This was the last sighting.

The *Merida* made another 35 miles before succumbing to the angry lake approximately 60 miles east of Southeast Shoal. Three days after the storm, the steamer *V. D. Mathews* recovered the first three bodies wearing *Merida* life jackets. The fate of Captain Harry Jones and his crew of 23 was no longer in doubt.

A few days after the storm, Port Stanley fish tugs recovered the floating wheelhouse with her brass bell still attached. Not until 60 years later was her exact location pinpointed.

The Wreck Today:

This awesome shipwreck lists slightly to port as she rises from the silty bottom of Lake Erie. Plan on two dives if you want to see the entire wreck. When we first dove her, the entire ship sat above the bottom of the lake. Today, the mid section of the ship disappears into the silt. Most divers dive the stern section first, move the boat to the bow and make their second dive. The stern of the *Merida* is easily penetrated. Caution is required due to heavy silt conditions, depth and the ability to go down more than one deck level. At the bow, you will find heavy damage to her decks and penetration is far more difficult.

Shipwreck penetration is dangerous. It should only be attempted by divers who are properly trained and equipped for wreck penetration.

The Merida as she appeared before her 1909 rebuild. Note the upper pilot house is open and the aft cabin is further forward. Photo from the Remick Collection.

MICHIGAN TRANSPORTATION BARGE #3 & #4

Official #:   #3: 67317   #4: 67318   **Site #:**   79

Location: 152°T 9.9 miles off Port Burwell, Ontario

Coordinates: Loran: 44388.4   58238.2   **DGPS:**   42 29.466   80 41.612

Lies: **Depth:**   65 feet

Type: wood railroad barge   **Cargo:**   pulpwood

Power: towed

Owner(s)   Lake Michigan Car Ferry Transportation Company

Built: 1895 at Toledo, Ohio by Craig Shipbuilding

Dimensions: 306.4 x 46.6 x 12.2   **Tonnage:**   1581 gross

Date of Loss: Tuesday, November 13, 1900

Cause of Loss: storm

Barge #4

Great Lakes Historical Society, Bowen Collection

Story of the Loss:

Michigan Transportation Company *Barges #3* and *#4* were built with four tracks to hold 28 railroad cars. They were originally intended to transport rail cars between Pestigo Harbor, Wisconsin and South Chicago. As this venture proved unprofitable, the barges were put in use for other cargo.

Loaded with pulpwood from Peshtigo, Wisconsin, *Barge #3* and *Barge #4* were in tow of the tug *Fisher* en route to Tonawanda, New York. To their misfortune, they encountered a mid-November gale, which forced everything on the lake that day to seek safe harbor. Oswego, Buffalo, and Harbor Beach, New York all reported record numbers of vessels to be sheltering from the storm. Caught off Long Point the tiny convoy had no safe harbor in which to hide.

As the gale winds blew over 70 miles per hour, the seas sweeping over the three vessels filled the holds of the barges and rapidly overcame the pumps ability to stay ahead of the onrushing water. When Captain Fred Johnson saw a distress flag raised on *Barge #4*, he began a desperate attempt to reach shelter around Long Point. As one approaches Long Point in a storm, the water action off the point creates mountainous rogue waves that come from different directions than the prevailing seas. The gale and the rogue waves proved too much for the 1½" steel towing hawser. It parted and the barges fell off into the trough of the sea.

Turning the tug first to *Barge #4*, Captain Johnson skillfully guided his vessel next to the barge in the wildly pitching waters. Seven crewmen on the barge managed to leap to the tug. The barge's cook was afraid to jump and had to be pushed off the sinking vessel to the relative safety of the tug. Captain Johnson then approached *Barge #3* and, in an extraordinary display of seamanship, brought his tug alongside the barge to rescue her crew. He then headed through the snowstorm to Erie, Pennsylvania.

The tug *Fisher* ventured out the following day to look for her tows, but they were never located. Captain Fred Johnson received a silver lifesaving metal for saving the crews from the two barges.

The Wreck Today:

We are not sure which of the two barges lies at the coordinates listed. They were both identical and the hull numbers have not been found. Maybe *Barge #3*, maybe *Barge #4*. Either way, she sits upright on a mud bottom. There are reports of additional wreckage ¼ mile west of the barge. This is believed to be either the other barge or part of the pulpwood cargo.

There is very little rise to this wreck and she is hard to see on a depth sounder. The easiest way to find her is to go down the pipeline marker line and follow the pipeline to the east. The pipe line runs direcly over the barge.

Barge #4

Great Lakes Historical Society, Bowen Collection

MUD WRECK

Official #:   **Site #:**   57

Location: 11 miles northeast of Erie, Pennsylvania

Coordinates: Loran: 44441.8   58581.3   **DGPS:**   42 15.06   79 57.06

Lies: **Depth:**   80 feet

Type: schooner?   **Cargo:**

Power:

Owner(s)

Built:

Dimensions: **Tonnage:**

Date of Loss:

Cause of Loss:

Story of the Loss:

Researcher Mary Howard tells us that, while it is certainly nothing definite, this wreck might be the *Rough & Ready*. She advises that her identification should be considered highly speculative as it is based only on the apparent age of the vessel and its location.

Laden with grain and barrels of flour, the *Rough & Ready* collided with the steamer *Constellation* on June 10, 1847. That same night, the steamer *Chesapeake* crashed into the schooner *Porter* and both sank. Each of these incidents occurred near Conneaut, Ohio.

While early reports had the *Rough and Ready* sinking immediately, two vessels reported seeing the partially submerged hull or floating cargo off Northeast, Pennsylvania. According to the June 16, 1847 *Conneaut Reporter*, the steamer *Champion* took the hull in tow below Erie, Pennsylvania and tried to make that port. However, the hull was too badly waterlogged and the effort was abandoned.

The U.S. Steamer *Michigan* recovered great quantities of flotsam from all three vessels. Stephen Champlin, Commander of the U.S. Steamer *Michigan*, reported as follows:

> "We left port on the 11th inst., after hearing of the disaster which had befallen the schooner *Rough & Ready*, laden with grain and flour consigned to R.H. Heywood, esq., of Buffalo, and after cruising about three hours came opposite Northeast, some 18 or 20 from this place (Buffalo, New York) , with floating pieces of wrecks and barrels of flour, some three miles from shore. We secured 132 barrels of flour, though we saw nothing if the schooner, which was reported drifting down the lake or gone to pieces in the late gale. We also picked up one satin vest, containing a gold pen and silver case, two sixpenny pieces, one led pencil and a black silk handkerchief, and a bill against Mr. Little, probably the steward of the *Chesapeake*. Also one black frock coat, containing two pairs of gloves, two pocket handkerchiefs, one tobacco box, and three yards of ribbon. Also three boxes of little or no value.

The Wreck Today:

According to those who have been on this wreck, there is only a one to four foot relief. The wreck rises off the bottom in three places. If you intend to search for this wreck, bring buoys and be prepared to do a bit of hunting.

From the looks of the site, early salvage attempts were made and these obliterated most of the vessel. Part of the bow protrudes above the silt and you'll be able to find an anchor and part of a mast. However, there is a reason it is called a mud wreck. The bulk of the remains are buried in the muddy lake bottom.

Visitors to the Erie area are often treated to the sight of the replica of Commodore Perry's Flag ship, *Niagara*.
Photo by Michael Wachter.

NIAGARA

Official #: C 73951   **Site #:** A

Location: 189°T 8 miles off Port Maitland, Ontario

Coordinates: Loran: 44719.8 58852.0   **DGPS:** 42 44.320 79 36.255

Lies: bow northeast   **Depth:** 90 feet

Type: wood propeller   **Cargo:** lumber, shingles

Power: steam

Owner(s) J. and J.T. Mathews of Toronto, Canada

Built: 1875 at St. Catherines, Ontario by Melancthon Simpson

Dimensions: 135.6' x 26.3' x 12.2'   **Tonnage:** 468 gross

Date of Loss: Wednesday, December 6, 1899

Cause of Loss: storm

Niagara

Private collection of Ralph Roberts

Story of the Loss:

On December 11, 1899 a bottle with a note was recovered by a fish tug off Port Colborne, Ontario. Unfortunately the message it contained was old news. "Expect to go down any minute. Captain McClory. Goodby." The other side of the note said "Steamer *Niagara* foundered about three miles from Port Maitland."

She had left Perry Sound in the Georgian Bay on November 28 loaded with wood for Tonawanda, New York. On Thursday, December 5, the hapless *Niagara* was observed off Long Point struggling through the snow and huge waves generated by 45 m.p.h. southeast winds. Three days later several vessels reported passing through great quantities of shingles and green and white painted timber. The *Niagara*, with her green hull, was the only boat missing. One of the vessels reporting the wreckage was the steamer *M.T. Green*. Ironically, the husband of Mrs. Annie Morrow, stewardess of the *Niagara*, was the mate on the *Green*. On December 11, the sighting of a piece of wreckage bearing the name *Niagara* confirmed her loss.

All sixteen of the crew were Canadians and the wife and children of Captain McClory lived in Port Colborne, near where the note in a bottle was discovered.

The Wreck Today:

The stern of the *Niagara* is broken, perhaps from the gale that sent her down. On the port side, there are mud grooves next to the wreck. That side has collapsed inward, while the starboard side has fallen to the outside of the wreck. Her bow stem rises intact out of the gloom. The windlass, a metal grate, and part of her foremast lay in the port bow. Forward of her engine is a winch and some of her cargo of shingles. The rudder and a bilge pump lie at the starboard stern.

Watch for a large quantity of fishnet at the stern.

Niagara's boiler, winch, bow rail, bow, and rudder post. Video captures by Mike Wachter.

NIMROD

Official #: 18773

Location: 151°T 22 miles off Port Stanley, Ontario

Coordinates: Loran: 44282.3 58052.8

Lies: bow southwest

Type: schooner

Power: sail, 3 masts

Owner(s) J. E. Lockwood, Ezra Fink, and Captain F.H. Wilcox

Built: 1873 at Milan, Ohio by Bailey Brothers

Dimensions: 172.3' x 31.7' x 13.4'

Date of Loss: Sunday November 8, 1874

Cause of Loss: collision with the schooner *Michigan*

Site #: 87

DGPS: 42 22.655 81 00.312

Depth: 71 feet

Cargo: corn

Tonnage: 559.31 gross

The anchor from the Nimrod sits at the base of the old Port Burwell Light, now part of a marine park.

Story of the Loss:

Occasionally, it appears one news article has it all. The Thursday, November 12, 1874 *Cleveland Plain Dealer* reported:

> "About 6 o'clock Sunday morning the schooner *Nimrod*, bound down, laden with 37,000 bushels of corn, consigned to Messrs. Marsh and Sternberg of Buffalo, was struck on the starboard side

between the main and mizzen rigging by the large new schooner *Michigan,* bound up. A heavy smoke-fog prevailed at the time and Captain Wilcox thinks it was but a few minutes after the *Michigan* was sighted that the collision occurred and in two minutes she was out of sight. He also says he was abreast of Port Stanley when struck and continued on sailing for an hour when his schooner sank in about 80 feet of water. The mate and four men took to the boat and the captain and the rest of the crew sought safety at the masthead. After she went down, the yawl returned and the entire crew remained in the exposed condition until eleven o'clock that night, when the weather became clear. They then started for shore in the boat, and about five o'clock Monday morning were picked up by the bark *Grantham* and taken to Port Colborne."

Two days later the *Plain Dealer* reported that Captain Kirby of the *Michigan* had no idea with which boat he had collided. He sent a letter to the owner in which:

"The captain reports having a collision with an unknown boat the night in question, the weather thick and foggy and of its result is unable to state what damages took place aside from his own vessel which has scarcely a mark on her."

The dense fog caused both vessels to be lost from view of the other after the collision. As a result, neither captain knew the fate of the other. The *Nimrod* was a typical two masted, white painted schooner of her day and as a result would have been indistinguishable in the fog. The *Michigan,* on the other hand, was easily distinguished. Captain Wilcox knew exactly what vessel had struck him.

The Wreck Today:

The *Nimrod* sits upright on in 71 feet of water, fairly well intact. The bow sprint was still standing until about 1997 when the weight of zebra mussels proved too much for it. There is one large anchor fluke sticking out of the mud on the port side. A second anchor is on display at the lighthouse in Port Burwell, Ontario. The bow section is pretty impressive with the windlass still in place and her stern has interesting detail. Much of the decking is lifted off. Regrettably, her steering gear was removed and placed on display in Tobermory, Ontario. Her wheel is at the marine museum in Port Burwell.

Nimrod
172.3' x 31.7' x 13.4'
by Georgann S. Wachter
not to scale

ONEIDA

Official #: 18888   **Site #:**   54

Location: 64°T 12 miles off Erie, Pennsylvania harbor entrance

Coordinates: Loran: 44454.1 58627.6   **DGPS:** boiler 42 13.966   79 51.583

Lies: bow south   **Depth:** 10 feet

Type: wood propeller   **Cargo:** light

Power: steeple compound engine with 20" and 40" diameter cylinders

Owner(s)   John Davidson of Bay City, Michigan

Built: 1862 at Buffalo, New York by William Crosthwaite

Dimensions: 200.3' x 31.7' x 21.1'   **Tonnage:** 719 gross 569 net

Date of Loss: Sunday, August 20, 1893

Cause of Loss: fire

Oneida

Private collection of Al Hart

Story of the Loss:

This was one snake bit boat. It appears that naming a vessel after an extinct Indian tribe is a bad omen.
Many of the vessels named Oneida have histories of frequent mishaps, but none was quite as accident
prone as this one.   She was built as a hogging arched package freighter to carry passengers and freight for
the railroads. She ran the Buffalo, Milwaukee, Chicago route in her early years. She managed to hit
several bridges, run aground numerous times, sink twice, and catch fire once before her final demise.

On her final voyage, she was under the command of Captain Thomas E. Black. They were upbound from Buffalo, New York to Bay City, Michigan and traveling light. The official story is that the boat was in mid-lake off Erie, Pennsylvania when the crew noticed smoke coming from the holds. The steam driven fire pumps were started and water was played on the fire as the ship was turned to shore. The crew fought a valiant, but losing battle against the spreading flames as the *Oneida* steamed toward shore. Realizing the flames would soon overwhelm them, the captain, 13 crewmen, one woman, and her child launched the yawl boats. By this time they were only two or three miles from shore and had no difficulty rowing to safety. The unofficial rumors are that the fire was an insurance job.

The crew beached their yawl boats as the thoroughly burned out hulk grounded near North East, Pennsylvania. The following morning the crew made their way to the rail station and were sent home by train. One of the crew supposedly absconded with the captain's papers, log, and gold watch.

Rumors of an insurance job were fuelled by the fact that the *Oneida* was the only vessel owned by John Davidson that carried insurance. Deliberate destruction of some aging vessels for insurance purposes was a common practice for those that would not pass inspection. The local papers hinted that the ship was deliberately torched to collect the money.

The Wreck Today:

Located about 500 feet north of Cemetery Road, it is possible to dive this site from shore if you are up for a bit of a swim. Not much remains at this shallow water site other than some ribs, the boiler, and part of her smoke stack. Scattered engine parts can be found buried in the sandy bottom. The boiler at this site posses a hazard to your propellers if you are approaching by boat.

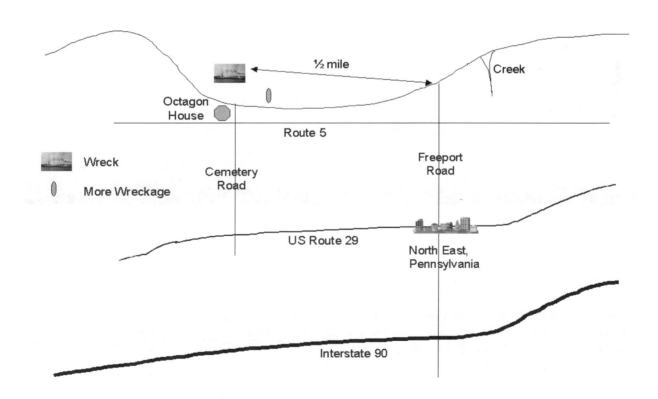

ONEIDA/ARCHES

Official #:	none	**Site #:**	50
Location:	8°T 20.9 miles off Erie Harbor	165°T 6.5 miles off Long Point Light	
Coordinates:	Loran: 44516.0 58586.9	**DGPS:**	42 27.476 80 01.021
Lies:	bow northeast	**Depth:**	160 feet
Type:	hogging arched package freighter	**Cargo:**	flour
Power:	Steam		
Owner(s)	O. A. Knight of Cleveland, Ohio		
Built:	1846 at Cleveland, Ohio by B.B. Jones		
Dimensions:	138'3" x 24'1" x 11'	**Tonnage:**	355
Date of Loss:	Thursday, November 11, 1852		
Cause of Loss:	storm		

Oneida

Great Lakes Historical Society, Bowen Collection

Story of the Loss:

Commonly known as the *"Arches"*, It has been speculated that this shipwreck off Long Point is one of three lost ships, the *Ohio*, the *Idaho*, or the *Oneida*. The Ohio was larger than the *Arches* and her boilers exploded. The *Arches* wreck's boilers are intact. Survivors from the *Idaho* clung to the ship's mast, which was above water after she hit the bottom. The depth of the *Arches* shipwreck precludes this possibility. On examining the holds of the *Arches* we find many barrel staves. This, along with the dimensions of the wreck, lead to current speculation that the *Arches* is the propeller *Oneida*.

The propeller *Oneida* left Cleveland Harbor laden with 3,500 barrels of flour, 1,100 on her decks. She was bound for Buffalo, New York. Had her crew of 20 to 25 men realized they were sailing into the teeth of a storm that would result in the complete or partial loss of 55 vessels, they may well have stayed in port. Every member of her crew was lost. As such, no one will ever know the precise events leading to her end.

On Monday, November 15, 1852, the *Cleveland Morning Leader* published this brief notice:

> **Propeller Wrecked!** – We learn by a private dispatch received in the city today, that a propeller is in sight off of Erie, bottom side up. She is supposed to be the *Oneida*.

Two days later the *Plain Dealer* printed:

> There is little or no question that the propeller *Oneida* is lost with all on board. Her books, papers and portions of the wreck are said to have floated ashore near Erie.

It remains to be proven that the *Arches* wreck is in fact the *Oneida*. However, we anticipate this speculation will be confirmed in the near future.

The Wreck Today:

Sitting in 160 feet of water, this dive is beyond the limits of sport diving as defined by all major certifying agencies. It should only be attempted by very experienced divers with specialized training for depths in excess of sport diving limits.

The *Arches* is considered to be one of the best examples of an early package freighter in Lake Erie waters. A tie in line is usually affixed to the engine. On a typical day, the visibility decreases as a diver descends though the first 90 feet of water.

Engine and starboard arch of the Oneida. Photo by Tom Wilson.

As you go beyond 95 feet, the wreck opens up below you. Her upper decks are gone; otherwise, she is intact and upright. The wreck rises to the 127' depth at the start of the hogging arch. Her boilers, machinery and anchors are present and waiting to be explored. Her lower holds are in excellent condition and the remains of the barrels that held her cargo can be seen through the hatch openings.

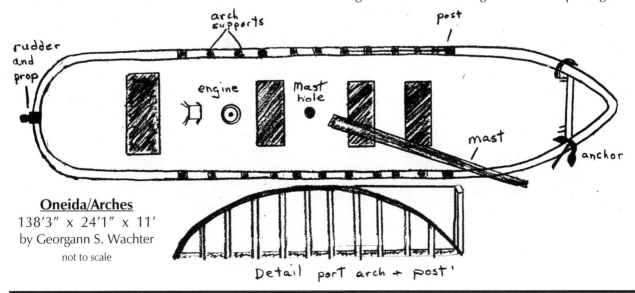

Oneida/Arches
138'3" x 24'1" x 11'
by Georgann S. Wachter
not to scale

Detail port arch + post

LOUIE O'NEILL

Official #: 14654

Location: 172°T 16.2 miles off Port Stanley, Ontario

Coordinates: Loran: 44269.2 57975.8

Lies: bow west

Type: schooner barge

Power: sail/towed

Owner(s) Robert Holland of Marine City, Michigan

Built: 1862 in Cleveland, Ohio by Presley and Stevens

Dimensions: 196′ x 31′ x 13′

Date of Loss: Friday, April 29, 1887

Cause of Loss: storm/collision

Site #: 88

DGPS: 42 25.443 81 10.319

Depth: 65 feet

Cargo: coal

Tonnage: 523

Louie O'Neill as S.D. Caldwell

Lower Lakes Historical Society

Story of the Loss:

Until recently this wreck was commonly known as "the Stanley Coal Schooner." Research by Port Stanley charter operator Wayne Hopper identified it as the *Louie O'Neill* (formerly known as *S.D. Caldwell*). In the Tuesday, May 3, 1887, *Cleveland Plain Dealer*, Captain Thomas E. Walker describes the sinking as follows:

"The tug *Swain* left Buffalo on Wednesday, the 27th of April, having in tow the schooners *H.W. Sage*, *Thomas L. Parker*, *D.S. Austin*, *Louie O'Neill*, and the *Riverside* in the order named. The *O'Neil* and *Riverside* were bound for Toledo and the other three to Lake Michigan ports. We had fair sailing until last Thursday night. Along about midnight, the sea became very heavy. Half an hour before the accident happened, the *Riverside*, which had been the last boat in the tow, let go of the tow line and concluded to care for herself. We were then the last boat in the tow and the *Parker* was the second boat ahead of us. The storm increased and began blowing a heavy gale.

The tug did much shifting in her course. You can imagine what a sea it was when I tell you that our boat took water over the weather rail and heaved it over the stern rail. All hands were on deck and hard at work when the tow broke up about five to eight miles off Port Stanley at 2:30 a.m. Friday. The towline between the O'Neill and the Austin did not part, but of course it was let go and the Austin was allowed to go on caring for herself. The Austin had scarcely been freed when we found the Parker's jibboom in our rigging. She had shifted her course and come up to our starboard. Her jibboom brought down our mainmast and it was broken in three pieces. With her port side to our starboard, the two vessels began pounding together. I ordered the mate to take his men forward and drop the port anchor. While this was being done, the mate of the Parker came aboard of our boat and requested that the same be done. The anchor immediately caught and held the O'Neill, but in a minute or two, we were again foul of the Parker, doing damage to her, but in return a large hole was stove in our stem. I went forward with a light and saw that the boat was bound to go down, although I do not now think it was the hole in her bow that caused her to sink. We had been struck amidships when the Parker first came upon us. I ordered the men aft to get the boat ready and the woman cook and one man were first put into it. The other men followed and when all was ready, I got in and ordered the yawl lowered. We placed a light on the davits, and that was about all we cared to find time to do.   Every order was obeyed promptly and to the letter and to this we owe our lives. On being launched into the heavy sea, we put the boat's nose to it. We had passed but a few of the swells when we saw the schooner go down."

When morning came, the Swain conducted an unsuccessful search for the O'Neill. Having no success, she picked up the Sage and the damaged Parker and proceeded to Amherstburg. The Riverside and Austin continued to their destinations on their own. Captain Fitch of the Parker expressed great concern for the crew of the O'Neill. He felt none could have survived the seas that night in a small boat. He was wrong. All that night and through the next day, a heavy sea from the northwest carried the small boat down the lake. Against the heavy sea, all they could do was run with it. At 9:00 p.m. Friday the Conneaut light was sighted. As the seas had subsided and they had no food, the crew determined to make for the light. Landing about one half mile east of the light, they were refused shelter at the first house they encountered. At the second home they came to they were offered shelter and a warm meal that "was relished all around."

The Wreck Today:

This wire rigged vessel lays on a mud bottom. Several nets and a fair current make this a tricky dive. A huge pile of anchor chain lays on her starboard bow. There is a capstan, a double block, and a pump lying on its side toward the stern. The hole that sunk her can be found on her starboard side and her starboard anchor is partially buried in the silt.

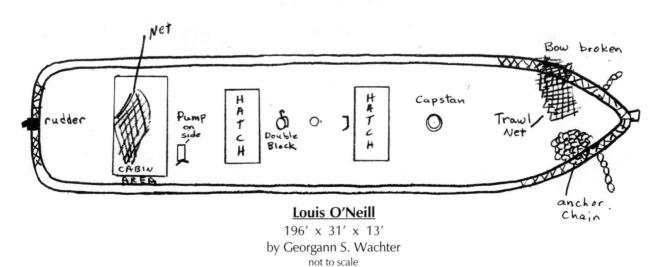

Louis O'Neill
196' x 31' x 13'
by Georgann S. Wachter
not to scale

ONTARIO

Official #:	none	**Site #:**	71
Location:	Long Point Bay		
Coordinates:	Loran: 44511.9 58436.6	**DGPS:**	42 38.11 80 22.02
Lies:		**Depth:**	8 feet
Type:	schooner, 3 masts	**Cargo:**	lumber & railroad joiner plates
Power:	sail		
Owner(s)	Henry Waters of Chatham, Ontario		
Built:	1851 at Quebec City, Quebec by A. St. Jean		
Dimensions:	130' x 23'	**Tonnage:**	415
Date of Loss:	Friday, August 27, 1858		
Cause of Loss:	storm		

Ontario center board box

John Veber

Story of the Loss:

Though some think this vessel is the remains of the *George McCall* sunk in 1906, diver and photographer John Veber believes these to be the remains of the schooner *Ontario*. The wreck's dimensions match those of the *Ontario;* she carried three masts, two center boards, and her cargo is correct.

The *Ontario* was caught in a raging windstorm in the inner bay. The crew, consisting of nine men and one woman, took to the rigging to save themselves. For seven hours, they clung to the masts as the wind and waves pounded their vessel to pieces. Finally, the *Star of Hope* spotted Captain Muir and the imperiled crew of the *Ontario*. Having brought first hope, and then rescue to the bedraggled crew of the *Ontario*, the *Star of Hope* transported them to Port Colborne, Ontario.

The Wreck Today:

Because she lays in the sand in shallow water, many items have been removed from this wreck. Both centerboards are on shore at Long Point and her anchor sits in a yard in Port Rowan, Ontario. Many other items such as bottles, a stove lid, railroad tongs, and padlocks have been taken from this site.

The wreck is covered in dense weeds and is home to huge bass. In the summer months, divers can easily get tangled in the weedy overgrowth at this site. Fortunately, the surface is only 8 feet away.

Ontario main mast step

John Veber

S. S. Osborn

Official #: 23361   **Site #:** 17

Location: on Cassaday Reef, east of Port Colborne, Ontario

Coordinates: Loran: **DGPS:** 42 51.93   79 12.69

Lies: east/west   **Depth:** 14 feet

Type: barkentine, 3 masts   **Cargo:** iron ore

Power: sail

Owner(s)   B. O. Wilcox of Fairport, Ohio

Built: 1867 at Fairport, Ohio by Bailey Brothers

Dimensions: 186′ x 35′ x 14′   **Tonnage:** 655 net

Date of Loss: Monday, November 3, 1874

Cause of Loss: fog

3 Masted Barkentine

Drawing of the barkentine Saint Louis from the Remick Collection

Story of the Loss:

Lasting for several days, a dense fog made it impossible for skippers to see past the bow of their vessels.

"Reports continue to come in of additional disaster resulting from the fog which has hug over the lake for several days. Such thick weather has not been known for more than twenty years."

— Detroit *Free Press*, November 9, 1873

The fog hung over the lake like a billowing cotton comforter. It muffled sounds, impaired vision, and wrecked ships. The newspapers reported a lengthy string of fog related mishaps. The schooner *Harriet Ross,* bound from Erie to Detroit, ran ashore four miles east of Port Colborne and was abandoned to the underwriters. The schooner *Miami* was aground on Long Point and filled with water. The schooner *Francis Palms* was on shore at Long Point. The barge *Detroit* went ashore near Point Abino and was "gone to pieces". Several Welland Canal schooners lost their way in the fog and were forced to anchor. The *Wild Rover* was lost 10 miles from Long Point Light. The scope of the losses was so great that all available steam pumps were tied up by the wreckers working to save stranded vessels.

In the midst of this long list of disasters is a one sentence notation. "The names of the vessels in difficulty reported here are the *Francis Palms* and *Miami* on Long Point, the **S.S. Osborn**, *Twin Sisters,* and *Bolivia* and one unknown ashore between Port Dover and Grand River …"

Such irony. The *S.S Osborn* was lost in pea soup fog on Monday, November 3, 1873. Her story was lost in the dense fog of reports on shipping disasters resulting from the thick weather.

She was bound from Escanaba, Michigan to Buffalo, New York with iron ore. Fortunately, there was no loss of life in this incident, but salvagers could not release her before other storms battered her beyond salvage.

The Wreck Today:

Very little is left of the *Osborn*. The keel and some hull planking are located on the east side of Cassaday Reef. They willl look something like the picture below.

Remains of one of the many ships lost in the foggy waters off Long Point.
Author's collection.

OXFORD

Official #: none   **Site #:** 35

Location: 25°T 24.7 miles off Erie Pennsylvania harbor entrance

Coordinates: Loran: 44558.7 58671.7   **DGPS:** 42 28.855   79 51.843

Lies: southeast/northwest   **Depth:** 160 feet

Type: two masted brig   **Cargo:** iron ore

Power: sail

Owner(s) Hoag Strong and Company of Cleveland, Ohio

Built: 1842 at Three Mile Bay, New York by A. Copley

Dimensions: 114' x 24' x 9'   **Tonnage:** 254

Date of Loss: Friday, May 30, 1856

Cause of Loss: collision with steamer *Cataract*

Tiller of the Oxford

Underwater video capture by Mike King

Story of the Loss:

The *Oxford*, a classic, tiller-steered brig, was upbound from Ogdensburg, New York with a load of iron ore for Toledo, Ohio. Captain John Lee's wife and young daughter had come with him this trip and he was enjoying the summer crossing and the calm Lake Erie water. At the same time, the propeller *Cataract*, of the American Transportation Company, was downbound from Toledo, Ohio with a cargo of flour and miscellaneous freight for Buffalo, New York. Both vessels were having an uneventful passage, cutting smoothly through the water as dusk became darkness and the sky filled with stars in the gentleness of the night.

The lookouts on the *Oxford* had been diligent that night. They had observed the lights of the *Cataract* from a considerable distance and, as the *Oxford's* lights were burning brightly, they were sure the steamer's lookouts could see them. Confident in their visibility, the brig held its course as the steamer bore down on them.

It was 2:00 in the morning when, just off Long Point, the onrushing steamer collided with the little brig, slicing her starboard side to the waterline abaft the foremast. Knowing his small ship would not survive, Captain John Lee rushed below to save his sleeping wife and child. He was never seen again. He, his wife, child, and two crewmembers perished as the *Oxford* fell beneath the waters in less than three minutes. Only three members of the *Oxford's* complement survived the collision.

Having sustained no significant damage, Captain Hunt and the *Cataract* continued on their journey, arriving at Buffalo in the evening.

The Wreck Today:

This wreck lies in 160 feet of water. It is beyond the limits of sport diving as defined by all major certifying agencies. It should only be attempted by very experienced divers with specialized training for depths in excess of sport diving limits.

The *Oxford* rests on a mud bottom with her masts reasonably intact. Her large tiller is another prominent feature of the wreck and before her identity was known she was called the *Tiller Wreck*. Although there is no crows nest, she was also referred to as the *Crows Nest*, probably due to the crosstree on her forward mast. Owing in part to her depth, the ship is remarkably preserved. While there is damage at the starboard bow from the collision that sank her, her two large anchors sit prominently on the bow. Moving toward the stern, her windlass, bilge pumps, offset centerboard, and rigging winch are sitting in place, ready for use, as though she might one day sail again.

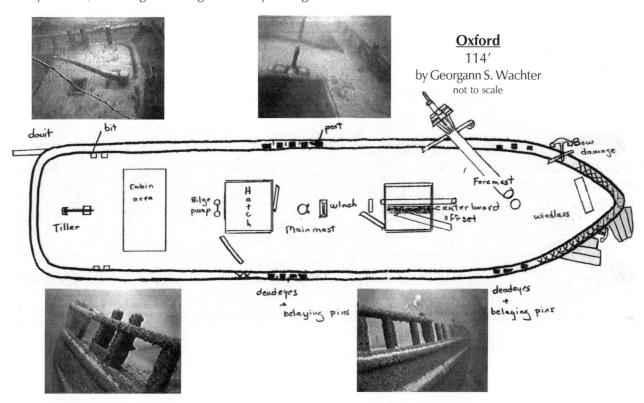

Underwater video captures by Mike King.

PASSAIC

Official #: 196991

Location: 261°T 6.1 miles off Dunkirk, New York

Coordinates: Loran: 44648.5 58883.2

Lies: bow southwest

Type: propeller package freighter

Power: vertical direct acting engine

Owner(s) Homer Blodgett of Detroit, Michigan

Built: 1862 at Buffalo, New York by Charles Bidwell

Dimensions: 198'3" x 27'7" x 11'4"

Date of Loss: Saturday, October 31, 1891

Cause of Loss: storm

Site #: 28

DGPS: 42 28.748 79 27.769

Depth: 80 feet

Cargo: lumber

Tonnage: 531 gross 411 net

Passaic

Remick Collection

Story of the Loss:

Originally built as a package freighter at 654 gross tons, the *Passaic* was typical of her class. She had high "hogging arches" to stiffen her spine, engines aft, and ornate pilot house, and limited passenger cabins on the upper deck. During her early years, she ran between Buffalo or Dunkirk, New York and various ports on Lake Michigan for the Erie Railroad. Upbound trips carried manufactured goods and downbound trips carried agricultural and farm commodities. In 1877 the *Passaic* was acquired by Homer Blodgett who removed her passenger cabins and converted her for use in the lumber and course freight trade between Michigan and Tonawanda, New York. These modifications reduced her gross tonnage to 531 tons.

Diver Georgann Wachter examines the Passaic's engine.
Video capture by Mike Wachter.

Nearing her 30th year in service, the *Passaic* had seen better days, but was still considered an economically viable vessel as she worked her way down the lakes in late October of 1891. She and her four consort barges, *Elma*, *Hattie*, *B.W. Jenness*, and *Superior* were laden with lumber for Tonawanda, New York. As evening approached on October 31, the ships encountered a brutal gale. They plowed on through the heavy seas and the *Passaic* labored against her load through the long night. Finally, off Erie, Pennsylvania, Captain Canastney decided the strain was too much for his aging vessel and let go the four tows. However, the die was already cast ... the *Passaic's* seams had opened. She struggled on toward Dunkirk, New York as water flowed through the open seams in her hull faster than her pumps could remove it.

Within sight of the safety of Dunkirk, the final calamity struck. The rising waters extinguished the fire in her boiler and the *Passaic* was left powerless against the seas.

Captain Canastney and crew climbed on the pilothouse and launched the yawl boat. One crewman refused to board the yawl until the last second. He then leapt into the raging waves and had to be pulled into the boat by his fellows. The fifteen crewmen pulled for the *Hattie*, which had anchored nearby. The tremendous seas prevented them from boarding the vessel. After being dashed against the sides of the *Hattie* during several attempts at boarding they sought limited shelter under her stern and stayed secured to her by a line. Tossed throughout the night and bailing with their hats and their cupped hands, the men suffered terribly from the cold and the yawl nearly swamped on several occasions. By 9:00 Sunday morning the waves finally subsided enough for the exhausted men to be brought aboard the *Hattie*.

Scattered remains of the Passaic.
Video capture by Mike Wachter.

Owner Homer Blodgett dispatched the tug *Hebard* to recover the stranded barges. She was joined by tug *Gee*. Each took two barges in tow and brought the suffering sailors to Buffalo, New York. When the *Passaic* crew were paid, they were docked for the two days from the sinking until their rescue.

The Wreck Today:

Mudpuppy
Video capture by Mike Wachter.

Salvors mistook the *Passaic* for the *Dean Richmond* and dynamited her in an effort to get at the *Richmond's* reported treasures. As you proceed from the stern, her rudder has fallen to starboard; there is a four bladed propeller, a capstan on its side, the engine, firebox, boiler, gears, and stem post. Her starboard side was obliterated by the dynamite. On the port side, her hogging arch lies with huge beams on a sand and mud bottom. We found a mudpuppy on this wreck - unusual for that depth.

Persian

Official #:	150064.	**Site #:**	37

Location: 16°T 29.1 miles off Erie, Pennsylvania harbor entrance, 82°T 7.1 miles off Long Point Light

Coordinates:	Loran: 44581.3 58661.3	**DGPS:**	42 33.781 79 54 696
Lies:		**Depth:**	195 feet
Type:	wood propeller with four masts	**Cargo:**	wheat and corn
Power:	steam engine		

Owner(s) R.R. Winslow of Cleveland, Ohio and H.S. Winslow of Buffalo, New York

Built: 1874 at Cleveland, Ohio by Quayle & Murphy

Dimensions:	243' x 40' x 19'	**Tonnage:**	1630 net
Date of Loss:	Thursday, August 26, 1875		
Cause of Loss:	fire		

Caledonia
Caladonia, pictured here, and the Raleigh on page 158 are very similar to the Persian.
Remick Collection

Story of the Loss:

When she left the ways, she was the largest propeller sailing the waters of Lake Erie. When she was lost one year later she was second only to the *Commodore* in size.

Loaded with 15,000 bushels of wheat and 50,000 bushels of corn, the *Persian* left Chicago, Illinois on Sunday, August 22, 1875. Bound for Buffalo, New York, she had fair weather and smooth sailing until 9:30 p.m. Thursday when fire was discovered by the mate and watchman. The call of "FIRE" brought all hands on deck to fight the blaze. Appearing to have started in the coal bunkers, the fire quickly burst out through the upper deck, over the boilers on the port side. The engineer stopped the engines and attempted to start the pony boiler to run the pumps. It would not start. Chased from the engine area by the raging fire, Captain Sam Flint and the crew attempted to fight it with the forward pumps, but the fire hose was too short to reach the flames.

By the time the crew realized the *Persian* was lost and they could only save themselves, the boats had all been burned. Ripping the hatch covers from the flaming pyre, they cast them to the water to use as rafts. The 16 member crew and three passengers abandoned ship and took to their makeshift rafts. Blessed by calm waters they floated next to the flaming ship for two hours. All agreed that, were it not for the calm waters, they would surely have perished in the open lake.

First to arrive at the scene was the yawl boat from the schooner *Montana*. Arriving about the same time was the tug *Merrick*, which had abandoned her tows and rushed to the rescue when she saw the fire. The entire ship's complement had been recovered when the propeller *Empire State* came on the scene. After boarding the *Empire State*, Captain Flint called the roll. When none were found missing, many expressions of joy and thankful prayers were offered. With the help of the *Persian's* crew, the *Empire State* attempted to extinguish the flames on the stricken vessel. Failing in this, an effort was made to tow the *Persian* toward Long Point and ground her. Straining for 2½ hours, the relatively small *Empire State* made no progress with the behemoth *Persian*. Finally, the flames burst through the pilot house and threatened to leap to the *Empire State*. Cutting the flaming ship free, the *Empire State* continued her voyage, transferring the passengers and crew of the *Persian* to the barge *Anna Smith* at Point au Pelee. The *Smith* carried the survivors to Cleveland, Ohio.

The crew lost all of their personal effects. The only woman on board, the engineers wife, saved only her night clothes, and they were partially burned. The female passengers on the *Montana* provided her with a complete outfit from their wardrobes. Fortunately, all of the 16 crew members and 3 passengers aboard the *Persian* survived.

The Wreck Today:

Today, the charred remains of the *Persian* lay near the deepest part of Lake Erie in 195 feet of water. She has a huge boiler and engine and her prop sticks prominently out of the bottom. There is often a current at this site.

This dive is beyond the limits of sport diving as defined by all major certifying agencies. It should only be attempted by very experienced divers with specialized equipment and training for depths in excess of sport diving limits.

While her engine is largly intact, nets drape her gunnels and extensive fire damage is evident on the remains of the Persian.
Photos by Tom Wilson.

PASCAL P. PRATT

Official #: 150424   **Site #:**   E

Location: 16.3 miles 160°T from Port Dover, Ontario, 2.3 miles 294°T from Long Point Light.

Coordinates: Loran: 44541.7 58568.9   **DGPS:**   42 33.682   80 05.429

Lies: bow south   **Depth:**   20 feet

Type: propeller   **Cargo:**   coal

Power: 700 HP fore & aft compound engine

Owner(s) Lake Erie Transportation Company

Built: 1888 at Cleveland, Ohio by Thomas Quayle & Sons

Dimensions: 272' x 40'6" x 23'   **Tonnage:** 1,947 gross 1642 net

Date of Loss: Wednesday, November 18, 1908

Cause of Loss: fire

Pascal P. Pratt

Great Lakes Historical Society

Story of the Loss:

In freshening wind, the *Pascal P. Pratt* left Buffalo, New York on Monday, November 16, 1908. She was bound for Milwaukee, Wisconsin with 2,500 tons of anthracite coal.

When she was off Mohawk Island, several miles out of Buffalo, Captain W.E. Moore decided that the 65 mile per hour winds and building seas were more than the ship could handle. He ordered a course change to duck behind the protective arm of Long Point. His would not be the only vessel seeking shelter from the tumultuous waters. On arrival, Captain Moore noted 13 other vessels were sheltering behind the point. Now resting in the lee of the point, the *Pratt* remained sheltered for a day as the seas began to moderate. When dawn broke on Wednesday morning, winds were still gusting to 40 m.p.h., but the lake was no longer the tempest that had driven the *Pratt* to shelter. Captain Moore had the crew make ready to depart. Finally, at 9:00 in the morning, the engine room was signaled to get under way. However, as soon as the order was given, Chief Engineer F.E. Doyle ran from the engine room shouting that the ship was afire! Flame lashed out behind him as the engine room was completely engulfed by the inferno.

For three hours the crew fought valiantly to save their ship. Fire hoses poured streams of water into the engine room and billowing clouds of steam and black smoke enveloped the stricken *Pascal Pratt*. Beneath the mantel of steam the fires gained energy from the stiff winds fanning the blaze. Even as it became increasingly apparent that the fire would win the battle, the crew struggled on. Captain Moore moved his vessel closer to shore. This would give all aboard a fighting chance at survival should the fires eventually drive them into the sea. With but a single yawl for their escape, the captain knew it would take two trips to carry his entire crew.

"Instantly, flames rushed from the engine room", Captain Moore reported, "and I knew we had to do some tall hustling. All hands were ordered to the pumps. We were about one and a quarter miles from shore. The blaze lighted up the water for a great distance and the stiff wind fanned the flames until it soon became suffocating aboard. The men were loath to quit, but when I saw it was utterly impossible to save the ship, I told them to save what they could and get into the yawl."

The *Pratt* was beached and a yawl boat landed half the 17 crew and returned for the others. Then, as the remaining crew rushed aboard the yawl, Captain Moore decided to return to his cabin to collect the ship's documents. Ignoring the plaintive cries of his crew, the captain rushed back aboard the *Pratt*. Through the suffocating smoke and scorching flames he could be seen entering his cabin, most assuredly never to return again. However, fate would not take the captain this day. He emerged unscathed from the conflagration with the ship's documents in hand. When back aboard the yawl, all rowed safely to shore.

The steamer continued to burn until the flames reached the waters edge. Then, in a great billowing cloud of hissing steam, she slipped beneath the water and the flames were finally extinguished .

Sheldon Cook, the lighthouse keeper at Long Point had tried to single handedly launch a boat when he discovered the burning steamer but was turned back by the heavy surf. He cared for the crew at his home until they could take the lighthouse launch to Port Dover, Ontario. Once there, the crew boarded a train for Buffalo.

The Wreck Today:

The *Pascal Pratt* was salvaged in 1909 and some of the machinery and much of her coal was removed. Later salvors dynamited her. She lies widely scattered on a sand bottom. One boiler, a propeller, and some machinery remain. Her stern rises some 10 feet off the bottom and the structure attracts many fish to the site.

RALEIGH

Official #: 110154   **Site #:** 16

Location: 87°T 5 miles off Port Colborne, Ontario

Coordinates: Loran: 44868.9   59104.2   **DGPS:** 42 51.893   79 09.264

Lies: bow northeast   **Depth:** 30 feet

Type: propeller   **Cargo:** pulpwood

Power: steam engine

Owner(s) Windslow Fleet, Henry Wineman, Jr. of Detroit, Michigan

Built: 1871 at Cleveland, Ohio by Quayle and Martin

Dimensions: 227'3" x 34' x 15'   **Tonnage:** 1205 gross 1140 net

Date of Loss: Thursday, November 30, 1911

Cause of Loss: storm/grounding

Raleigh rafted out

Private collection of Ralph Roberts

Story of the Loss:

The *Raleigh* survived several groundings before her last encounter with a Great Lakes shoreline.

The wood steamer had left Quebec City with a load of pulpwood destined for the Hammermill Paper Company of Erie, Pennsylvania. As she left the Welland Canal, she was caught in a ferocious gale. About midnight her rudder broke. From that point on, the situation grew worse by the hour. At 3:30 a.m., the *Raleigh* lost her pumps and equipment started washing away. Though her anchors were lowered, they eventually broke. Finally, she grounded about ½ mile from shore at Shislers Point. The lifesavers at Buffalo were notified, but they were unable to brave the mountainous seas.

During the vessels distress, the captain had made preparations to try and save the crew. The lifeboats had been made ready for the moment when the boat would eventually sink. As an anxious crowd watched from shore, Captain Beauvais ordered the first lifeboat lowered. The local papers reported that: "Tossed about by the irresistible waves, the little craft dashed toward shore, every minute bringing a miraculous escape for its occupants as the big rollers broke about them. When a short distance from shore, the boat was swamped, and the five men were thrown into the icy water." However, "eager watchers rushed into the icy waters and dragged them from what otherwise might have been their watery graves."

The captain, the steward and his wife, the mate, and two deck hands then set out in the second lifeboat. It had barely left the *Raleigh* when it was overwhelmed by an enormous wave and capsized. All were dragged ashore except for cook Wise and his wife. On surfacing, Wise saw his wife struggling in the water and swam to her. A strong swimmer, he cut through the towering waves and reached her just as she was lost to sight of the people on shore. They were not seen again until, some time later, they drifted ashore, locked in each others arms. A local physician, Dr. Snyder worked valiantly to revive them, without success.

Chief Engineer Pritchard had refused to board either lifeboat. He clung to the bow of the *Raleigh* and would occasionally wave to the onlookers, demonstrating that he was still alive. The lifesaving station attempted to reach the stricken vessel, but was forced, by the power of the seas, to turn back. Tugs were dispatched, but they too were thwarted by the fury of the waves. Before the lake settled sufficiently for rescuers to reach the *Raleigh*, Chief Engineer Pritchard had perished.

The Wreck Today:

One anchor, gauges, the capstan cover, wheel, and other artifacts were recovered in the mid-1970's. They were put on display at the Port Colborne Marine and Historical Museum. The sides of the *Raleigh* have opened up. Her engine and boiler can be explored, as well as a large windlass and her propeller. An anchor chain leads off the bow to an anchor to the south of the wreck.

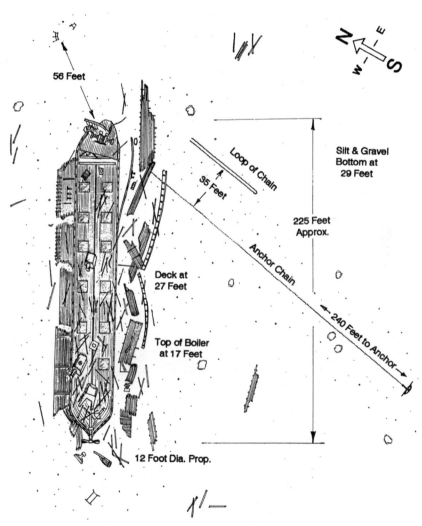

Raleigh wreck site drawing by Doug King, Sr.

Local divers often set a tie in line off the boiler of the wreck. There is a great deal of boat traffic in this area and divers are cautioned to fly a dive flag.

JAMES H. REED

Official #: 77589   **Site #:** 81

Location: 0°T 24.2 miles off Ashtabula, Ohio

Coordinates: Loran: 44277.8 58139.9   **DGPS:** 42 16.168 80 47.770

Lies: bow southeast   **Depth:** 70 feet

Type: steel propeller   **Cargo:** iron ore

Power: quadruple expansion engine

Owner(s) Interlake Steamship Company, Cleveland, Ohio

Built: 1903, Detroit Shipbuilding Company, Wyandotte, Michigan

Dimensions: 455'2"' x 52'2" x 24'9"   **Tonnage:** 5625 gross 4205 net

Date of Loss: Thursday, April 27, 1944

Cause of Loss: collision with propeller *Ashcroft*

James H. Reed

Great Lakes Historical Society

Story of the Loss:

The *James H. Reed* was typical of the iron ore and grain trade steel freighters of her day. Originally owned by the Provident Steamship Company, the *Reed* was one of over a dozen ships purchased from various fleets to form the Interlake Steamship Company in 1913. Thirty one years later, the world was at war. Our nation's survival depended on iron ore to fire the steel plants. This created heavy early spring traffic on the lakes in support of the war effort. So it was that the *James Reed* found herself creeping through a soupy gray fog in April 1944.

With fog horns and bells sounding from every Coast Guard station, the fleets went forth to carry the iron ore needed to build the nation's war machine. Many people died to win this war and on this foggy morning 12 seafarers on the *Reed* would give their lives to the war effort without a shot being fired.

Downbound from Escanaba, Michigan, the *Reed* carried iron ore for Buffalo, New York. She and the Canadian propeller *Ashcroft* had been blowing fog signals every minute as they proceeded. Distortion of these signals in the dense fog off Ashtabula Harbor eventually led to the collision at 5:00 in the morning.

Shortly before the collision, the mate standing watch awakened Captain Brightstone. The mate thought he had heard another ship in the area. Brightstone ordered engines stopped and signals blown. He explained, "As soon as the *Reed* signaled, we heard signals close by from another boat. I ordered sounding of the alarm bells and told the mate to get crewmen out of the forward end of the ship. We then saw lights of another vessel on the starboard side of the bow. The wheelsman and I grabbed life preservers and just as we stepped from the pilothouse to the texas deck, the ships collided. The forward end started sinking immediately, the water sweeping up over the texas deck and smashing us up against the pilot house."

As the two ships were locked together, steam poured from amidships on the *Reed*. There was no time to lower the lifeboats so the davits were loosened to allow the boats to float free when the *Reed* sank. As she went under, many were sucked down with her. Those with life jackets on were brought back to the surface and most survived. Others leapt to the safety of the *Ashcroft*, which sent its lifeboat out to rescue the poor souls cast into the frigid waters. People kicked their way free of the wreckage and held on to anything that would keep them afloat. The survivors were brought aboard the *Ashcroft* and taken to the engine room, where they received hot coffee and dry clothes. Five of the men were badly battered and bleeding from the nose and mouth. The crew worked on them for several hours with no reward. These five died of injuries suffered in the collision and seven others drowned.

Two of these were the cook, Ray W. Losey and his wife, assistant cook Camille Losey. The Loseys had recently finished paying for their home on Randal Drive in Toledo, Ohio and had planned for this to be their last season on the lakes. Camille could not swim and Ray chose to stay with her. According to one survivor, "She was afraid to go overboard so he stayed with her. His arm was around her as they drowned." Many of the 24 rescued seamen were taken by the *Ashcroft* to Ashtabula where they were treated for hypothermia.

On the same day on fog-shrouded Lake Erie, the *Phillip Minch* rammed the *Frank E. Vigor*. The *Vigor* sank, but all were rescued from the icy lake.

The Wreck Today:

There is much to see on the wreck site, but it can be somewhat confusing. The wreck was dynamited in November 1944 to provide 45 feet of shipping clearance. As a result, her remains are spread across a large area. Following his first dive on her, one of our friends commented "they used every bit of dynamite available on that sucker."

Keep in mind that the bow lies to the southeast and you'll be better oriented to the wreck. Her machinery is scattered and her hull is blown apart, creating a wonderful fish habit and fascinating exploration. There is much to see and half the fun is sorting out what is what after everything was blown apart.

As she lies directly in the middle of the shipping lanes, a good watch is essential while diving this site.

W. C. Richardson

Official #: 81816   **Site #:** 4

Location: 207°T 1.6 miles off Buffalo Harbor, New York east harbor entrance

Coordinates: Loran: 44923.0 59229.0   **DGPS:** 42 51.074 78 54.776

Lies: bow east   **Depth:** 40 feet

Type: steel freighter   **Cargo:** flax seed

Power: steam engine

Owner(s) Captain W. C. Richardson

Built: 1902 at Cleveland, Ohio by American Shipbuilding

Dimensions: 354' x 48' x 28'   **Tonnage:** 3,818 gross 2,841 net

Date of Loss: Wednesday, December 8, 1909

Cause of Loss: storm

W. C. Richardson

Great Lakes Historical Society

Story of the Loss:

December 9, 1909 saw one of the most ferocious storms in the modern history of Lake Erie. The storm took over fifty lives on three large vessels sunk that day. Lost in this giant of a storm were the 241 foot iron propeller *Clarion*, the 350 foot steel car ferry *Marquette and Bessemer #2,* and, largest of the three, the 354 foot steel freighter *W.C. Richardson.*

The *Richardson* had almost completed her late season voyage from Duluth, Minnesota to Buffalo, New York when the southwest storm overtook her. The storm made it impossible for the *Richardson* to enter the harbor. She set her anchors near Waverly Shoal and was pounded by gale force winds through the night. At one point, her cargo shifted in the heavy seas, allowing the vessel to take on water. Captain Enos J. Burke failed in his efforts to dissuade four of his crew from launching a lifeboat. These four; engineer Sam Mayberry, second mate E.J. Clery, deckhands Ed Gramsey, and Sidney Smith died before their lifeboat reached shore. Mrs. John Bratford, wife of the steward, was attempting to go forward from the aft end when she was washed off the steamer and lost.

Soon the distress flairs and fire signals of the foundering *Richardson* attracted the attention of another vessel, the *W. A. Paine*. Captain Emil Detlefs of the *Paine* gave a graphic description in the December 13, 1909 *Cleveland Plain Dealer*:

> "We sighted the *Richardson* just off Buffalo. She was in distress and was sending up rockets and burning fire to attract attention. Just before this, the *Paine* had dropped her wheel cables off the quartering and was steering badly. We weren't sure that we would be able to weather out the storm ourselves.

> When we saw the *Richardson* in distress, we blew and sent up rockets to attract the attention of the lifesavers and the tugs, but no one came. It was blowing so hard and the sea was rolling so high that, with the *Paine* disabled, we couldn't go to the *Richardson* that night. We lay to and waited until daylight Thursday morning. When we first saw her, she was resting on her stern, with her bow out of the water. On her pilot house, huddled together like sheep, were the men, we couldn't tell how many.

> We went to her, keeping the *Paine* out of the trough of the sea as best we could. We were dragging one anchor, and when we had drifted near enough to her we let over the other anchor and kept the engine working all the time. It was pretty careful work, but finally we got near enough so that the bow of the *Paine* touched that of the *Richardson*. Then we put a ladder over and pulled the men aboard.

> The men were in poor shape. Some of them we had to fasten lines around and pull them over in that way. Others could walk. They were almost frozen and exhausted, as they had had no fire nor heat for more than twenty-four hours. The men were wet with the spray and at times the sea had washed over them. Their clothing was frozen stiff. They were absolutely helpless when we found them and made a happy crowd when we got them aboard the *Paine*."

In all, fourteen exhausted and near frozen men were rescued by the *Paine*. The *Paine* was so dangerously close to Waverly Shoal that she could not be brought in until the seas subsided the next day. She was finally towed into Buffalo by the tug *Cascade*. Captain Emil Detlefs received a gold watch for "courage and seamanship" for his rescue of the 14 seamen of the *Richardson*.

The Wreck Today:

Salvage attempts by the Great Lakes Towing Company and Reid Wrecking Company failed. The *W. C. Richardson* was dynamited in October of 1913. Today, the dynamite having pretty well leveled her, she rises about eight feet off the bottom. There is a sizable debris field to the east. The site usually has a slight current from the south. Watch for heavy boat traffic. A dive flag is recommended.

DEAN RICHMOND

Official #: 6102   **Site #:** 53

Location: 38°T 11.6 miles off Erie, Pennsylvania harbor entrance

Coordinates: Loran: 44471.0 58602.8   **DGPS:** 42 18.430   79 55.859

Lies: bow east   **Depth:** 110 feet

Type: wood twin propeller   **Cargo:** flour, meal, oil cake, pig lead, spelter, and package freight

Power: vertical direct acting steam engine

Owner(s) Huron Transportation Company, East China, Michigan

Built: 1864 at Cleveland, Ohio by Quayle and Martin

Dimensions: 238′ x 35′ x 13′5″   **Tonnage:** 1432 gross 1257 net

Date of Loss: Sunday, October 15, 1893

Cause of Loss: foundered in storm

Dean Richmond

Great Lakes Historical Society

Story of the Loss:

Those who traffic in superstition would have you believe the *Dean Richmond* was destined to be a casualty of the lakes. She was the fourth Great Lakes vessel to carry the name of the president of the New York Central Railroad.

All three of her predecessors had met with disaster. The original *"Dean"*, a schooner, was wrecked off Racine, Wisconsin in 1855. *Dean #2*, also a schooner, sprung a leak and foundered during a gale in Lake Huron. The first steamer named *Dean Richmond*, caught fire and burned to the waterline on the Saint Marys River. When the fourth of the *Deans* sailed her final voyage, she departed with a female crew member on Friday the 13th. Surely, this was tempting the fates too much! Those who are less inclined to superstition question why she ventured into the teeth of a gale with a rudder that was known to be damaged and 100 to 200 tons of pig zinc in her belly.

Captain George Stoddard

The *Dean Richmond* was operating under charter to the Clover Leaf Rail company as one of a fleet of package freighters carrying rail freight between the ports of Toledo, Ohio and Buffalo, New York. Her sailing times were scheduled to get freight to and from the trains waiting at either end of her route. As such, there was no question of whether or not Friday the 13th was a good day to depart. The schedule required it. Her rudder had been damaged earlier in the season, but the demands of the shipping schedule kept her from the dry docks. Much needed repairs would have to wait for the winter lay up.

Under command of Captain George Stoddard, the Richmond had arrived in Toledo Thursday evening and laborers had worked through the night to offload her westbound cargo and bring aboard Toledo cargo bound for the east. Into her holds they first loaded the heavy bars of pig zinc, placing them in the lowest levels of the hold to act as ballast. Flour, bagged meal, oil cakes and other miscellaneous light merchandise followed these. Nowhere on her manifests is there any mention of the copper that would have treasure hunters seeking her remains for the next ninety years. As the loading process was completed, Chief Engineer and part owner, John Hogan, turned his responsibilities over to Frank Hilton. Hogan was off to the Chicago Worlds Fair.

Lifeboat washed ashore near Dunkirk, New York. Remick Collection.

Hilton had been off the lakes for weeks due to illness. In offering to relieve his friend Hogan, he had signed up for a date with death.

Knowing the winds were strong and the waves were high, Captain Stoddard and his crew of 18 men and one woman cast off the lines and made their way up the Maumee River and into Lake Erie. As soon as they entered the lake, they encountered heavy weather, and as they traveled eastward through the night the winds continued to build. When dawn broke on Saturday, the *Dean Richmond* was encountering gale force winds from the southwest at 60 miles an hour. Whitecapped waves, three stories tall, battered the ship as it struggled on toward Buffalo. Mid-morning, she was sighted off Erie, Pennsylvania by the upbound propeller *Helena*. Both masts and one stack were down and she appeared to be having difficulty maneuvering. With a stack down, she would have been taking water into her boilers and having trouble keeping up steam. If her rudder had gone she would be without control. With no steering and little steam, she was already in serious trouble, but the *Dean Richmond* struggled on. As the sun set on Saturday, she was sighted by the Schooner *Neosho,* reportedly 40 miles off Buffalo with both stacks down and rolling in the troughs. With both stacks down, she would not be able to keep steam up. The *Dean Richmond* was in intense danger. Somehow she survived until the middle of the night before Walter Goodyear and Captain Stoddard went into the water at 12:20 a.m. We assume it was about that time that the ship rolled and sank. Having fought valiantly through the storm, she finally found calm water 110 feet below the surface.

The following morning, farmer Frank Boling, was first to discover the wreckage of the *Dean Richmond* washing ashore eight miles west of Silver Creek, New York. The beach was filled with paste from the cargo of flour. Buried in the wreckage were the bodies of Andrew Dodge, from the galley crew, and Walter Goodyear, the first mate. Dodge carried a letter from a Michigan girl accepting his invitation to a dance on Saturday night. Goodyear wore a watch that had stopped at 12:20. Later in the day a boat recovered the body of Captain Stoddard. He also wore a watch that had stopped at 12:20.

Treasure Hunters:

Immediately following her loss, there were several search efforts mounted to recover her cargo. While the flour would be ruined, the pig zinc in her holds was worthy of salvage. Much to the dismay of the insurance companies, the wreck could not be found.

Propeller removed from the Dean Richmond shortly after she was found.

Through the course of years, the *Dean Richmond's* story grew. The longer she went unfound, the greater were the rumors of her treasure. Rumors developed that she had been carrying copper, not pig zinc. Her holds were full of the stuff. Copper, now that's a treasure worth finding. The *Dean* became the most sought after ship in Lake Erie. Finally in 1965, 72 years after her loss, she was reported to be found. Salvors discovered what they believed to be the *Dean Richmond* 3 miles off Van Buren Point. So certain were they of their find that they dynamited the wreck attempting to retrieve her treasure. We now know the wreck they dynamited was the single screw wood propeller, *Passaic*. The search continued and the rumors grew. Stories developed that she also carried gold bullion.

In 1974, Garry Kozak began what would prove to be a nine year search for the *Dean*. Using side scan sonar, Kozak covered 550 square miles and charted twenty eight new shipwrecks before finally locating the *Dean Richmond* on July 15, 1983. Ninety years after her last voyage her holds were entered in search of her hidden treasurers and all that was found was the pig zinc listed on her manifests ... no copper, no gold, no fortune.

The Wreck Today:

Lying upside down in 110 feet of water, the *Dean Richmond* is an imposing sight as the diver descends the tie-in line attached to her port propeller shaft. One propeller is still in place. The other has been removed. Her hull is breached on both sides at the stern, making it easy to enter the wreck. Entering the wreck is dangerous and should only be attempted by very experienced divers with specialized training and equipment for shipwreck penetration. There are few things more hazardous than an upside down shipwreck.

A sizable debris field lies to the north. Many zinc ingots and ship parts can be found in this debris field. Don't go looking for the ship's compass. Some years ago a compass believed to be off the *Dean* was raised in a fisherman's net and is now in a private collection.

Above: remaining wheel, top right: engine room hatch, middle right: blast hole from salvage operation, bottom right: debris field. Videocaptures by Mike Wachter.

SAINT JAMES

Official #: 22417   **Site #:** 67

Location: 353°T 20.5 miles off Erie, Pennsylvania, 209°T 7.6 miles off Long Point Light

Coordinates: Loran: 44491.0 58530.4   **DGPS:** 42 27.104 80 07.331

Lies: **Depth:** 165 feet

Type: schooner, two masts   **Cargo:** wheat

Power: sail

Owner(s) C.M. Reed of Erie, Pennsylvania

Built: 1856 at Milan, Ohio by Gay & Merry

Dimensions: 118' x 25'   **Tonnage:** 226 76/100 gross

Date of Loss: Late October 1870

Cause of Loss: unknown

Saint James

Watercolor as she looks today by Georgann Wachter

Story of the Loss:

Like many vessels lost in Lake Erie, the loss of the *Saint James* is shrouded in mystery. The ship left Toledo, Ohio on October 23, 1870 with the steady hand of Captain James Burrill at the helm. With a crew of seven men and 14,000 bushels of wheat in her holds, the staunch craft was bound for Oswego,

New York. She would never be heard from again. Had there been no problem, her trip would have taken her through Port Colborne to enter the Welland Canal. The *Buffalo Courier* reported, on November 4, 1870, that nothing had been heard from her at either Toledo or Port Colborne. The ship, her cargo, captain, and crew were gone to the bottom of Lake Erie with no one surviving to tell her story.

Was she in a collision? Did she founder in a Lake Erie storm? Did she spring a leak? No one knows. However, observation of the wreck today gives some answers. The only damage to the wreck is a broken corner on the wheelhouse, possibly caused by a falling boom when she went down. There have been no human remains found on the *St. James*. And, she appears to have been under full sail when she sank. As there is no damage, there was no collision. She sailed in late October and the history of Lake Erie shipwrecks is filled with storm losses at that time of year. However, one would not expect her to be under full sail in a storm. In all likelihood she simply sprung a leak. One imagines her crew fleeing to the yawl boat as the holds filled with water and the vessel slowly sank. Think of being one of seven men in a yawl in the middle of Lake Erie, searching in vain for a rescue that never came their way.

The Wreck Today:

This dive is beyond the limits of sport diving as defined by all major certifying agencies. It should only be attempted by very experienced divers with specialized training for depths in excess of sport diving limits.

When she was found she was also shrouded in mystery. No one knew her identity so she was called *"Schooner X"*. Sitting with a slight list to port in 165 feet of water, she appeared to still be under way with her anchors in place, her masts rising eighty feet from the bottom of the lake, her wheel and cabins ready for action, and the silt forming waves around her hull. She had a unique scrolled figurehead and both a wooden bilge pump and a newer cast iron bilge pump. Then, divers discovered her tonnage numbers carved in a main beam — 226 76/100. Armed with this information, many measurements, and descriptions of equipment, marine historian Art Amos was able to identify her as the schooner *Saint James*.

The *Saint James* is commonly considered to be the best preserved example of a 19th century schooner anywhere in the Great Lakes. It is an absolute must dive for anyone with the proper training and equipment.

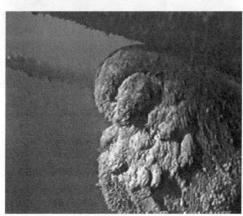

From top to bottom the photos on the right show: diver exploring the wheel and stern cabin, deadeyes amidships, and ram's head figurehead.

Video captures by Mike King.

Official #:

Site #:   43

Location: 139°T 11.7 miles off Port Dover, Ontario   359°T 7.1 miles off Long Point Light

Coordinates: Loran: 44585.0   58602.8   **DGPS:**   42.39.103   80.03.145

Lies: bow south   **Depth:**   105 feet

Type: schooner   **Cargo:**

Power: sail, 2 masts

Owner(s)

Built:

Dimensions: 77'   **Tonnage:**

Date of Loss: unknown

Cause of Loss: fire?

Cornelia

At 86' x 21' x 8' she is about the size of the 17 Fathom Wreck.

Great Lakes Historical Society, Bowen Collection

Story of the Loss:

Other than the fact that she appears to have had a fire on board, little is known about this small sailing vessel. With increased interest in discovering the name and history of the unknown shipwrecks off Long Point, we hope more will be learned about this site in the near future.

A letter from Port Dover, dated April 20, 1962, appears to refer to the discovery of this vessel:

> "Our fishermen are busy again. For the last 2 or 3 years some of them have been experimenting with trawling and I believe have been very successful. Sometimes they bring up unexpected things. … This week the *Lynn Dover* brought to the surface the end of a spar, which they towed into port. When they got to shore they found they had a mast nearly sixty feet in length and nineteen inches in diameter where it had broken off at deck level. Part of the crosstree was still in place. On the afterside, where the boom and gaff would rest against the mast, it was protected from chafing by sheets of leather tacked on, and the leather was in excellent shape. Captain Robert Simmons said that their depth sounder showed something lying in 17 fathoms of water, which he supposed might be a hull.
>
> It was found about fifteen or eighteen miles southeast of Port Dover and almost in line from the east end of Long Point to Nanticoke on the north shore. .."

The Wreck Today:

Lying on a silt bottom at 105 feet, this ship sits with a slight list to starboard in usually crystal clear water. Because the water clarity is normally very good, the entire wreck may be viewed as one descends the line. The mooring block is set on the starboard side amidships and a trail line leads from the block to the wreck. Nearby, you may discover the trawl doors from a fishing vessel.

Seventeen Fathom Wreck
77' x ??'
by Georgann S. Wachter
not to scale

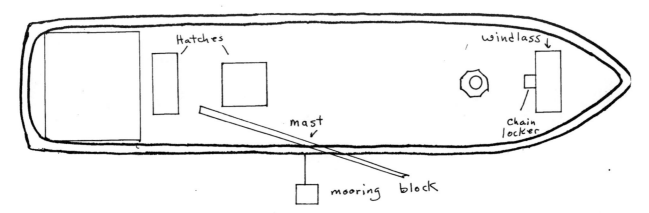

SIBERIA

Official #: 115848   **Site #:** 44

Location: 164°T 15 miles off Port Dover, Ontario   on Bluff Bar 4 at Long Point

Coordinates: Loran: 44538.6 58562.0   **DGPS:**

Lies: scattered   **Depth:** 18 feet

Type: wood propeller   **Cargo:** barley

Power: 720 horsepower steam engine

Owner(s) Gilchrist Transportation Company of Cleveland, Ohio

Built: 1882 at West Bay City, Michigan by James Davidson

Dimensions: 272' x 30' x 18'   **Tonnage:** 1618 gross 1222 net

Date of Loss: Friday, October 20, 1905

Cause of Loss: storm

Siberia

Private collection of Al Hart

Story of the Loss:

One of the paramount storms in Great Lakes' history occurred in October 1905. Such was the ferocity of this storm that vessels were lost and grounded throughout the Great Lakes. Among the vessels lost or grounded in Lake Erie were: the schooner *Yukon* off Ashtabula, Ohio, steamer *Sarah E. Sheldon* off Sheffield Lake, Ohio, schooner *Tasmania* off Pelee Island, steamer *Wisconsin* at Lorain, Ohio, schooner *Mautenee* off Erie, Pennsylvania, and the steamer *Siberia* off Long Point.

Bound for Buffalo, New York with a load of barley, the *Siberia* took a severe beating in the storm. Off Long Point, her steam pipes were battered apart by the seas. This rendered her pumps inoperable. With 11 feet of water in her holds, she raised distress signals in hopes of gaining assistance from other steamers nearby. Seeing her distress signals, the steamer *Wilkinson* went to her aid and provided escort to the lee waters around Long Point. Assuming her to be safe, the *Wilkinson* continued on. The *Siberia* was anything but safe. Having insufficient steam to run her pumps, the vessel was towed aground by the steamer *Wade*, which was sheltering under Long Point. Captain Benham lowered his lifeboats and transferred his crew to the *Wade*.

Following the sinking, Benham charged the steamer *George W. Peavey* with failing to respond to his distress signals. Captain Boyce, of the *Peavey* responded with the following statement:

"About 6:20 a.m. on October 20, when 25 miles above Long Point, we sighted a steamer which proved to be the *Siberia*, with her ensign hoisted right side up, apparently at full height in the foremast. We were then about four miles outside, or south of her, and two miles astern. At the same time, the steamer *H.S. Wilkinson*, which passed us during the night, was nearly abreast of the *Siberia*, and as it looked to us, quite near her. At the time we saw the flag, the *Wilkinson* was hauling toward the *Siberia* and seemed to be under check.

Before we were abreast of her, which took an hour, the *Wilkinson* had dropped into the *Siberia's* wake. We kept close watch on both boats with our marine glasses and did not see nor hear any more signals from either boat. We were ready at any time to go to their assistance, although our engine was partially disabled, one cylinder being useless. Our engineer said that any extra strain on the engine was liable to cripple it entirely.

My idea, as I told my mates, was that a steamer, in order to render any effective assistance in time of trouble, would have to be head to wind and sea, in which position I could have placed my steamer at any time. From our position, the danger did not appear to be imminent, as the *Siberia* kept on her course, making fair time, with the steamer *Wilkinson* following for company.

When we first saw the *Siberia* signal we decided that, as the *Wilkinson* was nearest to her it was the *Wilkinson's* place and duty to go to her, but if she did not go we would. Until we saw the *Siberia* turn under Long Point we stood ready to go to her.

I have sailed on the lakes for forty years and have never deserted a shipmate in time of trouble or refused to render assistance when needed. A man who would do so is not worthy of the name sailor. I always think it may be my turn next to call for help, but in this case I could not see where we could do anymore than to stand ready to give aid when needed."

After her grounding, an attempt was made to salvage her. While the attempt was underway, another storm came up. This storm pounded the stranded vessel to pieces and ended any thoughts of salvaging her.

The Wreck Today:

In addition to having been dynamited, this shallow site is regularly swept by waves, ice, and wind; leaving little of the wreck intact. The wave action at the site stirs the silt making for very poor visibility. Her keelson can still be found and the boiler is near the shore. The *Siberia's* remains are often covered by silt. Divers who discovered her in the 1960's drew the map to the left.

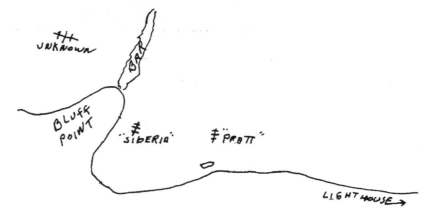

SMITH

Official #: C 138371   **Site #:** 51

Location: 295°T 21.6 miles off Barcelona, New York, 146°T 6.1 miles off Long Point Light

Coordinates: Loran: 44530.0 58607.1   **DGPS:** 42 28.486 79 59.061

Lies: southeast/northwest   **Depth:** 165 feet

Type: tug   **Cargo:** light

Power: fore and aft compound engine

Owner(s) Sinmac Company of Montreal, Canada

Built: 1881 at Buffalo, New York by Union Dry Dock Company

Dimensions: 120' x 22' x 10'   **Tonnage:** 218 gross 155 net

Date of Loss: Saturday, October 25, 1930

Cause of Loss: foundered

Smith

Private collection of Ralph Roberts

Story of the Loss:

The tug *Smith* was built in the United States as the *Albert J. Wright* official number 105993. Her first power plant, a high-pressure noncondensing engine, was removed in 1883. The *Albert J. Wright* was renamed *Smith* in 1907. In 1917 she was changed to Canadian registry under the new ownership of the Reid Wrecking Company.

Approaching the ripe old age of 50 years, the *Smith* was sold to the Sinmac Company of Montreal, Canada. On thorough examination, the new owners determined that significant repairs were required and made arrangements for the work to be done in Sarnia, Ontario. The *Smith* was sitting in Port Colborne, Ontario and was taken in tow by the *Manistique* for the trip to Sarnia. The vessels left for Sarnia on a blustery day Friday, October 24, 1930 and were off the tip of Long Point when, at 2:00 a.m. Saturday, October 25, the *Smith* foundered in one of the deepest points of Lake Erie. The *Manistique* rescued the four crewmen.

The Wreck Today:

Today the *Smith* rests in 165 feet of water with a slight list to port. Her wheelhouse is intact and the beautiful spoked wheel and chadburn sit in place at the helm. Her stack is fallen. Be sure to check out her whistle, which lies loose on top of the pilothouse. A mushroom anchor is on the port side. When you scrape away the zebra mussels at the stern, her name and port of registry can easily be read.

This dive is beyond the limits of sport diving as defined by all major certifying agencies. It should only be attempted by very experienced divers with specialized training for depths in excess of sport diving limits.

The wheel and chadburn still stand in place in the pilot house

Video captures by Mike King

STEEL PRODUCTS

Official #:   161876   **Site #:**   15

Location: 87°T 5.7 miles off Port Colborne, Ontario

Coordinates: Loran: 44870.7 59111.6   **DGPS:**   42 51.891 79 08.455

Lies: scattered, bow east   **Depth:**   10 feet

Type: propeller   **Cargo:**   light

Power: steam

Owner(s)   Marine Salvage Limited of Port Colborne, Ontario

Built: 1901 at Lorain, Ohio by American Shipbuilding Company

Dimensions: 346' x 48' x 28'   **Tonnage:** 3719 gross 2766 net

Date of Loss: Saturday, October 28, 1961

Cause of Loss: storm

Steel Products as Venus

Great Lakes Historical Society, Bowen Collection

Story of the Loss:

Christened the *Venus,* she sailed under that name for over fifty years. When she was sold to Steel Products Corporation, a subsidiary of Lake Shore Limited, she was renamed after the company, *Steel Products.* Befitting her new name, this crane equipped vessel often carried scrap steel.

In 1961, rolls were reversed and the scrap steel carrier was herself sold for scrapping. On October 26th the tug *G.W. Rodgers* took her under tow to be dismantled at the Dwor Metal Company. Due to heavy weather the ships sought shelter and anchored off Port Colborne, Ontario. Sometime during the night, the *Steel Products* slipped anchor and began to drift east. She continued to drift until she ran aground near Point Abino.

STERN CASTLE

Official #:   **Site #:**   48

Location: 4°T 24 miles off Erie, Pennsylvania harbor entrance, 170°T 3 miles off Long Point Light

Coordinates: Loran: 44530.0   58583.4   **DGPS:**   42 30.294 80 02.379

Lies: **Depth:**   185 feet

Type: schooner, 2 masts   **Cargo:**

Power: sail

Owner(s)

Built:

Dimensions: **Tonnage:**

Date of Loss: unknown

Cause of Loss: unknown

Story of the Loss:

Unknown.

The Wreck Today:

This site was nicknamed *"Stern Castle"* because the schooner's pronounced raised stern is her most prominent feature. Although the midsection of the wreck is almost entirely silted over, the bow and stern both rise out of the silt. In limited visibility, the heavy silt makes it easy to think you've lost the wreck. However, you can usually orient yourself by keeping an eye on her masts. Her wheel is in place and much of her running gear can still be explored.

At 185 feet, this dive is well beyond the limits of sport diving as defined by all major certifying agencies. It should only be attempted by very experienced divers with specialized training and equipment for depths in excess of sport diving limits.

STEEL PRODUCTS (CONTINUED)

With the onset of winter, the grounded vessel was frozen in. A crew of men was left on board as shipkeepers. They kept steam up on one boiler and tended to the boat through the winter. Come the spring of 1962, a decision was made to abandon her where she lay. In May 1962 a road was built to the ship to permit the vessel to be stripped for salvage. Over the course of several scrapping operations, her engines were removed and the hull was partially dismantled.

Steel Products trapped in winter ice.

The Wreck Today:

This site is close in and can be reached by boat or by swimming from shore. The salvage road is now underwater and many parts of the wreck have sharp jagged edges. Her prop remains as does a large navy anchor at the end of the steel cable trailing from the bow. Fish life abounds at this shallow water site. For those who do not scuba dive, it is easily toured by snorkel.

When diving by boat, watch your props.

WILLIAM H. STEVENS

Official #: 81120   **Site #:** 80

Location: 346°T 24.5 miles north of Conneaut, Ohio, position approximate

Coordinates: Loran: **GPS PA:** 42°19'30" 80°40'30"

Lies: bow east   **Depth:** 70 feet

Type: wood propeller   **Cargo:** flax seed, copper bars, flour

Power: 500 horsepower fore and aft compound engine

Owner(s) Union Transit Company of Buffalo, New York

Built: 1886 at West Bay City, Michigan by F.W. Wheeler and Company

Dimensions: 212' x 37' x 23'6"   **Tonnage:** 1332 gross 1025 net

Date of Loss: Monday, September 8, 1902

Cause of Loss: fire

William H. Stevens

Great Lakes Historical Society

Story of the Loss:

Loaded with 32,000 bushels of flaxseed, 9,000 barrels of flour, and 180 tons of copper, the *William H. Stevens* was downbound from Duluth, Minnesota to Buffalo, New York. Although Lake Erie was running a heavy sea, her passage had been reasonably uneventful until she reached a point 23 miles off Port Burwell, Ontario. Then, at 3:30 p.m., fire broke out on the *Stevens*. The crew fought the blaze until 1:30 a.m. before finally abandoning the vessel when she was afire fore and aft.

The crew left the doomed vessel in two lifeboats. Working against the heavy sea, the crews experienced a great deal of difficulty in reaching shore. After several hours, Mate Knapp and 11 crewmen made land. Searching along a fifteen to twenty-five foot high bank, they found a safe point to land near Clear Creek, Ontario. They then climbed the cliffs and built a signal fire to provide a beacon by which Captain John Tyrney and 8 others were able to land safely.

For a period of time, the remains of the *Stevens* were in a vertical position with her stern on the bottom and her bow floating. As a result, there was great concern about her as a hazard to other navigation. Apparently however, the action of the waves and wind finally sank her. A diver was sent to examine the hazard and reported that there was plenty of clearance over the burned out hulk. The flaxseed and flour were of no salvage value and the ship was obviously destroyed. However, 180 tons of copper bars were worth a small fortune. In July and August of 1904, the propeller *Snook* salvaged 160 tons of copper from the *Stevens*. Rumors persist that there is still copper to be found on the *Stevens*. We have one report of a diver finding a five-foot long ingot covered in hip deep flaxseed. Another diver reports large bars buried under coiled copper. But, you know how treasure stories go, the smaller the treasure the bigger the tale.

The Wreck Today:

The burned out remains of the *William H. Stevens* have been found and then lost again several times over the years. She is reported to have a six-foot rise at the bow and to be completely opened up. At this time, we are unable to divulge the exact coordinates to the wreck. For those who would like to do a little searching, here are some starting points. She is reported to be at 42°19′ north 80°40′ west, 23 ¾ miles off Port Burwell, 23 miles from the Long Point Cut Light, 30 ½ miles from the Presque Isle Light, and 35 miles southwest ¾ west of Long Point Light. Good hunting and give us a call when you find it.

Because of the heavy silt and jumbled coils of wire on this site, it is an extremely hazardous dive. Great caution needs to be exercised at this location.

U.S.S. MICHIGAN
Erie, Pa., Oct. 22nd, 1902

Sir:-

1. I have the honor to report that I buoyed the wreck of the steamer "STEVENS" yesterday. I found wreckers at work on her, and I was informed by them that the ship had settled to the bottom and nowhere was there less than about 48 feet of water over her. To assure myself of this, I sounded carefully and found it to be correct. She is therefore no longer a danger to navigation; but I placed a danger buoy right on her in 7 1/2 fathoms.

2. Owing to the fact that the day was somewhat hazy, and the distances from all points, I was unable to get my bearings; but the mean of two patent logs and a carefully corrected compass, both out and in from Erie, seems to put her a very little to the Eastward of her assumed position.

3. In addition to the buoy (red and black horizontal stripes) placed by me, there are two bouys marking her general direction placed by the wreckers.

Very Respectfully

Lieut. Commander, U.S. Navy,
Commanding

SUSQUEHANNA

Official #: none   **Site #:** H

Location: 330°T 4.5 miles off Elk Creek, Pennsylvania

Coordinates: Loran: 44271.6   58301.1   **DGPS:** 42 04.996   80 24.761

Lies: bow east   **Depth:** 55 feet

Type: two masted schooner   **Cargo:** coal and staves

Power: sail

Owner(s) Captain Campbell of Buffalo, New York

Built: 1846 at Huron Ohio by F.D. Ketchum

Dimensions: approximately 120 '   **Tonnage:** 195.20 gross

Date of Loss: Wednesday, August 23, 1865

Cause of Loss: leak

Foundering Schooner
Author's collection.

Story of the Loss:

It is said that there are two happy days in a boat owner's life -- the day he buys the boat and the day he sells it. Captain Campbell of the *Susquehanna* had only recently experienced one of those days. You see, he had only recently purchased her from General Reed of Erie, Pennsylvania.

The good captain had moved the vessel to his home port of Buffalo, New York, and he had plans to use her to haul bulk cargos and general merchandise across the Great Lakes. Unfortunately for the captain, his plans did not work out.

The *Susquehanna* departed Buffalo on August 21, 1865. She was only partially loaded with barrel staves to be delivered to the town of Saginaw, Michigan. On that same day, she made her first port of call at

Erie, Pennsylvania. In Erie she took on coal to be delivered to Chicago, Illinois. So far, Captain Campbell's venture was going well. He had a full load consisting of two separate cargos. This was going to be the first of what he anticipated would be many profitable trips.

Departing Erie on August 23, Campbell and his crew proceeded west toward the Detroit River. Regrettably, they had barely passed the town of Conneaut, Ohio when Captain Campbell's dreams of profits gave way to the first evidence of what would become a nightmarish disaster. The *Susquehanna* had sprung a leak just to the west of Conneaut. Campbell immediately made the decision to turn back toward Erie.

Of interest is the fact that *Susquehanna* was not the only ship to spring a leak off Erie that day. The steamer *Elm City* had also cleared Erie with a load of coal on August 23rd. Headed for Buffalo, she made it just past the town of North East when the crew discovered she was leaking. Her captain also made the decision to turn back toward the safety of Erie. Of the two vessels, only one would make it back to Erie, but neither would stay afloat. The *Elm City* made it into the harbor entrance before the water entering her holds took her to the bottom. Fortunately for her insurers, she sat in a location where she was protected from storms and where she could be easily raised.

Captain Campbell and the crew of the *Susquehanna* would not be so fortunate. They were about half way back to Erie when the schooner suddenly pitched down at the bow and did not recover. Within a minute, she dove bow first for the bottom of Lake Erie leaving only her topmast exposed. Quickly taking to the yawl boat, the crew barely saved their lives. They lost everything except the clothing they were wearing. Had Campbell not pulled one half drowned crew member into the boat, they would have lost one life as well. The captain lost everything when the ship went down. Not only were his dreams of profits now gone, but he and other crew members had to borrow hats, vests, and coats to get to Erie.

The propeller *Olean* passed upbound on Friday, August 25 and spotted masts sticking out of the water. Two gilt balls atop the main mast identified the wreck as the *Susquehanna*. With her location confirmed, the Home Insurance Company wrecking steamer *Magnet* was sent to remove her anchor, chains, and running rigging. Campbell's ship would not be raised. His ship and his dreams went down that day.

The Wreck Today:

The sharp vertical bow of the *Susquehanna* rises intact from the bottom. However, the rest of the wreck is rather broken up. As a canaller, she had a retractable centerboard that permitted her to transit the shallow canals of her day. Other features of note are the ship's stove and her cargo of coal. Many pieces of rigging and some artifacts of life aboard still adorn the wreck.

Do be careful, there is still gill netting floating off her gunnels.

Video captures of the Susquehanna by Larry Slomski.

Swallow

Official #: 115184

Site #: 38

Location: 14ºT 28.6 miles off Erie, Pennsylvania   5.5 miles east of Long Point light

Coordinates: Loran: 44572.1 58646.4 16486.6   **DGPS:** 42 34.892 79 56.455

Lies:

Depth: 190 feet

Type: wood propeller   **Cargo:** lumber and shingles

Power: steam

Owner(s) Carlos Siebert, Captain Quinlan, James & William Lennan

Built: 1873 at Trenton, Michigan by A. A. Turner

Dimensions: 133'8" x 25'8" x 10'8"   **Tonnage:** 256.67 gross 203.42 net

Date of Loss: Saturday, October 19, 1901

Cause of Loss: foundered in storm

Swallow

Private collection of Ralph Roberts

Story of the Loss:

Built for the Whiting Transportation Company, the *Swallow* first sank in October 1900 near Marine City, Michigan when the steamer *Seimens* struck her. She was raised that same year and returned to service.

A typical "lumber hooker", she carried two masts and a single stack. Lumber was carried in her holds and stacked on her decks between the raised pilothouse and crew accommodations at the stern.

The story of her loss is all too familiar in the annals of Lake Erie shipwrecks. The tale shares the four ingredients with many of the *Swallow's* lost brethren: an aging wood vessel, the fall of the year, gale winds, and the waters off Long Point.

Loaded with lumber, the *Swallow* cleared Emerson, on Lake Superior, Sunday, October 13, 1901. At Sault Ste. Marie, she picked up the barge *Manitou*, also loaded with lumber. Their passage toward Buffalo, New York had favorable weather until Friday, October 18, when they encountered 50 mile per hour gale winds on Lake Erie. As the steamer started leaking profusely at the seams, the crew of 11 worked to keep her afloat as she headed for the sheltering lee of Long Point. Engineer Frank Clark believed strongly that the ship would have made the shelter of Long Point had the consort been cut loose. This, however, was not to be the case.

Still over 20 miles from Long Point, the steamer was in danger of foundering and her crew of eleven abandoned her. Leaving her oil filled lights burning as a warning to other ships, they went by lifeboat to the *Manitou* and then cut the consort loose. The steamer continued to drift on the storm tossed seas until she finally foundered five and a half miles east of Long Point Light. Since the remains of the steamer are charred, we surmise that the oil filled lights ignited the steamer before she foundered.

With two full complements aboard, the *Manitou's* provisions would be rapidly depleted. The captain put up what little sail remained on the barge and attempted to head the boat toward Erie, Pennsylvania. He made no headway against the storm. With the gale continuing to pound away at her, the *Manitou* lost her deck load and was leaking badly. She drifted about the lake for 39 hours before the steamer *Scranton* come upon her, took her under tow, and brought her safely to Erie.

The Wreck Today:

Charter Captain Jim Herbert believes this wreck is the remains of the *Swallow*. The wreck shows evidence of a severe fire aboard her. The ship's bow stem is clad in steel and her anchor hangs loosely at the bow. Her boilers and engines stand proudly in place and offer interesting features, as do the small derricks on her rounded stern. Her rudder is almost completely buried. Divers need to watch for the large trawl nets on this wreck.

At 190 feet, this dive is beyond the limits of sport diving as defined by all major certifying agencies. It should only be attempted by very experienced divers with specialized training and equipment for depths in excess of sport diving limits.

The Lifesaving Station at Long Point was the last hope for many seafarers on Lake Erie.

Remick Collection

T-8

Official #:

Location: 3.15 miles, 39° from Long Point Light

Coordinates: Loran: 44566.7   58606.2

Lies:

Type: schooner, 2 masts

Power: sail

Owner(s)

Built:

Dimensions:

Date of Loss:

Cause of Loss: collision?

Site #:   40

DGPS: 42.35.226   80.01.335

Depth: 145 feet

Cargo:

Tonnage:

The Wreck Today:

Discovered in the 1960's, this site was nicknamed *T-8* because she was the eighth of many targets identified by a sidescan sweep of the area. She sits on the bottom with a severe list and many trawl nets and net floats pose potential hazards to divers. Her centerboard and distinctive carved wooden railing are prominent features. She exhibits obvious collision damage.

At 145 feet, this dive is beyond the limits of sport diving as defined by all major certifying agencies. It should only be attempted by very experienced divers with specialized training and equipment for depths in excess of sport diving limits.

The following photos from diver David VanZandt provide a diving tour of the *T-8*. From top to bottom we see the bow section, a diver exploring the starboard rail, the centerboard, the starboard railing, nets rising from the port rail, and the destruction at the stern.

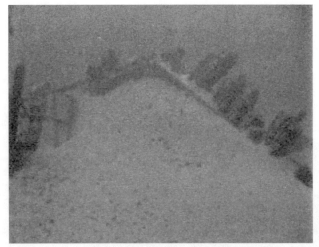

The bow is broken down and silted over.

Diver explores the starboard railing.

Underwater video captures courtesy of David VanZandt.

The centerboard provides a prominent point of reference.

This intact railing is in stark contrast to the rest of this badly damaged wreck site.

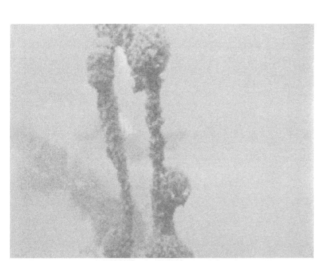

Fish floats from trawl nets that caught on this shipwreck still drape the structure.

Her stern is barely recognizable.

TONAWANDA

Official #: 24110   **Site #:** 7

Location: 10 miles off Buffalo, New York

Coordinates: Loran: 44902.2 59191.7   **DGPS:** 42 50.73   78 59.00

Lies: bow east   **Depth:** 48 feet

Type: wood propeller, package freighter   **Cargo:** flour, corn, pig lead

Power: two direct acting oscillating engines

Owner(s) Western Transportation Company, Buffalo, New York

Built: 1856 at Buffalo, New York by B.B. Jones

Dimensions: 202'3" x 32'3" x 13'3"   **Tonnage:** 936 gross 822 net

Date of Loss: Tuesday, October 18, 1870

Cause of Loss: foundered in storm

Tonawanda

Father Edward J. Dowling Collection, University of Detroit Mercy Library

Story of the Loss:

The package freighter *Tonawanda* was typical of the packet freighters of her day. She sported hogging arches on each side for structural support, had cargo openings along her sides, passenger accommodations on the upper deck, and carried two yawl boats. With a single mast forward and twin oscillating engines, she cruised the lakes at a rather leisurely pace by today's standards. She was based in Buffalo and routinely ran to various Lake Michigan ports and back.

She had come close to sinking on several previous occasions. She caught fire off Presque Isle on Lake Huron, July 6, 1857. The crew used axes to cut through the decks and fight the blaze. After five hours the fire was finally brought under control. On May 25, 1860, she and the propeller *Equinox* collided at Clay Banks, Wisconsin. This collision damaged her stern so severely that she was forced into the dry docks for repairs.

Tonawanda's final voyage began in Chicago, Illinois on October 12, 1870. Under command of Captain Bryant, she sailed to Milwaukee loaded with flour, grain, and miscellaneous merchandise. In Milwaukee she took on more cargo. On October 13, 1879, she left for Buffalo carrying 19,526 bushels of corn, 7,500 barrels of flour, and 750 pigs of lead. This was a massive load for a vessel her size and many believe the size of her load led to her eventual loss.

Off Point Abino on October 18 she was clobbered by a gale of great force. This storm had already driven three vessels ashore: the schooner *George Duncan, the schooner Emma Blake* with the loss of all aboard, and the schooner *Mary* with the loss of all aboard. Many vessels returned to port, unable or unwilling to face the fury of the storm. While fighting her way through the gale the *Tonawanda's* rudder was disabled, and she would no longer respond to the wheel. Now wallowing in the mountainous seas, the wave's brutal force battered in her amidships gangways. Already heavily laden, she began shipping water. Captain Bryan ordered the anchor lowered, but her chains separated and the vessel was again at the mercy of the lake. Now in a desperate effort to reach port, her foresail was raised and steam was brought up. As the seas broke over the ship, the water continued to rise until her furnaces were put out.

Knowing his ship was doomed; Captain Bryan raised distress signals and launched one boat. In it he placed his daughter, first mate, and 10 stout fellows to see her safely to shore. Working mightily against the gale, the small boat's crew rowed for 4 hours. Finally reaching the Canadian shore, they walked six miles to a rail station and boarded a train for Buffalo.

The tugs *F.L. Danforth* and *J.C. Harrison* did reach the *Tonawanda* and take her in tow. They had made five miles toward Buffalo when the package freighter listed heavily, rolled over, and sank. The remaining crew escaped to the safety of the tugs and were transported to Buffalo.

When the waters calmed the following morning, the final resting place of the *Tonawanda* was clearly marked by her foremast rising above the surface and hundreds of barrels of flour bobbing about on the waves.

The Wreck Today:

In 1871, the wrecker *Rescue* made several unsuccessful attempts to raise the *Tonawanda*. These efforts, and the removal of her boiler in 1875, damaged what was left of her hull beyond salvage. Today she lies on a mud bottom. Her bow is broken and part of the starboard arch lies inside the hull. There is always a slight current and she, like all wrecks in Lake Erie, is covered with zebra mussels. Lying in sight of Buffalo, this wreck is often buoyed by local divers. The buoy is commonly attached to her remaining boiler.

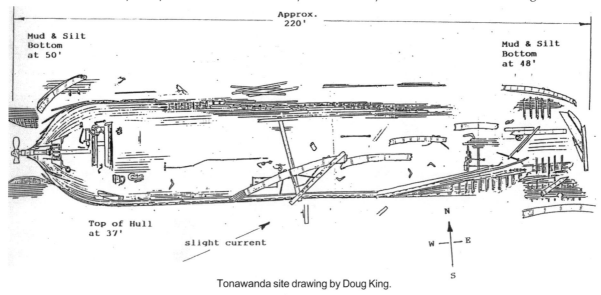

Tonawanda site drawing by Doug King.

TRADE WIND

Official #: none   **Site #:**   68

Location: 340°T 19.5 miles off Erie harbor entrance, 222°T 11.5 miles off Long Point Light.

Coordinates: Loran: 44463.5   58483.8   **DGPS:**   42 25.516   80 12.056

Lies: bow south   **Depth:**   120 feet

Type: bark, 3 masts   **Cargo:**   railroad iron, stoves, lifeboats

Power: sail

Owner(s) H.C. Walker and Company of Buffalo, New York

Built: 1853 in Buffalo, New York

Dimensions: 140'   **Tonnage:** 374.12

Date of Loss: Friday, December 1, 1854

Cause of Loss: collision with bark *Charles Napier*

Vilora A. Hopkins, similar to Trade Wind

Remick Collection

Story of the Loss:

Little known to modern Lake Erie seafarers, for many years there was a natural cut in Long Point. Merchant vessels used it to shorten the route across Lake Erie. This cut was initially opened by a strong Lake

Erie storm in November of 1833. In 1865, another storm created an even larger cut to the west of the first one. However, what the lake gives, the lake takes away. The cut was eventually eliminated by another strong Lake Erie storm in 1906. The Long Point cut plays a role in the loss of the *Trade Wind*.

The bark *Trade Wind* had left Buffalo, New York and was traveling upbound. She was loaded with 200 tons of railroad iron, 1000 stoves, and two U.S. government lifeboats destined for Chicago, Illinois. For the entire trip, the crew had complained about the bulky lifeboats being carried as deck cargo and how difficult it was to work with them in the way. The lifeboats would prove to be a fortunate cargo to have on board. As they traveled toward Long Point, the bark encountered a heavy snow that dangerously limited visibility. Some distance above Long Point cut, the bark *Charles Napier* was making an opposite tack in the thick snowstorm in an effort to run to the cut. The two vessels collided in the blinding storm.

The collision ripped a gaping hole in the side of the *Trade Wind* and destroyed her yawl boat. The captain of the *Charles Napier* reported that he remained by the *Trade Wind* a few minutes and inquired of them what damage they had sustained. He received no answer and, when the snowstorm cleared away, the other vessel was not to be seen. He then proceeded on toward the Welland Canal for repairs.

Captain Eastwick and the crew of the *Trade Wind* did not have the time or opportunity to respond to the hails of the *Napier*. Their yawl boat was destroyed, and their vessel was rapidly sinking. The only chance of survival was the cargo of two U.S. Government lifeboats. They quickly launched the boats and used them to take themselves to the safety of land.

The *Trade Wind* was barely a year old when she sank. Her loss was valued at $13,000 and her cargo at $50,000 — huge sums of money in those days.

The Wreck Today:

The *Trade Wind* sits on a mud bottom in 120 feet of water. Her cargo of railroad iron is widely scattered around the wreck and on the deck. Her fore rigging was heavily damaged in the collision on her starboard side and lays across the decks. A beautiful spoked wheel is has fallen below decks and many stove parts can also be found in her holds. Her capstan and much of her deck gear remain in place. Her three masts have fallen to the port side.

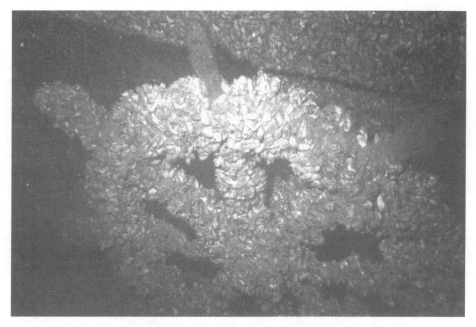

Wheel of the Trade Wind. Photo by Tom Wilson

U.S. 104

Official #: 167718

Site #: 1

Location: 359°T 1.2 miles off Buffalo, New York east harbor entrance, just outside Black Rock Canal

Coordinates: Loran:

DGPS: 42 53.420 78 53.920

Lies: northwest/southeast

Depth: 12 feet

Type: barge – concrete

Cargo: oats

Power: towed

Owner(s) New York Canal and Great Lakes Corporation of New York City

Built: 1919 at Detroit, Michigan

Dimensions: 149.3' x 21.1' x 10.3'

Tonnage: 306 gross 274 net

Date of Loss: Friday, July 15, 1921

Cause of Loss: foundered

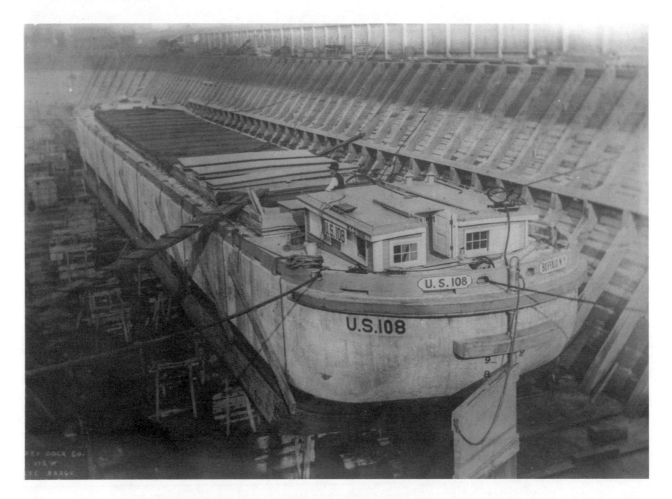

U.S. 108 was identical sister ship to U.S. 104

Private Collection of Ralph Roberts

Story of the Loss:

The *U.S. 104* was one of a series of ten steel reinforced concrete barges built by the United States Government for the canal trade. They served to transport bulk cargo, grain, and other agricultural commodities.

Having left Buffalo, New York loaded with 416 tons of oats, she was part of a five barge tow that departed on July 14. Some barges would go to Troy, New York and others, laden with corn, would travel down the Hudson River to New York City. As the convoy closed on the Black Rock Ship Canal on July 15, the *U.S. 104* struck a rock. She took on water rapidly and sank. While her cargo of oats was quickly salvaged, attempts to raise the barge were unsuccessful.

The Wreck Today:

Today, the *U.S. 104* rests exactly where she sank almost 80 years ago. Divers will find some current flowing to the north and a lot of boat traffic at this site. Her exterior is fractured open revealing the steel reinforcing rods used to build her.

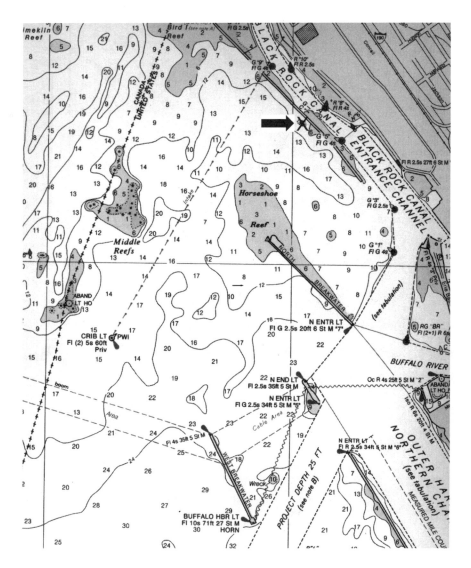

The location of U.S. 104 close to the breakwater at the Black Rock Canal is marked on charts of the area.

SIR C.T. VAN STRAUBENZIE

Official #:	C 75632	**Site #:**	52
Location:	93°T 6.4 miles off Long Point Light		
Coordinates:	Loran: 44571.0 58651.4	**DGPS:**	42 32.611 79 55.448
Lies:		**Depth:**	200 feet
Type:	barkentine	**Cargo:**	light
Power:	3 mast sail		
Owner(s)	Pittsburgh and Erie Coal Company, Ltd.		
Built:	1875 at Saint Catherines, Ontario by Louis Shickluna		
Dimensions:	127.7′ x 26.2′ x 12′	**Tonnage:**	317 gross
Date of Loss:	Monday, September 27, 1909		
Cause of Loss:	collision		

Sir C.T. Van Straubenzie
Lower Lakes Marine Historical Society

Story of the Loss:

When first discovered, this vessel was nicknamed the "10 Volt Wreck" and the "Yawl Boat Wreck". At this time, several researchers who have studied the wreck are of the opinion that it is the *Sir C.T. Van Straubenzie*.

The *Sir C.T. Van Straubenzie*, under command of Captain Thomas Horne, was in collision with the passenger steamer *City of Erie*. She filled so quickly that two men and one woman of her crew of 6 were lost.

The *Van Straubenzie's* starboard (green) light was not burning at the time of the accident. As a result, Captain James Stone, Supervising Inspector of Steamboats, found the pilot of the *Erie* blameless in the collision.

The Wreck Today:

At 200 feet, this dive is well beyond the limits of sport diving as defined by all major certifying agencies. It should only be attempted by very experienced divers with specialized training and equipment for depths in excess of sport diving limits.

Her wire rigged forward mast is still standing. Collision damage can be seen on her starboard side and her cabin is collapsed. There is a wheel, and the cast iron bell is in the bow of the wreck. Alas, there is no name on the bell. Trawl nets have dragged the port anchor to the starboard side. The ship's yawl boat layes against the stern on the starboard side.

In addition to the depth, divers need to be mindful of the steel net cable that is draped across the site.

The Van Straubenzie wheel and yawl boat make for an awesome dive. Photos by Tom Wilson.

WALK-IN-THE-WATER

Official #: none   **Site #:** 9

Location: near Point Abino, Ontario

Coordinates: Loran: DGPS:

Lies: salvaged   **Depth:** on shore

Type: sidewheel steamer/schooner   **Cargo:** passengers

Power: two masted schooner rig with cross head engine & side paddle wheels

Owner(s) Lake Erie Steamboat Company of Buffalo, New York

Built: 1818 at Black Rock in the Niagara River by Noah Brown

Dimensions: 135' x 32' x 8'   **Tonnage:** 339 tons

Date of Loss: Wednesday, October 31, 1821

Cause of Loss: storm

Walk-in-the-Water

Great Lakes Historical Society

Story of the Loss:

Walk-in-the-Water has the unique distinction of being the first steam-powered boat above the Niagara River. None other than Robert Fulton, inventor of the steamboat, installed her steam engine. At 135 feet in length and an 8 foot draft, she is small by today's standards, but was too deep to enter some of the ports of her day.

Launched at Black Rock, she needed to navigate the current of the Niagara River in order to reach Lake Erie. Her small steam engine was not strong enough to overcome the current and a team of fifteen oxen was used to tow the steamer to the lake. Undaunted, the steamboat stood off of Buffalo, New York and took on her first 29 paying passengers destined for Detroit, Michigan. Under command of Captain Job Fish, she steamed successfully across the lake. Three primary stops at Buffalo, Cleveland, and Detroit were featured and the vessel made stops at many other small ports along the way. She left Buffalo at 1:30 the afternoon of August 23rd and arrived in Detroit the morning of August 26th, after spending the night waiting in the river so she could have a proper reception on her arrival in Detroit.

Walk-in-the-Water continued to serve for four years as the only steam propelled vessel on the inland seas. In 1819 she steamed across Lake Huron and offloaded passengers and troops at Mackinaw Island. Her crowning cruise was later in 1819. She sailed from Buffalo to Detroit, then on to Mackinaw, and down to Green Bay on Lake Michigan. The one way trip took a mere eight days. Thus began the steam era of Lake Erie shipping.

On October 31, 1821, *Walk-in-the-Water* departed Buffalo on schedule at 1:30 in the afternoon. She had a full complement of passengers and ventured into troubled, but not unmanageable, seas. Shortly into her journey she encountered a storm, which rapidly built to gale force. With her 22 foot paddlewheels thrashing at the angry waters, the steamer ventured on against the elements. As night fell she was off Point Abino, but the vessel could no longer make headway against the towering waves. The force of her wheels against the waves was beginning to pull the ship's timbers apart. She was taking on water.

Unable to continue on, Captain Rogers turned his ship back toward Buffalo. In the tossing seas, his vessel was thrown off course, and he lost his bearings. In addition, the primitive boiler was not strong enough to run the engine and the pumps at the same time, and it was clear the ship was in great peril. Needing to run the pumps, the anchors were lowered and the steam pumps worked against the rising waters in the hold. Passengers and crew joined the bailing effort as torrential rains swept over the ship. Her anchors held, but the strain against the lines was ripping the vessel apart. Water rose faster than the bailing efforts could handle.

At 4:00 a.m., Captain Rogers called the passengers and crew together to advise them they were going to cut the anchor lines so the boat could drift to shore. He then set his ship free of its anchors and allowed it to drift at the mercy of the gale. She was driven ashore near the mouth of Buffalo Creek, and a sailor secured her to a tree on shore. The passengers and crew were able to reach shore on the yawl boats. Once aground, succeeding swells drove the *Walk-in-the-Water* further ashore and up on the beach.

The Wreck Today:

The engine of *Walk-in-the-Water* was salvaged and used in the steamer *Superior*, which replaced her. She was washed completely ashore by the gale, and souvenir hunters removed what was not salvaged of the wreck. The *Superior* continued in service, using the *Walk-in-the-Water's* engine, for ten years.

There is a story that, when *Walk-in-the-Water* first entered the Detroit River, a local farmer exclaimed to his wife "Jean! Jean! Look at the river! These yankees are sending us a sawmill!" He had never seen a steamboat before. However, his observation eventually proved true. Entrepreneur Harvey Williams acquired the engine from the *Superior* and used it to power a steam driven sawmill in Saginaw Valley, Michigan. The sawmill operated for 20 years until it was destroyed by fire on July 4, 1854. A crude early steam engine had served continuously for 36 years. Sure wish we could get a modern automotive engine to do that.

WILD ROVER

Official #: 26283   **Site #:** 69

Location: 10 miles west of Long Point Light

Coordinates: Loran: 44502.5 58476.7   **DGPS:**

Lies: scattered   **Depth:** 17 feet

Type: schooner   **Cargo:** cut stone

Power: sail

Owner(s) Captain Webb of Ashtabula and L.B. Easer of Cleveland, Ohio

Built: 1855 at Milan, Ohio by Evaline Bates

Dimensions: 117' 7" x 24' 8" x 10' 11"   **Tonnage:** 213 gross

Date of Loss: Sunday, November 2, 1874

Cause of Loss: fog

Wild Rover anchor chain

John Veber

Story of the Loss:

The *Wild Rover* was rebuilt at Fairport, Ohio in 1865.

The "smoky weather" fog that prevailed at the eastern end of Lake Erie for several days the early part of November 1874 was responsible for many accidents and total losses. The *Harriet Ross*, bound from Erie to Detroit ran ashore four miles east of Port Colborne and was abandoned to the underwriters. The schooner *Miami* was aground on Long Point and filled with water. The schooner *Francis Palms* was on shore at Long Point. The barge *Detroit* went ashore near Point Abino and was "gone to pieces". Several Welland Canal schooners lost their way in the fog and were forced to anchor. The *S.S. Osborn* was on Cassaday Reef, 2 miles off Port Colborne, Ontario. The scope of the losses was so great that the wreckers working to save stranded vessels tied up all available steam pumps.

Among the many vessels lost in this fog was the *Wild Rover*. Guided by Captain Webb, the *Wild Rover* was bound from Cleveland, Ohio to Toronto, Ontario with block stone. Feeling her way through the fog, she was trying to successfully navigate her way into Long Point Cut when she ran aground.

The boat was partially insured and, owing to her age, a decision was made to strip her of her gear and abandon her. Two years later, the *Monitor* salvaged her stone cargo.

The Wreck Today:

The *Wild Rover* rests on a sand bottom in shallow water along the shore of Long Point. Stripped of much of her gear and cargo years ago, the capstan, rudderpost, some chain, and a few deadeyes still remain. Her wood timbers and steel spikes attract fish to the site.

Do be careful of your boat at this shallow site. We wouldn't want you to join her.

Wild Rover deadeye ring

John Veber

HUNTER WILLIS

Official #: 140288   **Site #:** 64

Location: 500 feet west of United Refining Dock in Erie Harbor, Pennsylvania

Coordinates: Loran: GPS: 42 07.776 80 06.830

Lies: bow east   **Depth:** 10 feet

Type: wood tug   **Cargo:** light

Power: steam engine

Owner(s) Frank J. Tollon of Erie. Pennsylvania

Built: 1878 at Sandusky, Ohio by John Monk

Dimensions: 86.6' x 19.3' x 8.1'   **Tonnage:** 83 gross 43 net

Date of Loss: Thursday, October 22, 1931

Cause of Loss: fire

Hunter Willis as Louise

Private collection of Ralph Roberts

Story of the Loss:

Built at the foot of Meigs Street at Sandusky, Ohio and launched on March 19, 1878, the *Hunter Willis* spent most of her career under her original name, *Louise*. She had been named after the wife of one of the first owner's, Louise Biemiller. Her end came when she caught fire on October 22, 1931 and she was towed to her present location. However, she lead a storied life during her 53 years of service as the *Louise*.

For her first forty years, she ran between Sandusky, the Lake Erie Islands, and Canada hauling fresh fish and transporting sport fishermen to private clubs on the islands. On July 22, 1894, while cruising off Pelee Island, she was boarded by a heavily armed detail from the Canadian fish patrol steamer *Petrel*. Accused of having undersized fish aboard, the vessel was impounded at Amherstburg, Ontario and her engine crosshead was removed to prevent the boat from leaving under its own power.

In 1919 she was acquired for use in the excursion trade around the Chicago, Illinois lakefront. This venture proved not to be profitable, and she returned to Lake Erie under ownership of the Kolbe Fish Company of Erie, Pennsylvania. Again she was employed in freighting fresh fish, this time from Port Burwell, Ontario to the ports of Buffalo, New York and Erie, Pennsylvania.

We should note that the Prohibition Era began January 16th, 1920, when the United States ratified the 18th Amendment, which prohibited the manufacture and sale of alcohol. While we have no definitive proof of this fact, the *Louise* is rumored to have participated in "rum-running" during this time. This would have been a far more profitable activity than hauling fish. Prohibition led to several ill effects including corruption at every level of government and an astounding death toll resulting from the alarming rate of crime surrounding selling illegal alcohol. Prohibition was repealed by the 21st amendment in 1933.

Beginning in 1925 the *Louise* lay idle until she was purchased in the spring of 1931. She was cut down and converted to a towing tug. At this time she was renamed *Hunter Willis*. After one season as the *Hunter Willis*, she caught fire on October 22, 1931.

The Wreck Today:

Resting in only 10 feet of water, not much remains of the *Hunter Willis*. The boiler is present and pipes and engine parts are scattered about the site. Most of the hull is broken down. However, there is some relief at the stern and her starboard side.

This is often done as a shore dive from the nearby piers. Caution is required due to heavy boat traffic in the area and often limited visibility. A dive flag is highly recommended.

The Hunter Willis lays 500 feet west of the United Refining Dock in Erie Harbor.

WILMA

Official #: 130236   **Site #:** 42

Location: 122°T 10 miles off Port Dover, Ontario

Coordinates: Loran: **DGPS:** 42 42.150 80 02.068

Lies: bow northwest   **Depth:** 75 feet

Type: tug   **Cargo:** fish

Power: steam engine

Owner(s) Wilma Fish Company of Port Dover, Ontario

Built: 1911 at Collingwood, Ontario

Dimensions: 67.9' x 16' x 6.7'   **Tonnage:** 42 gross 20 net

Date of Loss: Tuesday, April 14, 1936

Cause of Loss: cut by ice

Wilma

Private collection of Frank and Nancy Prothero

Story of the Loss:

Early in the spring, the *Wilma* set off for the fishing grounds off Port Dover, Ontario. The crew under Captain McLeod was at breakfast when ice punched out a plank near the boiler on the tug's starboard side. Efforts to stem the leak by packing blankets in the splintered side failed. An urgent SOS was sent out as the crew lowered the lifeboat. This cry for help brought Captain McCaulay and the crew of the *Margaret L* to the rescue. Before departing the sinking *Wilma* the crew was able to retrieve the compass and a few belongings.

The Wreck Today:

Sitting upright in 75 feet of water, the *Wilma* is a popular dive site out of Port Dover. The main features of the wreck are the stack that lays along the port side, the boiler, and the forward hatch with ladder leading below. Care should be taken due to the fish net around the wreck.

Underwater photo of the bow of the Wilma courtesy of Long Point Divers, Port Dover, Ontario

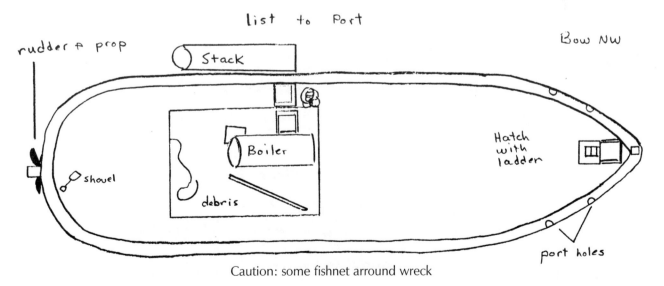

Caution: some fishnet arround wreck

Wilma
67.9' x 16' x 6.7'
by Georgann S. Wachter

not to scale

ANNABELL WILSON

Official #: 106475   **Site #:** 25

Location: 316°T 0.5 mile off Dunkirk, New York

Coordinates: Loran: 44682.8 58945.3   **DGPS:** 42 29.911 79 21.117

Lies: bow south   **Depth:** 50 feet

Type: Schooner, 3 masts   **Cargo:** coal

Power: sail/towed

Owner(s) Thomas Lannan of Port Colborne

Built: 1887 at Mount Clemons, Michigan by William Dulac

Dimensions: 174' x 32'2" x 12'   **Tonnage:** 490.63 gross 467.27 net

Date of Loss: Saturday, July 12, 1913

Cause of Loss: storm

Annabell Wilson

Great Lakes Historical Society, Bowen Collection

Story of the Loss:

Under tow of the tug *Meteor,* the *Annabell Wilson* was bound from Erie, Pennsylvania to Port Colborne, Ontario with a load of 1,000 tons of coal. Encountering much larger waves than they had expected, the two vessels had decided to turn and seek safe harbor at Dunkirk, New York. Just as shelter was in her grasp, the cargo aboard the *Annabell Wilson* shifted in the heavy seas, sending the vessel to the bottom with little notice.

Captain Barney McIntyre of Toronto rushed to his cabin to retrieve personal effects as the other three members of his crew abandoned ship and were saved by the tug *Meteor*. As the *Wilson* lurched toward the bottom, Captain McIntyre's wife, Elizabeth, stood in the passageway calling for him. He was never seen again. Elizabeth was later picked up by the *Meteor*. She was floating face down in the water, but still showed signs of life. She was rushed to shore and taken to Brooks Memorial Hospital. There, physicians worked over her for more than two hours before she was declared dead at 4:00 p.m.

Surviving the sinking were James Mullin of Kingston, Ontario, Henry Simmons of Erie, Pennsylvania, and Albert Blundem of Port Robinson, Ontario.

The Wreck Today:

The *Annabell Wilson* lies in the heavily trafficked approach area of Dunkirk Harbor. Due to heavy boat traffic, caution and a dive flag are essential at this site. Following the loss, her masts were removed and some of her cargo was salvaged. The site has considerable amounts of wood and iron parts strewn about.

The Annabell Wilson lays one half mile off the Dunkirk, New York harbor entrance.
Photo by Georgann Wachter

WOCOKEN

Official #: 80778   **Site #:** 78

Location: 1 ½ miles east of Clear Creek, Ontario

Coordinates: Loran: **DGPS:**

Lies: bow east   **Depth:** 50 feet

Type: wood propeller   **Cargo:** coal

Power: 1281 horsepower steam engine

Owner(s) Mitchell & Company, Cleveland, Ohio

Built: 1880 at Cleveland, Ohio by Thomas Quayle and Sons

Dimensions: 256.6' x 37.2' x 18.5'   **Tonnage:** 1400 gross 1179 net

Date of Loss: Saturday, October 14, 1893

Cause of Loss: storm

Wocoken

Great Lakes Historical Society

Story of the Loss:

The *Wocoken* was one of many victims of the great storm of October 13 to 15, 1893. Among the vessels lost in this monstrous storm were the *Dean Richmond*, the *C.B. Benson*, and the *Riverside*.

Captain Albert Meswald had his wife along on this fateful journey. They had been visiting Mrs. Meswald's brother, Captain John Mitchell, who was a part owner of the *Wocoken*. The vessel had taken on her cargo of coal at Ashtabula, Ohio and stopped at Erie, Pennsylvania to pick up her consort, the schooner barge *Joseph Paige*. Both were upbound for Milwaukee, Wisconsin when disaster struck. The first indication of the loss came when the fish tug *Bacon* found lifeboats bearing the *Wocoken's* name.

The tale is best told by First Mate J.P. Saph, one of only three survivors from a crew of 16.

"On October 13ᵗʰ last, we left Erie at 12:00 pm with the vessel *Joseph Paige* in tow. The weather was fine and the wind southeast light. About 5 o'clock, the wind shifted to the northeast and it commenced to rain. On Saturday morning I was on my bunk, Mrs. Meswald called me, and she wanted to know if the dummy light was in sight. I put my rubber boots on and went up on deck. It was blowing hard, so hard we could hardly stand on deck. A large sea was rolling, we kept the *Wocoken* headed into the wind, then she turned around on us and played into the trough of the sea. Dunnage, yawl boats, water barrels, boxes were scattered. We threw the dunnage overboard so it wouldn't tear our hatch cloths. She had one foot of water on the deck all day. The sea became larger and started to sweep clear over the deck. Mrs. Meswald was in the aft cabin where she could not hear the roar of the wind or sea. Fearing that the cabin would get washed off, I told the captain he better go back and get his wife. We both carried Mrs. Meswald foreword into his rooms. It became dark and the sea grew larger. We then struck land off the sand hills, we were headed for Long Point.

"The sea was boarding her more and more, but she was not leaking much. I told the captain to watch the wheelsman while I went forward, Henry Krantz came and told me the cabin washed in and the steam pipes were broken. The engineers stood by until the sea drove them out of the engine room, and the firemen out of the firehole. We strapped our life preservers on good, while the *Wocoken* was sinking. Three deck hands took to a small boat, the boat got into the water, but they had to be rescued. The water started to foam on deck and I knew it would be soon she would go down.

"Mrs. Meswald was leaning on my arm and I had to go down on deck and meet Henry Krantz, and told him we better take to the riggings. As Henry started ahead of me, he was washed overboard, also the pilot house, and texas, carrying the entire crew overboard, including Captain Meswald and his wife.

"By the time the sea struck us, the *Wocoken* was on the bottom, the water half covering me. I got high enough in the rigging and looked around. I saw nothing, no cry, no sound, only the roar of the sea. I climbed to the crosstree where two other men were. The lifesaving crew took us off and 400 people lined the beach. They have been hunting bodies ever since."

The schooner *Joseph Paige was towed in the following morning with five feet of water in her hold. The Paige is pictured with the Raleigh on page 158.*

The Wreck Today:

We know of no one who is currently diving the *Wocoken*. A diver who was searching for bodies of the lost crewmen visited her right after her loss. He reported that there was little left but the bottom of her hull.

She rests in a fairly remote part of the lake. Good hunting!

WONDER

Official #: 81794   **Site #:** 85

Location: inside the outer breakwalls of Ashtabula Harbor, Ohio

Coordinates: Loran: 43851.2 57184.0   DGPS: 41 54.77   80 46.89

Lies: north/south   **Depth:** 12 feet

Type: wood sandsucker   **Cargo:** sand

Power: steam

Owner(s) Ashtabula Sand and Gravel Company of Ashtabula, Ohio

Built: 1889 at New London, Wisconsin

Dimensions: 94.5' x 19.5' x 5.1'   **Tonnage:** 99 gross 78 net

Date of Loss: Sunday, September 6, 1908

Cause of Loss: stranded in storm

John R. Emery

Built in 1905, the Emery is a sandsucker similar to the Wonder.
Photo by Mike Wachter

Story of the Loss:

Small ships and sudden storms rarely work well together. The *Wonder* had been working to the west of Ashtabula, Ohio when she and her crew of four were caught in a sudden squall. The little sandsucker ran aground and was unable to free herself. The crew was safely removed, and efforts were rapidly begun to salvage her. Tugs strained to free her from the sand bottom's powerful grasp. However, the efforts of tugs to remove her were unsuccessful. She was left to rest on a sand bottom while her owners arranged to get her off without serious damage.

Throughout the following week, efforts continued to salvage the stranded vessel. She was lightered, pumped out, and successfully refloated. With victory in their grasp, the salvage crews were, once again, disappointed. Before she could be moved to a dock she sank again, just east of the harbor off the Pennsylvania Lakefront Slip. With little further hope that she could be saved, the company abandoned her as a constructive total loss.

The Wreck Today:

The *Wonder* lays on a sand bottom with two other wrecks inside Ashtabula Harbor. The remains of the *Wonder*, *Joy*, and *Gulnair* form what is commonly called the "Harbor Wrecks". Little remains of these three wrecks other than their timbers and a few metal parts. Because the site is shallow and attracts many fish, this is a popular night dive for divers in the Ashtabula Harbor area.

As the summer progresses, weeds grow up from the sandy bottom.

Divers who discovered the *James F. Joy* in 1960 developed the map to the right. They thought the wreck was in three sections. In reality, there are three wrecks, *Joy*, *Gulnair*, and *Wonder*. These three "Harbor Wrecks" can all be covered in a single dive. The *Wonder* lies furthest to the west. *James Joy* is the furthest east. Furthest south is the *Gulnair*.

A dive flag float and a good lookout are necessary due to the heavy boat traffic at this site.

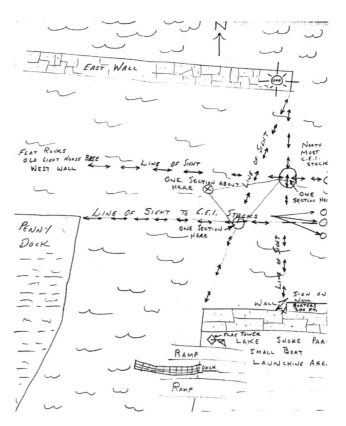

Drawn by divers who rediscovered the James F. Joy in 1960, this map shows the location of the three "Harbor Wrecks". Wonder is furthest section to the west.

BIBLIOGRAPHY

BOOKS

Barry, James P. Wrecks and Rescues of the Great Lakes, A Photographic History. La Jolla, California: Howell and North Books, 1981

Beesons Marine Directory of the Northwest Lakes (various years). Chicago, Illinois: Harvey C. Beeson.

Bowen, Dana T. Shipwrecks of the Lakes. Cleveland, Ohio: Freshwater Press, 1952.

Diving in Ohio. Rootstown, Ohio: Ohio Council of Skin and Scuba Divers, Inc., 1976.

Doner, Mary Francis. The Salvager. Minneapolis, Minnesota: Ross and Haines, Inc., 1958

Frohman, Charles E. Milan and the Milan Canal, 1976.

Great Lakes Red Book (various years). Saint Clair Shores, Michigan: The Fourth Seacoast Publishing Company.

Greenwood, John O. Namesakes 1930 - 1955. Cleveland, Ohio: Freshwater Press, Inc., 1995.

Greenwood, John O. Namesakes 1920 - 1929. Cleveland, Ohio: Freshwater Press, Inc., 1984.

Greenwood, John O. Namesakes 1910 - 1919. Cleveland, Ohio: Freshwater Press, Inc., 1986.

Greenwood, John O. Namesakes 1900 - 1909. Cleveland, Ohio: Freshwater Press, Inc., 1987.

Greenwood, John O. Greenwoods Guide to Great Lakes Shipping (various years). Cleveland, Ohio: Freshwater Press, Inc.

Heden, Karl E. Directory of Shipwrecks of the Great Lakes. Boston, Massachusetts: Bruce Humphries Publishers, 1966.

Heyl, Eric. Early American Steamers, Vols I - VI. Buffalo, New York: published by the author at 136 West Oakwood Place, 1961 - 1969.

Inches, H. C. The Great Lakes Wooden Shipbuilding Era. Vermilion, Ohio: The Great Lakes Historical Society, 1976.

Kohl, Chris. The 100 Best Great Lakes Shipwrecks, Volume I & II. West Chicago, Illinois: Seawolf Communications, Inc., 1998.

Kohl, Cris. Dive Southwestern Ontario!. Chatham, Ontario: published by the author, 1985.

Kohl, Cris. Dive Ontario Two! More Ontario Shipwreck Stories. Chatham, Ontario: published by the author, 1994.

Kohl, Cris. Dive Ontario. Chatham, Ontario: published by the author, 1990 revised 1995.

Lakelore. Simcoe, Ontario: circa 1974.

Lytle, William. Merchant Steam Vessels of the U.S. 1807 - 1868. Mystic, Connecticut: Steamship Historical Society of America, 1952.

MacDonald, Robert J. and David Frew. Home Port Erie. Erie, Pennsylvania, Erie County Historical Society, 1997.

Mansfield, J.B., ed. History of the Great Lakes, Two volumes. Chicago: J.H. Beers and Company, 1899. Reprint edition, Cleveland: Freshwater Press, 1972

Meakin, Alexander C. The Story of the Great Lakes Towing Company. Vermilion, Ohio: The Great Lakes Historical Society, 1984.

Merchant Vessels of the U.S. (various years). Washington: Government Printing Office.

Mills, John M. Canadian Coastal and Inland Steam Vessels, 1809 – 1930. Providence, Rhode Island: The Steamship Historical Society of America, Inc., 1979.

Prothero, Frank. The Good Years. Bellville, Ontario, Mika Publishing, 1973.

Prothero, Frank and Nancy. Tales of the North Shore. Port Stanley, Ontario: Nan-Sea Publications, 1987.

Prothero, Frank and Nancy. Memories, A History of Port Burwell. Port Stanley, Ontario: Nan-Sea Publications, 1986.

BIBLIOGRAPHY

Shaefer, Mary Louise. <u>Mitchell Steamship Company 1800's to 1900's, A Great Lakes Saga</u>. Avon Lake, Ohio: self published.

Stone, David. <u>Long Point, Last Port of Call</u>. Erin, Ontario: Boston Mills Press, 1988.

Swayze, David D. <u>Shipwreck!</u>. Boyne City, Michigan: Harbor House Publications, Inc., 1992.

Van der Linden, Rev. Peter J., ed. and the Marine Historical Society of Detroit. <u>Great Lakes Ships We Remember</u>. Cleveland, Ohio: Freshwater Press, 1979 revised 1984.

Wendt, Gordon. <u>In the Wake of the Walk-in-the-Water</u>. Sandusky, Ohio: Commercial Printing Co., 1984

PERIODICALS

Many articles from newspapers throughout the Great Lakes region were used to gather data for this book.

MISCELLANEOUS

Database of Walter Lewis: www.hhpl.on.ca/GreatLakes/.

Database of David Swayze: www.ghost-ships.org/swayzedb.asp

"Master Sheets", Historical Collections of the Great Lakes, Bowling Green State University, Bowling Green, Ohio.

PHOTOGRAPHS & DRAWINGS

In addition to pictures from our private collection, photographs and drawings for this publication were provided by:

Buffalo & Erie County Historical Society. Buffalo, New York.

Ralph Deeds. Birmingham, Michigan.

Father Edward J. Dowling Collection. University of Detroit, Mercy Library. Detroit Michigan.

Bill Duff. Sisters, Oregon

Skip Gillham. Vineland, Ontario.

Great Lakes Historical Society. Vermilion, Ohio.

Al Hart. Bay Village, Ohio.

Mike Hirsch, Erie, Pennsylvania

Historical Collections of the Great Lakes. Bowling Green State University. Bowling Green, Ohio.

Doug King, Sr. Blasdell, New York

Mike King. Cleveland, Ohio.

Lower Lakes Marine Historical Society. Buffalo, New York.

John Mathews. Port Dover, Ontario.

Milan Historical Society. Milan, Ohio.

John Misner. Port Dover, Ontario

Frank and Nancy Prothero. Port Stanley, Ontario.

Ralph Roberts. Saginaw, Michigan.

Larry Slomski, Sagertown, Pennsylvania

David VanZandt. Lakewood, Ohio.

John Veber. Brantford, Ontario.

Tom Wilson. New Market, Ontario.

Georgann and Mike Wachter have been diving around the world since the early 1970's. They discovered diving while snorkeling in the Mediterranean Sea in 1972 during a backpacking trip through Europe. Since that time, they have visited many sites in the Caribbean, Atlantic, Pacific, and Great Lakes. However, nowhere else in the world have they discovered the kind of pristine and perfectly preserved shipwrecks that lie in the fresh waters of the Great Lakes.

Living near Lake Erie led to the fascination with Lake Erie shipwrecks that drove the extensive research effort that is exhibited in **ERIE WRECKS EAST** and **ERIE WRECKS WEST**. Early on, guests diving aboard the Wachter's boat would ask about the details of a shipwreck while en route to the site. In order to answer these questions, Mike and Georgann began keeping a notebook on board that contained photos and information on many of the shipwrecks they were diving. This kept Mike from making up false stories to answer the many questions. As the notebook grew, many friends suggested that the book should be published. Once the decision was made to publish a book on Lake Erie shipwrecks, the real work began. What was once a part time hobby has become a full time investigation of the myths and realities behind the thousands of shipwrecks in the Great Lakes. The Wachters have published four books, and several magazine articles, but their work is only beginning. With over 2,000 ships known to have sunk in Lake Erie alone, we can look forward to many more articles, books, and shipwreck materials from this husband and wife team.

Georgann is an accomplished researcher who is sought after as a speaker on sport diving, Great Lakes shipwrecks, and aquatic life. Mike makes his living as a management consultant and public speaker. For both Georgann and Mike, their first love is shipwreck diving. The collaboration of Georgann's love of research and Mike's love of story telling provides the fuel for the Erie Wrecks series.

NEED ADDITIONAL COPIES?

Additional copies of *Erie Wrecks East, Second Edition* and *Erie Wrecks West* may be ordered directly from the publisher. *Erie Wrecks West* covers an additional 103 shipwrecks in the western half of Lake Erie.

Corporate Impact

33326 Bonnieview Drive, Suite 200
Avon Lake, Ohio 44012-1230

Phone: 440-930-2477
Fax: 440-930-2525
Email: Wachter@ErieWrecks.com
Web: www.eriewrecks.com